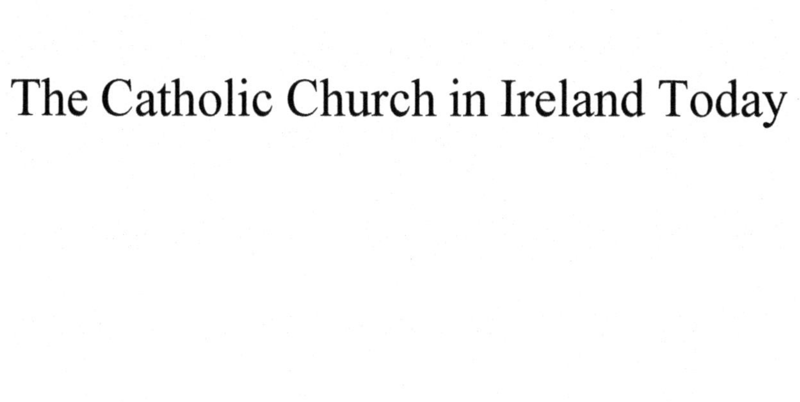

The Catholic Church in Ireland Today

The Catholic Church in Ireland Today

Edited by David Carroll Cochran
and John C. Waldmeir

LEXINGTON BOOKS
Lanham • Boulder • New York • London

Published by Lexington Books
An imprint of The Rowman & Littlefield Publishing Group, Inc.
4501 Forbes Boulevard, Suite 200, Lanham, Maryland 20706
www.rowman.com

Unit A, Whitacre Mews, 26-34 Stannary Street, London SE11 4AB

British Library Cataloguing in Publication Information Available

Library of Congress Cataloging-in-Publication Data

The Catholic Church in Ireland today / edited by David Carroll Cochran and John C. Waldmeir.
pages cm
Includes bibliographical references and index.
ISBN 978-1-4985-0252-8 (cloth : alk. paper) -- ISBN 978-1-4985-0253-5 (electronic)
1. Catholic Church--Ireland--History--20th century. 2. Catholic Church--Ireland--History--21st century. I. Cochran, David Carroll, editor.
BX1505.2.C37 2015
282'.41509051--dc23
2014044342

∞ ™ The paper used in this publication meets the minimum requirements of American National Standard for Information Sciences Permanence of Paper for Printed Library Materials, ANSI/NISO Z39.48-1992.

Printed in the United States of America

For William Lynch (Loras College, 1964) and the
Dubuque Sisters of the Presentation of the Blessed Virgin Mary

Contents

Preface and Acknowledgments

While books frequently open by claiming their subject is at a "moment of crisis" or a "crucial turning point," this is actually true of contemporary Irish Catholicism. From a Church that once enjoyed devotional loyalty, political influence, and institutional power unrivaled in Europe, one in which Archbishop McQuaid of Dublin could return from Vatican II and confidently report that "no change will worry the tranquility of your Christian lives," it now faces a collapse of institutional legitimacy, shrinking mass attendance, bruising political battles, and a devastating series of reports on sexual abuse.[1]

The contributors to this volume detail the stark realities of this current crisis, exploring its deep roots, unfolding dynamics, and varied manifestations. They also uncover areas of continuing, even surprising, resilience in Irish Catholicism. The role of the Catholic Church in Ireland has changed dramatically in the last several decades, but it is still an important one. And it is in this changing role that many of the chapters to follow see diverse signs of reform and renewal. Rather than a return to the triumphalist social, cultural, and political power wielded by an Irish Catholicism of the past, these signs point to a more humble, prophetic, and creative presence in Irish life.

The book's first part offers a broad overview of its topic. Eamon Maher surveys the current state of Irish Catholicism and the striking cultural shifts that have brought it about, drawing in particular on fiction, memoir, and political and social commentary for illustration and analysis. John Littleton follows by reflecting on how an Irish Church that is *in periculo mortis* (in danger of death) can heal itself by facing a series of core challenges with creative responses. In his response to Maher and Littleton's chapters, James Rogers extends their themes, calls attention to some additional dimensions, and draws some comparisons to Catholicism in the United States.

The book's second part offers a closer look at particular elements within contemporary Irish Catholicism. Michele Dillon's chapter uses sociological data, including comparisons to other countries such as the United States, to explore the comparatively rapid changes in Irish Catholicism during a period of "compressed secularism," as well as offering thoughts on the role of the Church in a "post-secular" Ireland. Elizabeth Oldmixon and Brian Calfano draw on survey data of clergy in Ireland to measure factors related to morale and burnout, comparing Catholic clergy to those in other denominations and examining how such factors impact the political role of clergy. Agata Piękosz also examines the lives and leadership roles of Catholic clergy, but her focus is on in-depth interviews with Polish Catholic priests recently arrived in Ireland to minister to an increasingly diverse Catholic population. While the 1932 International Eucharistic Congress was a landmark event in the consolidation of Catholic influence in the then-young Irish state, John Waldmeir's chapter uses the return of the Eucharistic Congress to Dublin in 2012 to explore today's much different religious landscape and the contrasting theological visions for the future of the Irish Catholic Church the meeting produced. Using two figures, one contemporary and one historical, Matthew O'Brien looks at how Irish American perceptions of Irish Catholicism have shifted over the last century. Andrew Auge draws on both historical practice and literary representation to explore the changing perceptions of Catholic missionaries from Ireland working abroad, especially how some contemporary missionaries have reversed the historical emphasis by focusing on how contact with countries in the developing world can enrich Irish Catholicism itself. Finally, Bernadette Flanagan closes the book by noting how Catholic renewal often comes from unexpected places—especially from the disaffected, overlooked, and marginalized—and how signs of this pattern are increasingly evident in a recovery and reformulation of Ireland's contemplative traditions.

Many people made this book possible. Our thanks, first, to the contributors, who were a pleasure to get to know and work with. Thanks also to Alissa Parra, Emily Frazzette, Meaghan White, and everyone at Lexington Books. Laurel Lloyd provided expert assistance in formatting graphs.

The book began its life as a symposium at Loras College in Dubuque, Iowa, one that would not have been possible without the generous support of William Lynch and the Dubuque Sisters of the Presentation of the Blessed Virgin Mary. We are deeply grateful to both. Our thanks also to Jim Collins, Carol Oberfoell, Mary Love, Sue Hafkemeyer, Rebecca Krapfl, Colleen McKenna, Jodi Cecil, Anne Vaassen, and Jackie Baumhover for their help with the symposium and book. Finally, thanks to Julie O'Callaghan and *New Hibernia Review* for permission to use selections from Dennis O'Driscoll's poem "Missing God."

NOTE

1. McQuaid quoted in Dermot A. Lane, "Vatican II: The Irish Experience," *The Furrow* 55 (2004): 67.

I

The Current Status and Future Directions of Irish Catholicism

Chapter One

"Faith of Our Fathers"

A Lost Legacy?

Eamon Maher

In the past few decades, Ireland has experienced seismic changes in terms of its social, cultural, and religious *habitus*. The burgeoning Celtic Tiger, with its promises of unimaginable wealth, full employment, an end to emigration, has been shown up for what it was: a chimera. The gap between rich and poor, between the haves and the have-nots, has widened inexorably, with all the potential for social disharmony that such a situation bodes for the future. Severe cuts to public sector pay, savage reductions in the amounts paid to the vulnerable, such as the sick and the elderly, increases in the pupil-teacher ratios in primary and secondary schools accompanied by the withdrawal of special needs assistants: all these measures have all been implemented with a view to recapitalizing the banks and paying back senior bondholders, the very people who played a significant role in exposing the country to untenable debt in the first instance. It is hard not to be disenchanted by what has unfolded in the last six to eight years.

What role, if any, has the Catholic Church been playing in this drama, you may well ask? Once a powerful force, often for good it should be pointed out, it has now been reduced to the level of other Irish elitist groupings such as politicians, the banks, and the legal profession that failed to justify the faith that was invested in them. The clerical abuse scandals have removed any real claim to moral authority that the Church once enjoyed, and a rising tide of secularization has had a negative impact on the status of organized religion in Ireland. Church and State were complicit in many initiatives that resulted in children and young women being exposed to rape and torture in places such as the Industrial Schools and Magdalen Laundries. People often ended up in these places for the simple reason that their parents did not have the wherewithal to feed and clothe them, or, in the case of women, if they found themselves pregnant outside of marriage. The pioneering journalist Mary Raftery, who sadly passed away in January 2012, was instrumental in exposing the hypocrisy and self-serving attitude of the religious orders that oversaw the harsh treatment meted out to the children in their care. She wrote at the time of the publication of the Ryan Report (2009): "When protecting their own (usually financial) interests, the religious orders displayed a zeal and even ferocity notably absent from their attempts down the years to control the criminal battery, assault and rape perpetuated by their member Brothers, priests and nuns against small children."[1]

Several other commentators were quick to point out a similar "groupthink" mentality among the Catholic hierarchy when revelations of sexual abuse of children by a small number of priests began to surface in the 1990s. Preservation of the institution took precedence over natural justice and the safety of children. The systemic attempt at damage limitation had the effect of leaving heretofore staunchly loyal Catholics feeling dismayed by the drip, drip revelations of the detailed knowledge the Church authorities possessed with regard to what exactly had been happening in the area of clerical sex abuse. Pope Benedict's long-awaited pastoral letter to the Catholics of Ireland was issued on the 20 March 2010. In paragraph 6, he addressed the victims of abuse and their families: "You have suffered grievously and I am truly sorry. You have been betrayed and your dignity has been violated. . . . I openly express the shame and remorse that we all feel."[2] Clearly, this was an unprecedented and historical apology, the sincerity of which might at first sight appear to be beyond doubt. But then Benedict began to examine what for him were the main causes of the abuse problem in Ireland. He cited the relativism that had taken hold of people's minds, which led to a blurring of the borders between right and wrong, the move away from family prayer and the sacraments, a failure of leadership among the Irish bishops in responding to allegations of misdemeanours by priests. Kevin Egan echoes the view of many in lamenting Benedict's failure to carry this line of thought through to its natural conclusion:

> In hindsight, I wonder will the Pope realise that his mistake was to stop there. His letter would have had much greater impact if he had gone on to acknowledge his own and his predecessor's failings in leadership in addressing this issue. The writers of a recent article in *Time* magazine entitled: "Why Being Pope Means Never Having to Say You're Sorry," pointed out the Pope in his letter was merely apologising for errors committed by the hierarchy of Ireland but not for anything he or the Vatican may have done.[3]

This type of double standard is what has fuelled the rage felt by many toward an institution that is supposed to stand for truth and integrity, justice and decency for all. Instead, it is now in danger of becoming a sad caricature of the aspirations of its founder. The result is a void that has not been adequately filled by any viable alternative. Material prosperity has been shown to foster greed and selfishness, to engender a deterioration in human relationships, as everybody attempts to climb over the next person only to arrive in a mythical El Dorado where everything, to contradict Voltaire's Dr. Pangloss, is far from being the best in the best of all possible worlds. The Benedictine monk, Mark Patrick Hederman, sums it up in the following manner: "We are living in spiritually destitute times. The institutional church, which was for many a bastion of dogmatic truth, a divinely appointed moral law, of sure and certain guidance toward the heaven we looked forward to, has been discredited in the short space of about thirty years, as the new century turned its course."[4]

Priests working on the ground in parishes the length and breadth of the country are probably the ones who are most adversely affected by the changed religious climate. The majority of them are now elderly, overworked, and appalled at how the institution to which they devoted their lives has failed them in their hour of need. The enthusiasm engendered by Vatican II, which would have been a seminal moment in the lives of the majority of these men, has been replaced by fatigue and disillusionment. One of the founding members of the Association of Priests of Ireland, Brendan Hoban, describes their predicament in the following manner:

> In present circumstances, disenchantment among diocesan priests in Ireland is predictable, understandable, even inevitable, given the accumulated wreckage of the last few decades: paedophile scandals, failures of Church leadership, vocations in free-fall, haemorrhaging of our congregations; rising age-levels of priests; the ever-increasing demands of our people; the perception of an anti-Church media bias; and, not least, the feeling that we have become endless and usually disparaging news.[5]

Hoban paints a far from rosy picture, but it is one that is reinforced by all the data currently available on the scarcity of priests in Ireland, a situation that is unlikely to improve given that the average age of priests is currently sixty-five, a stark statistic that poses many questions as to how an aging group will be in a position to continue saying Masses and administering the sacraments in another ten years' time. The cultural "habitus," to use the phrase coined by the French anthropologist Pierre Bourdieu, and applied to the Irish context by the sociologist Tom Inglis, is no longer favourable to those who are holding on to the Catholic faith by the tips of their fingers. It was in decline before the clerical abuse scandals, a fact that may well have prompted the visit by Pope John Paul II in 1979, but it is undeniably far more hostile at the moment. In this chapter, I pose the following questions: What has become of the faith of our fathers, that proud legacy which was so intimately associated with Irish identity? Has it been lost forever, or is it merely lying in wait of the spark that might reignite it?

Obviously, it is far from easy to assess something as personal and tenuous as religious sensibility. What people feel in their hearts and express publicly are often very different. When asked about one's faith in a survey or when filling out a census form, the answer given can reflect the feelings of a particular moment. For example, if one were to question people about their opinion of the Catholic Church shortly after the publication of the Ferns, Ryan, Murphy or Cloyne Reports, which depict heinous crimes against children, a betrayal of trust by certain priests and religious, it is unlikely that they would have anything constructive to say about the institution. But if, on the other hand, after a family bereavement or a wedding, one were to ask about the local priests, I think there would be a much more positive reaction. People definitely feel betrayed by the Church as an institution, but they still hold many of its ceremonies and rituals in high regard. The writer John McGahern (1934–2006) was disenchanted with the authoritarian and repressive form of Catholicism that he experienced growing up in rural Ireland during the 1930s and 1940s. And yet he regularly acknowledged his indebtedness to the sense of mystery and awe imbued in him by Catholicism:

> I have nothing but gratitude for the spiritual remnants of that upbringing, the sense of our origins beyond the bounds of sense, an awareness of mystery and wonderment, grace and sacrament, and the absolute equality of all women and men underneath the sun of heaven. That is all that now remains. Belief as such has long gone.[6]

He recalled the ceremonies of Christmas and Easter with particular fondness, the Stations of the Cross during Lent, the Corpus Christi processions. The smell of incense in the church, the beautiful flowers decorating the altar, the priest's ornate vestments, the congregation dressed in their best clothes: these were the things the writer missed when he ceased practicing his religion. He regretted how in Ireland, instead of espousing the Gothic form of Catholicism, with its church spires reaching toward the sky and raising Man's glance from the avaricious earth, the Irish opted instead for the Romanesque spirit—"the low roof, the fortress, the fundamentalists' pulpit-pounding zeal, the darkly ominous and fearful warnings to transgressors."[7] The contrast is stark between the beautiful flowers and uplifting liturgies and the iron-fist, patriarchal form of Catholicism that ruthlessly crushed any challenge to its authority with psychological and physical violence and imbued in people a negative image of themselves and of their bodies.

This dichotomy between the Gothic and the Romanesque was far from being unique to Ireland, however. Jean Rohou, a highly regarded specialist of seventeenth-century French history and someone with a solid grasp of the

Bible and the history of Christianity, recently published two studies that I found to be of immense interest to the Irish context. Although a self-confessed humanist, Rohou is well-disposed to many aspects of the Catholic religion to which he was introduced when growing up in rural Brittany. He talks of the way in which Catholicism was drummed into them: "*Apprendre sans comprendre*" (Learning without understanding) was the motto of the Church at the time.[8] A few quotes will underline the similarities between Rohou's portrayal of Brittany and the Ireland of a few decades ago:

> In the rural Léon district of my youth, religion inspired our thoughts and feelings: its rites structured our lives, and *Monsieur le curé* was our leader . . . God was a proven entity. There was no need to force yourself to believe: He thought for you. Our faith was not a cross we had to carry, as it is today.[9]

The priests in Brittany were powerful figures whom one opposed at one's peril. Like their Irish equivalents, they supervised the local dances, ensured that there was nothing untoward going on, and generally acted as a type of moral police force. Rohou was sad to lose his faith and does not look at the present religious landscape in Brittany with any degree of smug satisfaction. There are even fewer priests left in Brittany than there are in Ireland, religious practice is at an all-time low, and there would appear to be little likelihood of any reversal of this trend. When he read the New Testament for the first time after his arrival in university, Rohou could not believe how all the negative interdictions he associated with the Catholic faith, such as blind obedience, guilt, fear of Hell, the purifying side of suffering, were not to be found in it. Instead, he discovered an invitation to grow and develop in the love of God and His creatures, especially the poor and the downtrodden. Then, in 2011, he attended the funeral of his brother, an anticlerical unbeliever, and found himself transported back to the time of his childhood. The children of the deceased wanted a religious burial, which Rohou considered appropriate, as that was the local custom. There was no priest, but the congregation sang hymns, there were readings from the Gospel, poetry, prayers. It brought the community together in a non-sectarian way and Rohou found it comforting:

> The success of the occasion can be explained by a community of seventy-something-year-olds who knew each other intimately and who had shared a childhood nourished by religious ceremonies. They sang the Breton hymns with gusto; all the more so perhaps because they sensed vaguely that this burial was a prelude to the disappearance of their world, of their language, of their religion.[10]

The poet and Nobel Laureate Seamus Heaney, like McGahern and Rohou, a non-practicing Catholic who was far from convinced about the existence of God, was also buried in the traditional Catholic fashion, with a Mass and a decade of the Rosary recited at the graveside. After the passing of his friend McGahern, Heaney remarked about how appropriate the funeral service was. It had little or nothing to do with religious faith, however, and everything to do with local custom. In an interview with Dennis O'Driscoll, Heaney noted how understated the ceremony was, in spite of the fact that a writer with a world-wide reputation was being laid to rest:

> And no Latin either, just the vernacular parish mass—a low mass, as they used to call it—during which a tribute was spoken by the celebrant. No music, no addresses by friends or writers, the coffin carried down the aisle the same as at the funeral last week and last year and last century, the rosary said at the graveside and then local men shovelling in the mould.[11]

The same was true of Heaney's own funeral, which was a simple, local affair. The importance of tradition was paramount to both men, from whence the need for everything to be done in the same way as the ritual had been carried out for centuries. Hence it would have been unthinkable for these men to have a humanist ceremony. After all, the Catholic Church had been the language of their youth, its ceremonies had punctuated the calendar year and brought some beauty and comfort into what was a harsh life growing up in rural Derry or Roscommon/Leitrim. The faith of their forefathers, the faith that molded their thoughts and inspired their aesthetic appreciation of beauty and the sacred, was not something that could be discarded like a glove. It was an essential part of who they were.

The same reverence would not be evident in the next generation of Irish writers, who adapt a very different stance toward the Catholic faith. For example, Roddy Doyle's novels, often set in the fictional working class suburb of Barrytown, contain little, if any, reference to religious symbolism. The characters go about their lives without ever seriously questioning if their acts are right or wrong—Catholic guilt, the plague of so many of McGahern's characters, is the farthest thing from their minds. This undoubtedly has a lot to do with the particular experience of Catholicism that Doyle had. Rather than being sensitive to the beauty of the rituals, what struck him in particular was the attempt by the Catholic Church to control the moral and sexual lives of Irish people. During the 1980s, Doyle campaigned actively for divorce and found himself resentful of a certain Catholic mind-set that was opposed to change. Speaking of this period in Irish society in an interview, he remarked:

> It was basically the Catholic Church against everyone else. It was the insistence that if you're Irish, you're white and you're Catholic as well, and if you're not both of those things, then you're not fully Irish. Ultimately, that is what it (the divorce referendum) was all about . . . I felt it was a real fight, a

> fight for the future of my children and the future of the country. I was very, very emotionally involved.[12]

Another Booker Prize winner, Anne Enright, demonstrates a similar antipathy toward Catholicism, which she associates with hypocrisy and patriarchy. In her 2008 award-winning novel *The Gathering*, for example, the main character Veronica reflects on attending Mass with her father when she was young and realizes that he may well have shared his daughter's ambivalence toward what was taking place on the altar:

> Of course Mammy is a Catholic, in the way that Mammys are, but for fourteen years or so I sat by or behind my father, on a wooden church bench, every Sunday morning and in all that time, I never saw his lips move. I never heard him pray aloud, or saw him bend his head, or do anything that might be considered remarkable were he sitting on the top deck of a bus. When it was time for Communion he stood at the end of the bench as we trooped by, like letting sheep out at a gate, but I don't know if he ever followed us up to the Communion rail. My father attended church in his official capacity. If I went looking for his personal belief I would not know where to begin, or in what part of his body it might inhere.[13]

This idea of doing one's duty, of conforming to one's "official capacity," this non-questioning and artificial observance of religion is brought out in a stark manner by Enright. It is clear from interviews she has given and things that she has written that Enright has issues with the role that Catholicism played in Irish society in the past. In *The Gathering*, it is worth noting that there is no medium through which Veronica can articulate to anyone else the abuse of her young brother Liam by their grandmother Ada's lodger, a man called Nugent. This event, which she witnesses in the front room of Ada's house, was ultimately responsible for Liam's rather problematic life and eventual suicide. Veronica, on coming across the awful scene of Nugent's sexual deviance, does not raise her voice and come to the aid of her brother. Being young herself, she closes the door and abandons Liam to a horrible fate. Thinking back on the incident as an adult and a mother, Veronica observes:

> I don't know why his (Nugent's) pleasure should be the most terrible thing in the room for me. The inwardness of it. The grimace it provokes like a man with a bad fart making its way through his guts, or a man who hears terrible news that is nonetheless funny. It is the struggle on Lamb Nugent's face that is unbearable, between the man who does not approve of this pleasure, and the one who is weak to it.[14]

What is most significant about Veronica's description is the extent to which she can see that Nugent is in some way also a victim; he is conflicted in his sexuality, which his religious conditioning tells him is wrong, and he is incapable of overcoming his pedophile predilection, or weakness, as he would probably view it. Enright engages in a detailed description of what passes between the man and his young victim that spares the reader nothing of its sordidness and depravity. Just as happened in many instances of clerical sexual abuse of children, Nugent's crime was left unpunished because of society's silence or complicity, or its inability to imagine that horrific things like this could actually take place. The upshot of it all is that the hapless victim has no hope of being saved. Veronica thinks about what Liam must have been feeling:

> Now I know the look in Liam's eye was the look of someone who knows they are alone. Because the world will never know what has happened to you, and what you carry around as a result of it. Even your sister—your saviour in a way, the girl who stands in the light of the hall—even she does not hold or remember the thing she saw. Because, by that stage, I think I had forgotten it entirely.[15]

It was the stories that started emerging in the 1990s about what happened to children in the Industrial Schools and Magdalen Laundries, about the numerous instances of boys and girls suffering abuse at the hands of priests, that prompted Veronica to see that Liam was one in a long line of children whose lives were ruined because of what happened to them when they were at their most vulnerable. While pedophilia itself is a frightening concept to come to grips with, when it is carried out by a man or a woman of the cloth it becomes an even greater betrayal of trust. In his memoir of the abuse inflicted on him by Fr. Sean Fortune, a priest in the diocese of Ferns, Colm O'Gorman chronicles the huge difficulties he encountered in getting anyone to believe his story. He made a report to the police on February 9, 1995, about what he had had to endure, but neither the guards nor the Catholic Church authorities did anything significant to investigate his claims. It took a BBC television documentary, *Suing the Pope*, to bring the situation out into the open. O'Gorman notes:

> The problem wasn't simply that no one told about the abuse, but that no one in the Church was prepared to act. No one in authority did anything even when they did know. It's not enough to speak out. Others have to be prepared to acknowledge what they have heard. They have to believe it, no matter how threatening or troubling the facts might be. And, most importantly, they have to be prepared to act.[16]

Veronica's paralysis in the face of Liam's fate is prompted by an inability to comprehend what exactly is happening to him and by her powerlessness to do anything to protect him. It is likely that had she broken her silence about what she witnessed, no one would have believed her. Because theirs was an outwardly religious family, a family where silence was demanded around certain issues. Even Veronica's brother Ernest maintained the pretence that he was still a priest at his mother's deathbed and went so far as to give her a blessing. Veronica describes him as "the lying hypocrite bastard of lapsed-priest atheist," but one wonders if his dissimulation is any worse than her own unbroken silence over many years about what she witnessed between Nugent and Liam.[17]

These few examples are given by way of illustrating the changed climate in the wake of the revelations concerning previously unspoken horrors in Irish society through the medium of novels, plays, memoirs, and the independent reports set in train by various governments. A picture slowly began to emerge which was anything but favourable toward the Catholic Church in Ireland. Undoubtedly, the once-powerful institution was fatally damaged by the clerical sex abuse scandals and the various reports that have made public their findings. In July 2011, a landmark event took place when An Taoiseach Enda Kenny made a biting attack on the Catholic Church in the wake of the publication of the Cloyne Report into clerical sex abuse in that diocese. Kenny is a practicing Catholic and leader of Fine Gael, a centre right party with historically strong links to the Catholic Church. One wonders what his predecessors John A. Costello or Liam Cosgrave, both conservative, devout Catholics, would have made of the following pronouncement on the floor of the Dáil, as the Irish Parliament is called:

> . . . for the first time in Ireland, a report into child sexual abuse exposes an attempt by the Holy See to frustrate an inquiry in a sovereign, democratic republic.
>
> [Ireland is no longer a country] where the swish of a soutane smothered conscience and humanity and the swing of a thurible ruled the Irish Catholic world.
>
> This is the "Republic" of Ireland 2011. A republic of laws, of rights and responsibilities; of proper civic order; where the delinquency and arrogance of a particular version, of a particular kind of "morality," will no longer be tolerated or ignored.[18]

The interesting thing about these comments is that they mark a real break from a past characterized by deference by politicians toward the Catholic hierarchy. Kenny seemed to capture the *Zeitgeist* of the nation, if the public approval of his speech is anything to go by. People found his presentation of the situation accurate, even though there is scant enough evidence that the Holy See actually interfered with the workings of the Cloyne Report, as he claimed was the case. My reading of the public response is that the Irish nation needed to find expression for their pent-up anger at how the Church, and its bishops in particular, failed to accept responsibility for the cruel treatment of children for whom there were supposed to have a duty of care. In his Introduction to a recently published set of essays entitled *Broken Faith: Re-visioning the Church in Ireland*, Patrick Claffey sums up the current perception of Catholicism in Ireland thus: "[T]he public profile of the Church is all but non-existent, except in the most negative terms; and there is a perceptible rise in a sharp anti-clericalism which leaves clergy deeply demoralised and religious bodies more or less muted in public debate. . . ."[19]

The downside of this development is that the poor and the marginalized are losing their most influential advocate, and those wanting to belong to a vibrant Church are too often left disappointed by what they encounter during ceremonies that are often performed by weary priests who feel under siege because of the sordid actions of a few of their number. For Michael Cronin, the diminution of the Church's reputation had led to a fearful, distrustful society with CCTV cameras set up in many locations, more prison sentences being handed out, the emergence of a "garrison state" where people are being closely monitored in case there is a revolt against the surreptitious erosion of public freedom. The prevalence of suicide and self-harm, among young males in particular, is symptomatic of a shift in emphasis away from religion. Instead of being preoccupied by concepts such as sin and grace, the focus now tends to be on self-indulgent hedonism. Because fewer and fewer believe in an afterlife, earthly existence assumes greater prominence and pleasure is raised to almost divine status. In the Christian perspective, death takes precedence over life, which prompts Cronin to observe: "What is implicit in the recognition of the centrality of death in a human experience is the acceptance of human finitude. Taking human finitude seriously means taking human life seriously. It means focusing on ends, not means. It means focusing on what counts, not on what is countable."[20] Rediscovering the original messages of the Christian tradition, in particular what Cronin refers to as "the enduring contribution of hope to human betterment," could, in his estimation, help allay some of the fear that is currently paralysing the Irish psyche.

Louise Fuller, the foremost historian of Irish Catholicism from the second half of the twentieth century to the present, notes how Catholic culture was changing rapidly in the 1970s and 1980s in spite of high levels of religious practice. Young people, she notes, were abandoning Catholicism in large numbers, especially when it came to the moral teaching of the Church, which they found impracticable and out of touch with the reality of their lived experience. The prohibition of contraception and divorce caused many of them to question how they could stay within an institution that outlawed the recourse to two basic human rights. Fuller notes that the Family Planning Act was passed in Ireland just two months before the visit of Pope John Paul II in 1979. It was the first step in what she describes as "the process of dismantling of legislation and constitutional provisions which had underpinned the Catholic ethos in the Republic." There is an argument often put forward, and it is one to which I subscribe, that the Pope's visit was prompted by a realization on the part of Rome that Ireland was slipping into the grip of the same secular forces that dominated continental Europe, especially countries such as France and Germany. The hope was that John Paul's visit would encourage new vocations and stem the tide. However, Fuller concludes that although the 1980s saw the emergence of some influential conservative Catholic groups such as PLAC (Pro-Life Amendment Campaign), the tide had tilted noticeably in the direction of the liberal elements within Irish society. Fuller concludes: "The impressive crowds, who turned out at all the venues that pope John Paul II visited, might have conveyed the impression that nothing much had changed in Ireland—but much had indeed changed."[21]

Another brief example from literature will serve to underline the extent of this change. This time, it can be found in a short story by the Church of Ireland writer, William Trevor. "Justina's Priest" recounts the relationship between the middle-aged Fr. Clohessy and his young parishioner Justina Casey, who takes it into her head that she wants to visit her friend Breda Maguire in Dublin. The problem with this plan is that Breda is suspected of making a living through prostitution, something that Justina, who suffers from a learning disability, is incapable of understanding. In the end, she does not make the trip to Dublin, but Fr. Clohessy realizes that things have changed irreparably in his role within the community. In spite of still maintaining a certain level of respect and affection in the parish, he has become a rather peripheral figure:

> The grandeur might have gone from his church, his congregations dwindling, his influence fallen away to nothing, but there was money where there had been poverty, ambition where there'd been humility. These were liberated people who stood about in ways that generations before them had not. They wore what they wished to wear, they said what they wished to say, they stayed or went away.[22]

Trevor's description captures the marginal role now occupied by many Catholic priests in Ireland. Although they are necessary in times of sorrow and joy, to perform funerals and weddings, to officiate at First Communions or Confirmations, to say Mass and administer the sacraments, they no longer hold sway over the people in the way they would have done perhaps thirty or forty years ago. What I have attempted to do in this chapter is to provide a snapshot of how Irish Catholicism has evolved in the past few decades and how it appears now. The negatives are clear for all to see: falling numbers attending Mass and the sacraments, a crisis in vocations, a clergy that feels weighed down by an increasingly heavy workload and poor morale, a general antagonism toward organized religious belief, probably as a result of growing secularism and enhanced material wealth. Access to education has meant more questioning of their faith by even the most fervent Catholics, and an ability to see the contradiction between the message of love of self and one's neighbor contained in the Gospel and the Church's tendency to preach about laws and obligations. Earlier on, I quoted one of the founding members of the Association of Catholic Priests, Brendan Hoban, on the disenchantment of the diocesan clergy. In his book *Where Do We Go from Here: The Crisis in Irish Catholicism*, Hoban speaks to the findings of a survey carried out for the ACP by Amárach Research and observes: ". . . what Irish Catholics want is compassion and tolerance rather than the defence of absolute positions, local input rather than central control, a people's Church rather than a clerical Church."[23]

When reading through the text of Pope Francis's interview for Jesuit publications which was published in the journal *America* on September 30, 2013, and sent shockwaves through the Catholic world, I was struck by the way in which he identified many of the same issues as were highlighted in the ACP survey. He criticised clericalism and legalism, the neglect of the poor, the excessive pomp and ceremony that occlude rather than illuminate the Word of God. He described the Church as a "field hospital" and emphasised the need to bring healing to those who have been wounded. He continued:

> God is greater than sin. The structural and organizational reforms are secondary—that is, they come afterward. The first reform must be the attitude. The ministers of the Gospel must be people who can warm the hearts of the people, who walk through the dark night with them, who know how to dialogue and to descend themselves into their people's night, into the darkness, but without getting lost.[24]

While he is at a very early stage of his Pontificate, Pope Francis has already managed to transform the perception of the Catholic Church as a monolithic, patriarchal, legalistic institution. With him, we sense that a more person-centered, caring Church is about to emerge from the ashes of the scandal-torn establishment that existed before his election. In Ireland, as elsewhere, he may well be the spark that is needed to attract people back to the loving embrace of a Church that seems to have lost its way.

The highly regarded sociologist Tom Inglis would not underestimate the importance of the home and the Catholic school in creating an environment whereby being spiritual and moral becomes almost second nature to many children, which in turn imbued in them "a Catholic sense of self and way of behaving and interpreting the world." He continues:

> Being Catholic becomes a fundamental part of their social and personal identity—the way they are seen and understood by others and the way they see and understand themselves. This helps explain why, even though many Catholics may no longer practice as regularly as their parents, or adhere to fundamental

> teachings of the Church, they still regard themselves as belonging to an Irish Catholic heritage.[25]

This chimes with the idea the journalist John Waters often makes: In Ireland, although there are Catholics, lapsed Catholics, non-Catholics and anti-Catholics, there is no such thing as an ex-Catholic. Both Inglis and Waters would maintain therefore that even those Catholics who hit out most violently against the negative role that the Church has played, and continues to play in Irish society, still cannot escape fully from the remnants of a Catholic upbringing and education. While this will in all likelihood never lead to large numbers returning to religious services or abiding by Church teaching, it could indicate that the faith of our fathers may not yet be completely a lost legacy.

NOTES

1. Mary Raftery, *Do They Tink We're Eejits? A Selection of the Irish Times columns 2003–2009* (Dublin: The Irish Times, 2013), 156.
2. Cited in Kevin Egan, *Remaining a Catholic after the Murphy Report* (Dublin: The Columba Press, 2011), 39.
3. Ibid.
4. Mark Patrick Hederman, *Underground Cathedrals* (Dublin: The Columba Press, 2010), 10–11.
5. Brendan Hoban, "Disenchanted Evenings—The Mood of Irish Diocesan Clergy," *The Furrow* 64 (November 2013): 604–19.
6. John McGahern, *Love of the World: Essays*, ed. Stanley Van der Ziel, (London: Faber & Faber, 2009), 133.
7. Ibid., 145.
8. Jean Rohou, *Catholiques et Bretons Toujours? Essai sur L'histoire du Christianisme en Bretagne* (Brest : Éditions Dialogue, 2012), 38. All translations from this work are my own.
9. Ibid., 33–34.
10. Ibid., 445.
11. Dennis O'Driscoll, *Stepping Stones: Interviews with Seamus Heaney* (London: Faber & Faber, 2008), 473.
12. Liam Fay, "What's the Story?" *Hotpress*, April 3, 1996, 19.
13. Anne Enright, *The Gathering* (London, Vintage Books, 2007), 227.
14. Ibid., 144.
15. Ibid., 172.
16. Colm O'Gorman, *Beyond Belief* (London: Hodder and Stoughton, 2009), 224–25.
17. Enright, *The Gathering*, 207.
18. "Enda Kenny Speech on Cloyne Report," *RTE News*, July 20, 2001, accessed June 7, 2014, http://www.rte.ie/news/2011/0720/303965-cloyne1/.
19. Patrick Claffey, introduction to *Broken Faith: Re-visioning the Church in Ireland*, eds. Patrick Claffey, Joe Egan, and Marie Keenan (Oxford: Peter Lang, 2013), 18.
20. Michael Cronin, "Fear and Loathing in the Republic: Why Hope Matters," in *Broken Faith*, 120.
21. Louise Fuller, "Identity and Political Fragmentation in Independent Ireland, 1923–83," in *Irish Catholic Identities*, ed Oliver J. Rafferty (Manchester: Manchester University Press, 2013), 316.
22. William Trevor, "Justina's Priest," in *A Bit on the Side* (London: Viking, 2004), 57.
23. Brendan Hoban, *Where Do We Go from Here: The Crisis in Irish Catholicism* (Ballina: Banley House, 2012), 74.

24. "A Big Heart Open to God: The Exclusive Interview with Pope Francis," *America*, September 30, 2013, accessed June 7, 2014, http://americamagazine.org/pope-francis-interview.

25. Tom Inglis, "Catholic Identity in Contemporary Ireland: Belief and Belonging to Tradition," *Journal of Contemporary Religion* 22 (2007): 205.

Chapter Two

In Periculo Mortis

Can Irish Catholicism be Redeemed?

John Littleton

It is no exaggeration to say that the Catholic Church in Ireland is in crisis.[1] Indeed, many commentators suggest that Irish Catholicism is in meltdown and that disaster looms.

This is mostly because, since the 1980s, there have been recurring revelations of horrendous sexual and institutional abuses perpetrated by numerous clergy and religious. These revelations have resulted in a serious loss of moral authority—mainly self-inflicted, in fairness to the critics—by all levels of institutional leadership. They have consolidated the quite understandable demands from many people for the separation of Church and State, especially regarding schools and education provision, in a country where, traditionally, the Catholic Church's influence dominated. The child-abuse scandals have validated the negative opinions of many critics of the Church. This, in turn, has undermined the faith of countless ordinary Catholics, both laity and clergy, who are desperately struggling to make sense of what has happened to their Church.

Secularization is undoubtedly another notable factor in the general decline of religious practice and denominational affiliation in Ireland. Catholicism, the faith tradition of the majority of Ireland's population, has been severely affected by this trend. Ireland is becoming a more secular nation, with widespread calls for the total separation of Church and State coming from many sectors in society. The description of Ireland as the Land of Saints and Scholars has, by now, been relegated to the realm of nostalgia.

What, therefore, is the future for Irish Catholicism?[2] How can its credibility be restored and how might the Catholic Church in Ireland move forward? Not surprisingly, it is impossible to predict the future with accuracy, especially when people are seeking credible answers to increasingly complex and worrying questions. The reality is that it is not possible to be absolutely certain about the future. All that can be said with confidence is that the present has been shaped by the past. Similarly, the here-and-now is laying the foundations for what the future will bring. Therefore, the future of Irish Catholicism depends essentially on how it deals with the range of challenges currently confronting it.

IN PERICULO MORTIS

Soon after I was ordained a priest, I routinely began to record entries in baptismal registers, where I occasionally saw references to children who, some or many years earlier, had been baptized *in periculo mortis* ("in danger of death"). The phrase *in periculo mortis* was used to denote that an emergency baptism had occurred immediately or very shortly after a baby's birth because that infant was in imminent danger of death. Often, the child simultaneously received the sacrament of confirmation and, perhaps, what was then referred to as the Last Rites (that is, the sacrament of the anointing of the sick).

I often wondered what the outcome was for those new-born infants who were perilously close to death. Did they die—as was feared—or did they recover? Needless to say, in most instances I never discovered what happened. But in several cases, I actually met teenage and adult parishioners who, as babies, had been baptized *in periculo mortis* and who, thankfully, had recovered fully from the dangerous threat to life at the time of their birth. I contend that the phrase *in periculo mortis* (in danger of death) is applicable to Irish Catholicism at this time. It remains to be seen whether it will recover and, if it does, to what extent.

FROM PRESENT TO FUTURE

This chapter discusses several of the options for change and renewal that are necessary if Catholicism is to regain its credibility and remain relevant in contemporary Irish society. Central among them is a new approach to leadership that emphasizes repentance, accountability, and transparency. But this new style of leadership also needs to be sufficiently humble to acknowledge that the teaching Church (*Ecclesia docens*) is also the learning Church (*Ecclesia discens*): a Church that is capable of dialogue with diverse theological opinions.

In addition, the vision of the Second Vatican Council (1962–1965), especially with regards to the role of an educated and articulate laity, needs to be properly implemented.[3] Concerns about democracy (including the desire for greater consultation at all levels), ordained priesthood, the role of women, clericalism, liturgical celebration, the Church's engagement with the media, and racial and religious pluralism need to be addressed honestly and respectfully. Assimilation of the worldwide impact of the "Francis factor" is needed too.[4] Otherwise, the future of Irish Catholicism, which is already in grave danger, is bleak. In summary, the redemption, so to speak, of Irish Catholicism—at least in terms of the institution and the tradition—is indeed possible but not assured. It can be saved, although this is not to suggest, in a Pelagian sense, that it can save itself.[5]

In order to be saved from danger of death, Irish Catholicism must respond constructively to the following challenges:

1. Flourish in a post-Catholic milieu
2. Exist confidently within the separation of Church and State
3. Eradicate the difficulties caused by clericalism
4. Tackle the "vocations crisis" and work effectively with fewer priests
5. Empower an educated and articulate laity
6. Communicate an attractive and appealing faith to young people
7. Dialogue transparently with the news media
8. Organize a national assembly of the Church in Ireland

CHALLENGE 1: FLOURISH IN A POST-CATHOLIC MILIEU

Ireland is now a post-Catholic country. This means that it is no longer a Catholic country as was traditionally understood, where the Catholic Church and its controlling influence had been dominant in Irish society for centuries. Therefore, being Irish and being Catholic cannot be assumed to be synonymous, as in previous generations.

An obvious indication that Ireland is post-Catholic is that the Catholic Church is increasingly irrelevant for many people, and the authority of Catholicism has been dislodged by the loss of a sense of Catholic identity.[6] As already indicated, this is due in no small way to factors such as the growing worldwide influence of secularism and, undoubtedly, the massive damage done to the moral authority of the Church by the various abuse scandals. This has often led to people rejecting the Church, and even despising its beliefs and teachings, because they have experienced its culture and practices as being corrupt and lacking transparency—while the institution has protected itself at all costs.

The effects of the Celtic Tiger, and of its fatal demise, have also impacted on the place of religion in general and Catholicism in particular.[7] There is a common perception among many people that there is no need for God, simply because human beings are so sophisticated that they assume they are invincible. Consequently, they think that it is possible to survive and prosper without dependence on God or even reference to God. The attitude of many people can be summarized by the sentiment: "What good is God to us now, anyway? He's not going to get us out of this mess! We can manage things ourselves." However, it must be acknowledged that, while this comment is generally true of many people, there are notable exceptions where some people, with a renewed awareness of the vulnerability of human beings, are turning toward God in prayer once more—but almost as "lost souls."

Another dimension to this post-Catholic Ireland is the ever-evolving pluralist society characterized by multiculturalism and different religious traditions. For example, there is a growing Islamic population. Likewise, there is an emerging interest in the less structured and more evangelical expressions of Christianity, which are often quite attractive to young people and to disillusioned older Catholics.

There is arguably an anti-Catholic bias among much of the news media, which is not usually counterbalanced by articulate and media-savvy Catholic spokespersons.[8] Although much criticism of the Church is justified, some of the harshest criticism is often emotive and results in confusion, dismay, and even apathy among the general public. At the same time, those who critique the institutional/hierarchical Church out of a sense of love and loyalty are usually treated with scorn and ridicule by Church authorities. Unfortunately, they are largely ignored by Church leadership in Ireland while being disciplined and censured by Rome—which is indeed ironic!

This, then, is the context in which Catholicism finds itself in contemporary Ireland. As a result, Church leadership is perceived to be "on the defensive" much of the time and is confronted by a noticeable decline in the practice of the faith, particularly in urban and socially disadvantaged areas.

Of course, there are still many "cultural Catholics" in Ireland. These are people who identify with at least some Catholic doctrines and practices but who are not actively practicing Catholics. On a superficial level, this could give the impression that the situation is not as bad as it seems. But apart from important sacramental and ritualistic occasions (that is, baptism, first Holy Communion, confirmation, marriage and death) the reality is immediately obvious. Without wishing to be judgmental, or insensitive toward some of the devotional practices of many Irish Catholics, I periodically wonder about the significance of the huge numbers of people attending, for example, the Fiftieth International Eucharistic Congress in Dublin (2012), the annual Croagh Patrick climb in July (which has approximately 20,000 pilgrims), and the annual novenas (popularly known as festivals of faith) led by the Redemptorists in various locations around the country.[9] Similarly, the visit of the relics of Saint Thérèse of Lisieux to Ireland (2001) drew massive crowds of people to venerate her relics. But the numbers attending such events and gatherings seem artificially high because when other barometers of religious fervor are monitored—for example, pilgrimages to Lough Derg and to Knock, not to mention Sunday Mass attendance—a different reality is evident.

Simply put, this means that the rules of engagement have changed. The Church cannot assume that its message will be readily heard from Sunday to Sunday and its teaching welcomed and accepted without question. In these circumstances, there is nothing to be gained from wallowing in self-pity and claiming, for instance, that "the media is out to get us." This has all too often been the case, instead of acknowledging that the news media have a crucial job to do and that the institutional Church should be willing to engage with it. Thus, the present reality of a post-Catholic Ireland is a significant challenge to the future of Irish Catholicism.

The Catholic Church in Ireland needs to recognize and accept that it is but one voice among many—although this is not to suggest that it is merely another lobby group. If its voice is to be heard, it must be articulate, cogent, authentic, and have a worthwhile message. This means collaborating more with the other Christian traditions that have a broadly similar outlook, in the hope that a coherent Christian viewpoint is communicated during important public debates and discussions. In turn, this would involve the Catholic Church placing genuine ecumenical relations higher on its agenda—so often Christian unity is essentially armchair and tea-party ecumenism, confined to the annual week of prayer for Christian unity (18–25 January each year). In addition to these steps, the Church needs to work more effectively in interreligious dialogue, especially with Islam.

CHALLENGE 2: EXIST CONFIDENTLY WITHIN THE SEPARATION OF CHURCH AND STATE

The undefined "special position" afforded to the Catholic Church in the 1937 *Bunreacht na hÉireann*, the Constitution of Ireland, which enshrined some of the Church's moral and social teachings, was removed after a referendum to amend the Constitution in 1972. Since then, there have been repeated calls for the complete separation of Church and State.

Probably the most controversial example of this is to be found in education provision. Historically, education in Ireland, especially at primary level, has been denominational, with Catholic schools still comprising approximately 90 percent of all schools. Yet, substantial amounts of their funding are provided by the State. In an era of escalating pluralism and secularization, there is a strong and vociferous campaign for the Catholic Church to divest its so-called "patronage" of schools. Many interdenominational and nondenominational schools are now being opened. This has implications for the faith formation of Catholic students. There is also an ongoing debate about introducing "value-free" education in schools (of course, the question needs to be asked: where can there be a genuinely "value-free" approach to education provision—even in a pluralist society?).

In addition to education, there is the whole area of law and legislation, particularly with reference to the availability of abortion, and same-sex marriage and the consequent "right" to adopt children. All these concerns are now coming to the fore. Initially, they seem perfectly reasonable, being presented as situations where there needs to be a balancing of "rights" because all human rights are valid and must be respected. But there is a need for "Catholic voices" to be heard too. That is why Catholicism needs to be in the public square, presenting an equally reasonable and even more convincing contribution to the ongoing and often contentious debates.[10] For example, what about the Christian anthropology presented in the Second Vatican Council's *Gaudium et Spes*?[11] Authentic and credible Catholic voices are urgently needed to ensure that the Catholic position is not simply—and inaccurately—perceived and judged as "battening down the hatches" without any rationale.

For generations, the Catholic Church in Ireland relied on society in general to be an important vehicle for passing on the faith. However, this can no longer be taken for granted—nor should it ever have been. The Church now needs to learn how to exist comfortably and confidently within the separation of Church and State.

CHALLENGE 3: ERADICATE THE DIFFICULTIES CAUSED BY CLERICALISM

Clericalism is not easily defined, because of its insidious and ingrained nature. It is a cultural trait, an attitude, which enables clergy to exercise a domineering role within Church structures. As such, clericalism is a form of institutionalism. It is fundamentally about power—the wielding of power over others—and is frequently, but not always, exercised unintentionally. Clericalism often manifests itself as arrogance, superiority, and condescension. It is patronizing, and it contributes to the corruption and "structural sin" that is from time to time present in the heart of the Church.[12] It disenfranchises and inhibits lay people, effectively making them second-class members of the Church.

Ironically, in my experience, most priests today shun clericalism. Yet it is ever-present to some extent. There is plenty of anecdotal evidence available from lay people about how they have experienced clericalism from clergy. But clericalism also resonates from the laity. This form of clericalism is best caricatured by the phrase "Father knows best!" which expresses the obsequiousness often shown by some lay people toward their clergy. George B. Wilson expressed this succinctly:

> It would be a fatal mistake to view a view a clerical culture as being generated only by its clergy. Like any other cultures it is the product of everyone affected by it—or implicated in—its continuance. That includes equally those who are seen as laypeople vis-à-vis a particular body of clergy. Cultures are generated by the behavioral interactions *between* a particular clergy and its corresponding laity. The generation and continuance of a culture is a matter of relationships, a single reality mutually created by both sets of participants.[13]

Two personal stories may help to illustrate this. The first relates to my role as a substitute for other clergy at weekends when I visit the parishes where they minister. I always park my car on the street or roadside beside the parishioners' cars before walking into the church grounds. Invariably, people say to me as I walk alongside them toward the entrance to their church, "Why didn't you drive your car up beside the sacristy?" I reply, "Because none of the parishioners do it." Then they say, "But the priest always does that here." And I say to them, "I thought the Church was supposed to be egalitarian!" However, more often than not, they miss the point that I am making.

he second relates to my arrival, some years ago, as the newly appointed priest in several different parishes. When I arrived, I noticed that there was very little or no involvement of lay people in the various liturgical celebrations and parish structures. There were no readers, no cantors, no extraordinary ministers of the Eucharist, no ministers of hospitality—although, usually, there was a sacristan and a choir, and there were altar servers and collectors. Likewise, there was no parish pastoral council. When I began to encourage congregational singing and asked people to read the word of God during the celebration of Mass and lead the prayer of the faithful (that is, the general intercessions), when I encouraged them to participate in liturgical processions and to become members of the pastoral council, they often reacted negatively, at least initially, saying that the previous priest did not permit these roles. Sometimes they accused me of trying to upset the parish by changing "the way things have been done." This is a classic case of the priest inviting lay people to become more involved in parish life by exercising their baptismal dignity, and those people rejecting the opportunities being offered them. This is also clericalism—but in this case it originates with the laity.

The only way to eliminate clericalism is to go "back to basics," the basics of the Gospel, that includes a renewed understanding of and appreciation for the dignity of all the baptized who are made in God's image and likeness, and who have become brothers and sisters in and through Jesus Christ. Throughout this process, lay people need to become more assertive and claim their baptismal dignity and rights.

A few comments about the appointments of bishops are appropriate here, because the effects of clericalism are quite evident in episcopal appointments. There needs to be much wider consultation about the appointments of bishops, what might be termed a more collegial approach. The centralized approach that currently predominates is too introspective. In contrast, the collegial approach is, by its very nature, outward-looking—with an interest in the specific needs of the local diocese as well as satisfying the centralized authority. Though it is much more risky than the current methods of selection, the rewards could include the identification of candidates who understand more fully the struggles of Catholic individuals, families, and parishes. Throughout such a process, it might be helpful if Catholic leadership remember that the greatest risk-taker of all is God, who, at the Incarnation, sent his Son into the world to save human beings from the consequences of sin. Surely, the Church needs to imitate God's innovation in the appointment of its bishops—for the enhancement of all of God's people.[14]

CHALLENGE 4: TACKLE THE "VOCATIONS CRISIS" AND WORK EFFECTIVELY WITH FEWER PRIESTS

In 1984, there were 171 ordinations; those numbers were reduced to twenty-two in 2006. Most of the seminaries around the country have closed. The average age of priests is sixty-five years and, due to fewer numbers, there is an ever increasing workload for those in active ministry. Recently, headlines in some of the national newspapers have suggested that, within a short time, there will not be sufficient priests to officiate at the burial services of the deceased. This is because where, in the past, there was more than one priest in most parishes, there is now usually one. In addition to the extra work that such situations generate for individual priests, it must be acknowledged that they also present parishioners with a limited choice when seeking a priest who suits their circumstances and temperaments.

A variety of solutions to the shortage of priests are being implemented. In many dioceses, there is the "clustering" of parishes into groups with one or two priests servicing the needs of each parish from a central location within the cluster. One of the consequences of this, though, is that an increasing number of parishes do not have a resident priest. Additionally, there have been closures of churches and reductions in the numbers of Masses being celebrated. This inevitably causes disappointment among parishioners. It also results in reduced financial contributions because some parishioners may choose to go to a neighboring parish that has Mass at a more convenient time.

A more recent solution to the shortage of priests is the introduction of the permanent diaconate in several dioceses. However, deacons are not priests and, although they can preach, they cannot preside at the celebration of Mass or hear confessions. This means that the priest still needs to be available whenever the celebration of Mass is needed. Consequently, many priests are rather cynical about the introduction of permanent deacons as a genuine solution to the wider shortage. Therefore, it seems that catechesis of both priests and laity is necessary.[15]

Personally, I am not convinced about the sense of pessimism that usually accompanies discussions about the vocations crisis. I have suggested elsewhere that "the real crisis is arguably a crisis of ideas rather than a crisis in vocations."[16] For example, much of priests' time is often taken up with non-priestly activities such as routine administration, fund-raising, and committee work, and little effort has been made to reorganize parish structures.

Another thought for consideration is that perhaps parishes should no longer be defined as geographical areas. After all, many people go to a Mass that suits them—it may be that the time is more convenience than at the local parish, or they like the preaching or the music. Some innovative thinking by all those concerned with the vocations crisis might well lead to better and more effective pastoral co-ordination.[17]

CHALLENGE 5: EMPOWER AN EDUCATED AND ARTICULATE LAITY

In most respects, the future of Irish Catholicism depends on having a well-educated and articulate laity. This is not only because of the shortage of priests, but because of the dignity of all the baptized. Many commentators say that it is quite amazing that lay men and women have remained committed to the Church despite the clergy. For so long, members of the laity in Ireland did not have the possibility of studying their faith at a serious level. Consequently, they depended very much on the clergy to inform them about the Church's teaching and its application to daily living. Apart from teachers, the clergy were the only people trained to teach the faith. This was especially true in rural Ireland. Once people had finished school education, the only opportunity for most Catholics to develop their knowledge of the faith was through Sunday sermons.

In the past, Irish lay people were not involved in the Church's thinking and administration. Their role was to receive what was handed down to them. Because of this role, a perception even developed that the Church consisted solely of the clergy (pope, bishops, priests, and deacons) and that lay people were the passive onlookers and receptors. Some cynics even remarked that the purpose of the laity was "to pray up, pay up and shut up!"

Since the connection between going to church on Sundays and living a Christian life during the week was not always adequately emphasized, it was easy to compartmentalize different areas of one's life. The practice of the faith in Ireland was mostly confined to church-going, where people said their prayers and engaged in devotional practices. Over the second half of the twentieth century, however, attitudes changed. Today, many people are no longer interested in religion. Irish society has become increasingly secularized. The decline in the number of people attending church services and worship has been dramatic. Many people dismiss the Church and organized religion as irrelevant. The existence of God is constantly questioned, especially because there is so much suffering and misery around the world. Some go so far as to say that religion is dead, and God (if God ever existed) is dead too.

However, this is not the complete story. Nowadays, there are also many Irish people who appreciate the relevance—indeed the necessity—of linking belief in God with their religious practice and with all areas of their lives. Numerous people, conscious of their baptismal dignity, are again being motivated to think seriously about God and their faith. Moreover, a growing number of people are becoming committed members of their parish communities, particularly in those dioceses throughout the country that have developed pastoral plans for parish renewal, and they actively seek involvement in parish activities.

For them, participation in the Church's life and ministry is indeed worthwhile. They recognize that the Church to which they belong is "their" Church as well as God's Church, and that they are as important and as needed as the clergy. But many who seek to express their faith in this way do so in the midst of the pressures of a very busy world. And yet, the deeper questions about life—questions regarding the meaning and purpose of life—remain embedded in Irish people's minds and hearts.

Committed Catholics, if they are to contribute meaningfully to the Church's mission, need opportunities to learn more about Christ, the Gospel, and the Church's teaching. This is the basis for the rationale for providing lay people with serious opportunities to explore their faith. There are many instances of serious attempts to provide theological and ministerial formation for the laity. But these have varying levels of success. Nonetheless, proper collaboration between laity and clergy is required more and more.

CHALLENGE 6: COMMUNICATE AN ATTRACTIVE AND APPEALING FAITH TO YOUNG PEOPLE

People's hopes and dreams, and their unrealized aspirations, live on in those who come after them. This is one of the reasons that the Catholic Church needs to pay particular attention to the handing on of the faith to young people. Recalling an earlier comment in this essay, the Catholic Church in Ireland can no longer presume that the faith will be transmitted to the next generation through the school system. In the past that assumption held simply because the numbers of available clergy and the work of religious orders made it seem reasonable. But, in reality, the assumption always tended to exonerate parents from the responsibility to be, as the Rite of Baptism points out, "the first teachers of their children in the ways of faith [and also] the best of teachers, bearing witness to the faith by what they say and do, in Christ Jesus our Lord."[18] I believe that the ideals of the newer Irish catechetical programs for children, which call for a three-way partnership between home (parents), school (teachers), and parish (clergy), have not been satisfactorily realized. This is mainly because, increasingly, many younger parents have given up practicing their faith—it has no value for them anymore. How, then, can they be expected to pass on the faith that they do not possess?

But there is also confusion among those parents who are committed to Catholicism and practicing their faith. They are usually uncomfortable talking about their faith, and they do not always recognize what they could do as a family. For example, several years ago, I met a parishioner in the supermarket. She mentioned that I had not been to the school recently to hear the children's confessions and wondered when I planned to visit the school for the confessions. When I asked her why she and her children did not avail of confession that was readily available on Saturday evenings when they came to the church for Mass, she said that it had never occurred to her. This is an instance of a committed and caring mother abdicating her parental responsibility to be directly involved in the faith development of her children. For generations, Irish parents could presume that the faith formation of their children was being taken care of in school.

Another instance of such neglect of responsibility is often evident in Catholic secondary schools. In many of these the chaplains and the religious education teachers usually organize penitential services and class Masses at various times during the school year. While that is commendable, it also means that parents do not have to remind their teenage children to go to confession or Mass—because it is organized by the school. Then, when the teenagers complete their secondary education and go to university or begin work, often away from home, they may cease going to confession and/or Mass simply because no one else organized them, as was done during secondary school. This is how young adults easily develop the habit of not practicing their faith.

Thus, there is a serious challenge facing Irish Catholicism in dealing with the faith development of young people. The Church needs to investigate continually new ideas and strategies that present the Catholic faith, not only as attractive and appealing, but also as meaningful and worthy of effort.

CHALLENGE 7: DIALOGUE WITH THE NEWS MEDIA

The relationship between the Church and the news media in Ireland has, even at the best of times, been somewhat turbulent.[19] There is a major lack of trust and openness between them. The hierarchical Church seems to be always on the run from the media—the Church is seen as being reactive ("always on the back foot," as the saying goes), never responsive. It has to be remembered, too, that media organizations are in the business of getting "scoops" and driving the news agenda. Nevertheless, it has to be acknowledged that the news media have done a great service to truth, accountability, and transparency in Ireland and, in particular, in Irish Catholicism.

I spent six years (2001–2007) working with the National Conference of Priests of Ireland (NCPI), an organization that represented priests and their concerns. During that time, I had frequent dealings with the news media. Amazingly, some journalists used to tell me that trying to get an interview with the Catholic Communications Office was extremely difficult, like trying to "break into Fort Knox," as one reporter said.

During those years I always believed (and still do) that the Catholic Church has no reason to fear the media if the Church is honest, accountable, and transparent in its dealings. Engaging in dialogue with journalists during an era that is dominated by the sound bite, the Church needs to become more professional, competent, and confident. It makes sense to be proactive instead of reactive. By being proactive, Irish Catholicism could begin to exercise some control over how news stories develop.

CHALLENGE 8: ORGANIZE A NATIONAL ASSEMBLY OF THE CHURCH IN IRELAND

It seems to me that this challenge incorporates all of the challenges already discussed. Many religious affairs commentators and most thinking people in Ireland are currently advocating some kind of national forum for discussion in the Church.[20] I recall that, when I worked with the NCPI, I and others advocated that such an assembly become part of that organization's official policy. But during six years, the NCPI never succeeded in persuading the Irish Episcopal Conference to support the idea and become involved. The Bishops' Conference was too cautious; it seemed to be afraid that it would not be able to control such an event. However, dialogue between all the stakeholders in the Irish Church must eventually happen, and the stakeholders need to include those from other faith traditions and those who hold no faith at all. I suspect that the initial stages in organizing and implementing a national conversation could be quite acrimonious—and certainly scary for

Church leadership. But a key responsibility of leadership, in any sphere, is surely to listen, even if parts of the message are unpleasant.

There are currently several other campaigns to organize a national conversation about the future of the Irish Church. But without the bishops (who are the leaders of the Church, regardless of how some critics may feel about that reality), any conversation will be less than complete. I think that great leadership would be shown by the leaders of Catholicism in Ireland if they took the risk.

ADDITIONAL CHALLENGES

There are two further important challenges facing Irish Catholicism. One is the restoration of the Church's credibility in the aftermath of the appalling child-abuse scandals.[21] The other is the need for serious intellectual debate about theology in general and Catholicism in particular in Ireland.[22] These challenges are not discussed in this chapter, because they would need longer consideration than is possible here. However, it is appropriate, for the record, to state that, regarding the protection of children and vulnerable people, the Catholic Church in Ireland is now one of the safest places because of the implementation of carefully monitored guidelines and policies.

THE FRANCIS FACTOR AND THE FUTURE OF IRISH CATHOLICISM

Pope Francis is unquestionably a great sign of hope for the universal Church, and the Catholic Church in Ireland can learn from his leadership style. The primary characteristics associated with him include humility, mercy, conversion of heart, and simplicity. He unashamedly urges all Catholics to internalize the message of the Gospel.

Amid the positive impact that Pope Francis's words and actions are having on how the Catholic Church worldwide is perceived—and significantly by many people who have no allegiance to Catholicism or the Gospel—some critics are suggesting that the new pope's departure from the customs of his predecessors reflects merely differences in style but not substance because, to date, he has not changed or abandoned any of the Church's central teachings.

In response to those criticisms, it is helpful to recall the Catholic understanding of the sacraments: a sacrament is a sign that brings about what it symbolizes. That is why the sacraments are described as effective signs. That means that they bring about what they signify; they are spiritually transforming. Thus the simple realities of bread and wine, water, oil, the spoken word and various human gestures, when used in the Church's sacred rituals, facilitate people in personally meeting the risen Lord Jesus and in being transformed by these encounters.

Similarly, the compassionate, non-judgmental preaching of Pope Francis, and his many caring gestures—such as phoning some of the people who write to him about their worries, and embracing disfigured people during his public audiences—ensure that, as these people experience the Pope's radical imitation of Christ, they are transformed by their encounters with the Vicar of Christ on earth. In this way, the reassuring words and simple gestures of Francis bring about what they signify: God's merciful and unending love. So, regarding Pope Francis, it is not only about style instead of substance; it is about being transformed by encountering the risen Lord Jesus in simplicity and humility.

Another indication that the actions of Pope Francis reflect much more than mere differences in style from those of his predecessors is to be found in the teaching of Saint Thérèse of Lisieux about doing the ordinary things of life with extraordinary love. According to this teaching, the smallest act done with love is more important that the greatest act done for personal glory. The lesson of this is evident in the actions and gestures of Pope Francis, which, although ordinary and simple, are done extraordinarily well.

Many Irish Catholics look forward to Pope Francis introducing much needed change in the Church that, in their opinion, will lead it into the twenty-first century and thus into line with the popular approaches to equality, individual freedom, and human rights in contemporary society. Not surprisingly, their concerns relate mainly to the controversial topics of the ordination of women, married priests, same-sex marriage, reception of the sacraments by divorced and remarried people, and contraception.

A common presumption—but one that is not as straightforward as it sounds—is that Pope Francis who, as pope, has supreme authority in the Church, could, if he wished, unilaterally depart from two millennia of the Church's lived faith experience (that is, its tradition) and the crucial development of doctrine—without any reference to his brother bishops and the teaching of the ecumenical councils throughout the Christian centuries. Indeed, the most recent of those councils, the Second Vatican Council, considered carefully the concept of "collegiality," which describes how the responsibility for the entire Church is shared by the bishops around the world in communion with one another and with the Pope who is the head of the College of Bishops. The primary place for the exercise of collegiality is an ecumenical council, but collegiality is also exercised to some extent through synods of bishops and national bishops' conferences.

As Pope Francis, the Bishop of Rome, has stated repeatedly, he is implementing the teaching of Vatican II. Therefore, he will not—indeed, he cannot—unilaterally change central tenets of Catholic doctrine because to do so would be to contradict his commitment to the principle of collegiality or shared responsibility. Even so, he is listening attentively to what people are saying.

These, then, are some of the reasons why I believe that Pope Francis gives a renewed sense of hope to everyone in the Church—and to Irish Catholicism as it sails through choppy waters into the future.

CONCLUDING REMARKS

In conclusion, let me remain with the image of sailing through choppy waters. Each of the synoptic gospels contains the story about Jesus calming the storm on the Sea of Galilee while in a boat with his disciples.[23] During the storm, the disciples were afraid and not sure what to do. So they woke Jesus from sleep and appealed to him to save them. He calmed the raging storm and restored peace and tranquility.

The image of the boat is often used as a metaphor for the Church. We must never forget that Jesus is in charge of the Church—he is its Head—just as he proved that he was in charge of the boat on the Sea of Galilee. Sometimes Jesus is the only one who can restore harmony in a troubled situation. Of course, he expects us to cooperate with him. But a mistake that our Church leaders inevitably make is that they think that they must shoulder the burden alone. Instead, they need to do all that they can to guide and lead the Church through its various trials and tribulations. But they need to rely on the powerful presence of Jesus too, because he is in charge. And his presence is found in many places, including the voices and commitments of the laity.

In discussing the future of Irish Catholicism, one could adopt a business stance. The answer to the question "Is Irish Catholicism viable?" is undeniably "Yes." But the answer to the question "Is Irish Catholicism feasible?" is "No, unless it changes its approach." Changing its approach does not require that central beliefs and doctrines be jettisoned, but it does require responding with a true humility and greater pastoral sensitivity to the various challenges discussed in this essay.

So can Irish Catholicism be redeemed? Yes, but, as stated at the beginning of this chapter, it cannot redeem itself. It needs the enthusiastic efforts of all its members combined in faith with the grace of God. That is why there is need for renewal in the Irish Church. A key component of that renewal is to trust totally the words of Jesus: "For where two or three are gathered in my name, there am I in the midst of them" (Mt 18:20) and "I am with you always, to the close of the age" (Mt 28:20). Believing these to be true, we can, in the words of Saint Paul, confidently say: "If God is with us, who is against us?" (Rom 8:31).

This is the fundamental reality that is Catholicism within Irish society. It seems to me that Catholicism should always be struggling, because it is never possible for it to be comfortable if it takes seriously its mission to proclaim the Gospel authentically. In a real sense, then, Irish Catholicism should always be *in periculo* mortis—in danger of death—so that resurrection is never far away.

NOTES

1. This crisis is well documented. See, for example, Eamonn Conway and Colm Kilcoyne, eds., *The Splintered Heart: Conversations with a Church in Crisis* (Dublin: Veritas Publications, 1998); Brendan Hoban, *Change or Decay: Irish Catholicism in Crisis* (Kilglass: Banley House, 2005); and Brendan Hoban, *Where Do We Go from Here? The Crisis in Irish Catholicism* (Dublin: Banley House, 2012).

2. For detailed discussions about the future of Irish Catholicism, see Niall Coll and Paschal Scallon, eds., *A Church with a Future: Challenges to Irish Catholicism Today* (Dublin: The Columba Press, 2005); and Niall Coll, "Irish Identity and the Future of Catholicism," in *Irish Catholic Identities*, ed. Oliver P. Rafferty (Manchester: Manchester University Press, 2013), 362–76.

3. Much of the criticism of the Second Vatican Council is misplaced because many current dysfunctional liturgical and other practices attributed to the Council are distortions and aberrations of the renewal it espoused.

4. This is sometimes described as the "Francis effect." For an appraisal of Pope Francis's first year in office, see John Littleton and Eamon Maher, eds, *The Francis Factor: A New Departure* (Dublin: The Columba Press, 2014).

5. Pelagianism is a heresy concerning grace that was begun by the teaching of Pelagius, a fourth century monk, who claimed that human beings can attain salvation through their own efforts.

6. For a thorough discussion of Catholic identity, see John Littleton, "Catholic Identity in the Irish Context," in *Irish and Catholic? Towards an Understanding of Identity*, ed. Louise Fuller, John Littleton, and Eamon Maher (Dublin: The Columba Press, 2006), 12–30.

7. The term Celtic Tiger refers to the rapid growth in the Irish economy between 1995 and 2000. However, this growth underwent a dramatic reversal in 2008.

8. There is, however, an independent organization, Catholic Comment, recently established by a group of mainly lay Catholics. It is not an official Church organization, but provides comment on topical issues from a Catholic perspective. See their website at www.catholiccomment.ie.

9. I have occasionally met people at the large annual novenas who, when chatting, would say, "I don't ever go to Mass on Sundays, but I would never miss a day of the novena!" It is as if there is an element of superstition at work in their thought processes. This in not to suggest, of course, that all novena attendees think like that.

10. For example, Gerry O'Hanlon, *Theology in the Irish Public Square* (Dublin: The Columba Press, 2010).

11. *Gaudium et spes, Pastoral Constitution on the Church in the Modern World, promulgated by Pope Paul VI December 7, 1965*, par. 4, The Holy See, accessed July 31, 2014, http://www.vatican.va/archive/hist_councils/ii_vatican_council/documents/vat-ii_const_19651207_-gaudium-et-spes_en.html.

12. The term "structural sin" refers to the idea that there exists a larger, social dimension of sin beyond individual wrongdoing. Thus we can have corporate responsibility for sinful actions originating from social systems.

13. George B. Wilson, *Clericalism: The Death of Priesthood* (Collegeville: The Liturgical Press, 2008), 7.

14. That being said, it is worth noting that, during 2013 and 2014, several bishops have been appointed to Irish dioceses, and there is every hope that there is a new style of leadership emerging in the Irish Church. Time will tell.

15. Lay people often do not always appreciate that priests need to be catechized too!

16. John Littleton, "Being a Catholic in Ireland Today," in *Contemporary Catholicism in Ireland: A Critical Appraisal*, ed. John Littleton and Eamon Maher (Dublin: The Columba Press, 2008), 21. Also, for some provocative thoughts on the shortage of priests, see Brendan Hoban, *Who Will Break the Bread for Us? Disappearing Priests* (Dublin: Banley House, 2013).

17. See Tony Flannery, *The Death of Religious Life* (Dublin: The Columba Press, 1995) for an interesting account of one priest's experience of the decline of religious life. A related issue that merits comment is the so-called "death" of religious life, the almost total disappearance of religious communities of religious brothers or sisters. I often think that the presence of religious orders—and their ministries—was defined and understood by their functions instead of their witness. Both, of course, are related—but not always in people's perceptions.

18. Extract from the blessing for the parents at the end of the baptism ceremony. See Sacred Congregation for Divine Worship, *The Rite of Baptism for Children* (London: Geoffrey Chapman, 1970).

19. Eamonn Conway and Colm Kilcoyne, eds., *Twin Pulpits: Church and Media in Modern Ireland* (Dublin: Veritas Publications, 1997).

20. Gerry O'Hanlon, *A New Vision for the Catholic Church: A View from Ireland* (Dublin: The Columba Press, 2011), 107–14.

21. For wide-ranging discussions on the child-abuse scandals, see Andrew Auge, Louise Fuller, John Littleton, and Eamon Maher, "After the Ryan and Murphy Reports: A Roundtable on the Irish Catholic Church," *New Hibernia Review* 14 (2010): 59–77; Patrick Claffey, Joe Egan, and Marie Keenan, eds., *Broken Faith: Why Hope Matters* (Oxford: Peter Lang, 2013); Kevin Egan, *Remaining a Catholic After the Murphy Report* (Dublin: The Columba Press, 2011); Tony Flannery, ed., *Responding to the Ryan Report* (Dublin: The Columba Press, 2009); Brian Lennon, *Can I Stay in the Catholic Church?* (Dublin: The Columba Press, 2012); and John Littleton and Eamon Maher, eds, *The Dublin/Murphy Report: A Watershed for Irish Catholicism?* (Dublin: The Columba Press, 2010).

22. For a comprehensive discussion about the need for cultural and intellectual renewal if the Catholic Church in Ireland is to engage meaningfully with the challenges confronting it, see D. Vincent Twomey, *The End of Irish Catholicism?* (Dublin: Veritas Publications, 2003).

23. Mt 8:23–27, Mk 4:35–41, and Lk 8:22–25.

Chapter Three

Holy Unpredictable

A Response to Maher and Littleton

James Silas Rogers

I want to thank Dr. Maher and Father Littleton for opening two extraordinary windows on the current condition of the Catholic Church in Ireland. I've been asked to respond. To follow two of the most astute and respected commentators on the Church in Ireland, who know the Irish religious scene right down to the ground, is daunting at the outset. Further, I am speaking as an American outsider; I would like to think as an informed non-specialist, but by no means as an expert. Nevertheless, I might offer some additional areas for us to reflect on as we try to get a handle on the full extent of the Catholic moment today.

Both writers used the word "crisis," Fr. Littleton in his first sentence, and Dr. Maher in his conclusion. Perhaps crisis is the new norm, no longer worth remarking on. With differing stresses, each has presented a more-than-a-little dire portrait of the present state of Irish Catholicism. Each has, and I believe with absolute accuracy, made clear that the watershed events in the turning of Irish public opinion vis-a-vis the Church have been the abuse scandals, coupled with the fabulously inappropriate, self-protective, and inept response of the hierarchy. In the 2010 roundtable article "After Murphy and Ryan Reports," Fr. Littleton is a little more hesitant to say that any specific event caused a decisive turning; there, he wrote that "there have been many tipping points and their cumulative effect has been detrimental to the church's credibility."[1] It is probably the word "cumulative" that best sums up the effects of scandal.

Though here, too, we are not looking at a bolt from the blue. I was struck by Dr. Maher's comment, when discussing Taoiseach Endy Kenny's speech, that the Irish people needed to find "expression for their pent-up anger." That pent-up anger is very real indeed, and it has been steeping for a long time. Being Irish, everything seems to lead to a story, and here I was reminded of the story about the poet Patrick Kavanaugh being in England, where he met a young Irish child. Somehow, in the course of conversation, Kavanagh learned that the family no longer attended church because they not been invited to a church picnic, and "mother said we'd pack it."[2] In a sense, we might think of the recent scandals as having shifted that decision to "pack it" back into Ireland itself: the pent-up anger could be bottled up only so long, and its release was inevitable.

The abruptness with which great numbers of Irish Catholics have taken their leave of the Church has occurred in a remarkably compressed span. As recently as forty years ago, J. H. Whyte was able to say, in *Church and State in Modern Ireland*, that the first distinguishing characteristic of the Church in Ireland was its hold on the loyalty of the people. He was able to say as a matter of course that "one facet of this loyalty to the Church in their tradition is that they do not criticize their clergy in public."[3] That was then, though, as Dr. Maher has noted, it would be a mistake to characterize the relationship of ordinary Irish Catholics to their church—and certainly their relationship to the individual clergy who are the frontlines of that church—as one of unmixed contempt. Not at all. There are still many situations in which Irish Catholics are grateful for the Church, and many who respect and like their priests.

Here, a comparison with the American Church finds a very different experience. The wholesale turning away from Catholicism as an organizing principle of personal and public life in Ireland differs in many ways from the American experience. A fundamental dissimilarity is that we have never been a confessional state; indeed, the opposite is written into our Constitution.

Still less has America been a society of near total adherence. Fr. Littleton has spoken persuasively about the challenges and, yes, the opportunities of a post-Catholic milieu, urging the church to embrace that situation (about which, it seems to me, it will have little choice). But out-marriage, secularization, and apostasy have worried American bishops for a very long time; in the nineteenth century, the heroic age of Catholic immigration, Church leaders fretted about what they called "leakage," as in "leakage from the vessel of faith." (One of the most talked-about Catholic books of ninety years ago was Gerald Shaughnessy's *Has the Immigrant Kept the Faith?*)[4] It didn't worry all of the bishops to the same extent. Some of the great Irish American ecclesial leaders of that century, such as Archbishop John Ireland and James Cardinal Gibbons, understood that pluralism was the future and received ferocious pushback for their assertions. Yes, there were ghetto neighborhoods, and the siloization of American social life persisted longer than we might realize (as Herberg's *Protestant-Catholic Jew* of 1955 made clear) but this country never saw a birth-to-death Catholic environment.[5] In America, we were, to adapt the country and western song, "pluralist before pluralism was cool."

In our own time, despite scandal and a hierarchy with a chronic tin ear, Americans have not abandoned the Church in anything like the numbers in Europe, nor has the tailing off been an almost overnight phenomenon. It is easy to find astounding numbers over here, including the stunner that in a recent survey of the archdiocese of Boston only 15 percent of Catholics regularly attend weekly Mass.[6] Nevertheless, the fall-off does not follow on a period of deep investment, personally and nationally, in Catholic identity. The reasons why individual Catholics stop practicing in Ireland—the anger, the embarrassment, the irreconcilable cognitive dissonance—are, I suspect, not that different from those given by Catholics in the United States. But the decline has been a far more drastic turn in Ireland: a cliff, rather than a downward slope.

In this context, I want to float an idea that might be helpful as we try to understand the precipitousness of the changes in Irish practice. Specifically, it strikes me that the Irish experience of religious faith tends toward being more of an all-or-nothing matter. Or to put it another way, the Irish response to doubt runs to extremes. It is not a continuum in which faith is followed by weaker faith, but frequently, a breakdown in which faith is followed by something close to nihilism. This impression is repeatedly confirmed in my readings of Irish literature. The poet Seán Dunne, whose memoir *The Road to Silence* is a marvelous spiritual autobiography, describes the suddenness with which his faith collapsed: abruptly, he says, "I lost all sense of Catholicism as a positive thing."[7] Perhaps no one caught the intensity of the unbelieving former Irish Catholic better than Shaw, with the lapsed priest Fr. Keegan in his 1904 play *John Bull's Other Island* who is convinced that "this earth of ours must be hell."[8]

We all know, or course, about the legendary rigorism of Irish Catholic mind and practice in earlier eras. There is a wonderful scene in Sean O'Faolain's short story from 1953, "An Enduring Friendship," in which a prudish Catholic journalists declares that "if the priests of Ireland are hard on their own people, it's because they know that if they once took the lid off the pashuns of Irish men and Irish women, aye and of Irish children, the country would blow up!"[9] Such an embrace of a puritanical religion hardly seems credible now, but it was more than real. And I wonder if the Irish receptiveness to the enforced restrictiveness of a Jansenist Church was not in some a terrified response to swirling doubt; Beckett's bleakness was always near.

One place where the historic American experience might be relevant is in the future of the priesthood. Dr. Maher noted the graying and the sheer weariness of the clergy, and very important, has also reminded us that the dispiritedness of Irish Catholicism extends into the clerical ranks. As both speakers referenced, we are looking at the possible extinction of religious life among the orders and severely reduced numbers of diocesan priests.

There is sidelight to this that I haven't seen noted, but which to my mind marks a major shift in the mindset of ordinary Catholics: the unprecedented fact that most parents no longer want their children to become priests or nuns, and, indeed, that many would discourage them from such a career. This reverses a deep-seated pattern within Irish families, inscribed in hundreds of novels and in anecdotal accounts of the mother giving her pride and joy to the Church (one of the yet-to-be-written tragedies of Irish life must be the story of the priest whose vocation was not truly his own). We have a tendency, today, to think of the hierarchical Church as a machine that required *apparatchiks* to function, and perhaps that is true at some level. But we also forget how fully the Irish internalized the idea that theirs was a uniquely spiritual nation, called by God to be a Catholic city on a hill. Given that a vocation was, for generations of Irish Catholic families, the always-present ideal of a life to be aspired to, its departure from the "approved" list marks an enormous change, and something truly new.

Yet, the prospect of a church that was functionally without priests was a foundational experience on this side of the water. As James M. O'Toole notes in his brilliant book on the lived experience of American Catholics, *The Faithful: A History of Catholics in America*, colonial and frontier America was very much a place where Catholics practiced their faith without clergy (his first chapter is titled "The Priestless Church"). The church that America's first Catholics knew was largely one compelled to function without priests; Catholics "had to make do, holding onto their religious identity as best they could on their own, guided only in the most general way by a distant clergyman. This is what it was like to be an American Catholic in the priestless church."[10] O'Toole concludes that this condition "is once again becoming the case."[11] America and Ireland are both headed back to a functional priestlessness.

To turn to a more upbeat note, one of the striking commonalities here is that both Dr. Maher and Fr. Littleton recognized that the papacy of Francis is potentially a "game-changer," at a level perhaps not seen in our lifetime—certainly not seen since John XXIII. But will the game change as dramatically as we are sometimes led to believe—led by a media that, in many ways, is spectacularly ill-informed about the workings and the beliefs of Catholicism? And here, as ever, the answer is a resounding "maybe." For my part, I would recommend caution.

As Fr. Littleton noted, the Pope has stated repeatedly that he is "implementing the teaching of Vatican II. Therefore, he will not—indeed, he cannot—unilaterally change central tenets of Catholic doctrine because to do so would be to contradict his commitment to the principle of collegiality or shared responsibility." Personally, I happen to be one of those people to whom he referred, counting myself among those who believe that the Pope should bring the church "into line with the popular approaches to equality, individual freedom and human rights in contemporary society," and nowhere more so than in regard to mandatory celibacy. I'm not betting that won't happen; but neither am I betting that it will. Fr. Littleton has indeed said something important when he reminds us of the structural brakes on sudden change.

The current Pope, like his predecessors, clearly has a sense of himself as a shepherd of the people of God—the church as the "people of God" being in itself a radical re-thinking of ecclesiology set in motion by Vatican II. But being a world pastor doesn't mean that he isn't also the head of an institution. The fact of the matter is that one of the main purposes of any institution is to slow things down. And few if any institutions take the duty to slow things down more seriously than does the Roman Catholic Church. Once again, the best answer appears to be "we shall see." It is undoubtedly true, though, that prospect of a transformative papacy is real.

In that regard, though, I want to raise yet another caveat. I mentioned J. H. Whyte's insightful and still relevant 1971 book *Church and State in Modern Ireland*, which opens by suggesting five "traditions" of Irish Catholicism. These include the unique loyalty of the people, an occasional but persisting independence on certain issues (in which the people feel free to ignore the clerics), a sense of aloofness between Church and State, and a grip on the educational system. But the one that interests me is the fifth: the authoritarian strain in Irish life.[12]

In our time, we have come to look on the old Catholic Ireland as best represented by what sociologists term a "total institution": the industrial schools and the Magdalen laundries have come to stand in for the entire regime of restrictiveness that James M. Smith so memorably describes as "the nation's architecture of containment."[13] In the family, in the petty demands of autocratic civil servants, certainly in the school system, in the clericalism that Fr. Littleton has described as a "scourge," authoritarianism has been a powerful reality in Irish life. Is this one of the places where, as Louise Fuller put it, it is "necessary to consider the influence of Ireland on the church"?[14]

I would ask us to consider whether that authoritarianism has, in fact, vanished. And if it has not disappeared, where will it emerge? We know that in the United States, the men entering seminary are consistently more authoritarian, more pugnaciously orthodox, than the ordinary Catholics they will be asked to serve. In Ireland, the same pattern obtains; the drastically reduced pool of priests inevitably means that there will be some battlefield promotions. Those authoritarian young men will be moving into positions of authority sooner rather than later.

Fr. Littleton has charted a number of invigorating and ambitious ways in which the Church might re-imagine itself—become more transparent, become more democratic, become more nimble—and I quite frankly hope it comes about. But can such a Catholicism ever emerge if authoritarianism is one of its core traditions? And especially if it has the clerics—who are after all, the most ardent supporters of clericalism—in its grip? Here, the gap between priests and people may widen. It is clear from Dr. Maher's and Fr. Littleton's chapters that there is no prospect of an irredentist conservatism becoming the church triumphant in Ireland. The vast majority of Irish Catholics want a different future.

Just as an aside, I do think there is a brick-and-mortar question to address about that future. Catholicism has left an astonishing footprint on the built environment—all those convents, churches, schools, and the like that are no longer sustainable. Ireland has grown familiar with the spectacle of a "ghost estate," meaning the unfinished and now-deteriorating houses left behind with the crash of 2008. The actual infrastructure, the physical plant of the Roman Catholic Church, is going to be visible for a long time to come. The old physical plant will, so long as it stands, offer some sort of comment on the Ireland of the present. We don't know how that comment will be interpreted, but the next Ireland will not be bereft of reminders of the earlier dream. As buildings are repurposed—and they can't all be made into ironic discos and theme pubs, and in any case, the irony can only last so long—how will that comment be heard?

But more than the physical plant, it's the psychic geography that is altered in a post-Catholic milieu. And in this regard, I'm not an optimist. Too often, those who check "none" when surveyed about religious belief—who are the fastest growing religious segment of the United Stated, accounting for 20 percent of the population—live with an impoverished spiritual, and to my mind, emotional and imaginative vocabulary.[15]

As Dr. Maher observed, "it is far from easy to assess something as personal and tenuous as religious sensibility." I could not agree more: doing so requires that we turn away from survey reports and statistical analysis to look to much more exact sciences—like poetry.

No Irish poet more directly addressed the spiritual costs of modernity than the late Dennis O'Driscoll (who was not himself a believer), and nowhere more so than in his poem "Missing God"—a poem in which the diminishment of the modern spiritual vocabulary is rendered as, in a sense, its own elegy for the lost "Sea of Faith."

> His grace is no longer called for
> Before meals: farmed fish multiply
> without His intercession.
> Bread production rises through
> disease-resistant grains devised

scientifically to mitigate His faults.
Yet, though we rebelled against Miss Him
like adolescents, uplifted to see
an oppressive father banished—
a bearded hermit—to the desert,
we confess to missing Him at times.

"We confess to missing Him." In nineteen stanzas, O'Driscoll catalogs the anomie of an Ireland after God—the insufficiency of consumer culture, the bleakness of a wholly scientific universe, the awkwardness of art and ritual when they are abstracted from belief—and concludes that we can

Even feel nostalgic, odd days,
for His Second Coming,
like standing in the brick
dome of a dovecote
after the birds have flown.[16]

We have heard compelling, in many ways alarming, in not many ways surprising, readings of a Church in crisis. But O'Driscoll's acute reading imparts nothing of a "crisis." What it imparts, rather, is a sense of diminishment. Dr. Maher titled his chapter, "Faith of our Fathers: A Lost Legacy?" We do need to take note of the question mark.

The Irish Catholic Church now lives inside that question mark. It is in many ways a diminished church. Without question, some of that diminishment has been for the better; the power to silence all critique, however accurate and well-intended that critique may have been, should have been diminished long ago. In most ways, a humbler church is a more attractive church. As we saw in Dr. Maher's accounts of the funerals of John McGahern and Seamus Heaney, the Church's capacity to embody and express, through local custom, the most enormous questions of human existence, is an undisguised blessing. One surely hopes that this will survive, because we know that it must.

I will close with another caution as we look out at the church and ponder its future from inside that question mark. Let us remember that, in religious history as in history writ large, *diagnosis is not the same as prediction*. If we were to turn American religious history back a hundred years, and make diagnoses about America's religious future, how wrong we would have been! Who would have seen a Catholic president within fifty years? Who would have foreseen a wholesale evacuation of mainstream churches by the century's end? Who would have expected the evangelical denominations to have become a huge political and cultural force? The short answer is "no one."

Maybe the only Church we can respond to is the Church right now. The Church right now does indeed present a mixed picture: anger, loss, embarrassment, clumsy articulation of its thinking, yearnings in polar directions, and now and again, persisting hope. We should indeed be grateful for the perceptive readings of the present moment in Irish Catholic life that Eamon Maher and John Littleton have provided. But we must also bear in mind that the direction in which the Holy Spirit leads the church always has been and will remain, wholly (and holy) unpredictable.

NOTES

1. Andrew Auge et al., "After the Murphy and Ryan Reports: A Roundtable on the Irish Catholic Church," *New Hibernia Review* 14 (2010): 66.
2. Anthony Cronin, *Dead As Doornails* (Dublin: Lilliput, 1999), 173.
3. J. H. Whyte, *Church and State in Modern Ireland, 1923–1970* (Dublin: Gill and MacMillan, 1971), 7.
4. Gerald Shaughnessy, *Has the Immigrant Kept the Faith? A Study of Immigration and Catholic Growth in the United States, 1790–1920* (New York: Macmillan, 1925). Shaughnessy's conclusions on the persistence of Catholic practice are generally positive.
5. Will Herberg, *Protestant, Catholic, Jew: An Essay in American Religious Sociology* (Garden City, NY: Doubleday, 1955).
6. John C. Seitz, *No Closure: Catholic Practice and Boston's Parish Shutdowns* (Cambridge: Harvard University Press, 2011), 6.
7. Seán Dunne, *The Road to Silence: An Irish Spiritual Odyssey* (Dublin: New Island Books, 1994), 15.
8. George Bernard Shaw, "John Bull's Other Island," in *Bernard Shaw: Complete Plays with Prefaces*, vol. 2 (New York: Dodd, Mead, and Co., 1963), 585.
9. Sean O'Faolain, "An Enduring Friendship," in *Collected Stories of Sean O'Faolain* (Boston: Atlantic Little Brown Books, 1983), 541.
10. James M. O'Toole, *The Faithful: A History of Catholics in America* (Cambridge: Belknap Press of Harvard University Press, 2008), 12.
11. O'Toole, *The Faithful*, 305.
12. Whyte, *Church and State*, 1–23.
13. James M. Smyth, *Ireland's Magdalen Laundries and the Nation's Architecture of Containment* (Notre Dame: University of Notre Dame Press, 2007).
14. Auge et al., "After the Murphy and Ryan Reports," 63.
15. On the "nones," see *Nones on the Rise: One-in-five Adults Have No Religious Affiliation* (Washington, DC: The Pew Forum on Religious and Public Life, 2012), accessed April 10, 2014, http://www.pewforum.org/files/2012/10/NonesOnTheRise-full.pdf .
16. Dennis O'Driscoll, "Missing God," *New Hibernia Review* 6 (2002): 48–50.

II

A Closer Look at Specific Dimensions

Chapter Four

Secularization, Generational Change, and Ireland's Post-Secular Opportunity

Michele Dillon

The year 2013 was momentous for the Catholic Church. Pope Benedict, in a historically unprecedented move, resigned the papacy on February 11. And continuing the transformative nature of the year, the College of Cardinals elected the Church's first South American pope, and the Church's first Jesuit pope, Cardinal Bergoglio of Argentina. In the days and months immediately following his ascension to the papacy, Francis quickly demarcated a new style and tone for the Church. His friendly, humble and warm demeanor, the simplicity of his household arrangements, his preference for community and collegiality over pomp and ceremony, his denunciation of the grandiosity and narcissism of church officials, and his radical acknowledgment of the church's "obsession" with sexuality and abortion all pointed to Francis's commitment to shaking up the Church, even if doctrine per se remains unchanged.

The year 2013 was also momentous for Ireland. The State regained its economic sovereignty, yielded in 2008 as part of its desperate attempt to unload the stark failure of the Celtic Tiger that ran a course of unprecedented economic growth between approximately 1993 and 2007.[1] Recent economic reports from Ireland point to a slowly improving economy. Unemployment is down to 11.8 percent; this is the lowest the rate has been since mid-2009, and approximates the current EU average of 11.7 percent.[2] Irish public finances are on target to meet the government's targeted deficit reduction for 2013, and its gross domestic product has had an annual increase of 6.9 percent between 2008 and 2013.[3]

With Ireland's fractured economic conditions on the mend, plans are underway to re-open the Irish embassy in Vatican City, as well as to establish a diplomatic presence in global cities such as Hong Kong. The Vatican embassy was closed by the government in November 2011, ostensibly as a financial cost-cutting measure. It coincided, however, with an interval of unmatched public criticism in Ireland of the Vatican. In July 2011, Irish Prime Minister Enda Kenny publicly criticized the Vatican for its systematic failure to recognize, and to show accountability with regard to, the numerous cases of child sex abuse by priests and their cover up by church officials. Addressing his colleagues in the Irish Parliament, Kenny used sharply worded, unapologetic language to denounce what he referred to as the Vatican's culture of "clericalism, dysfunction, disconnection, elitism, and narcissism."[4]

The speech marked an unprecedented critique of Church authorities from an Irish politician, let alone a Taoiseach. And equally remarkable, Kenny's critique received widespread and resounding approval across Ireland. The Irish government withdrew its ambassador to the Holy See, and in turn, the Vatican recalled its ambassador (papal nuncio) from Dublin to Vatican City. The Vatican also issued a lengthy public statement defending its actions over the sex abuse crisis and challenged the Irish government's claims that it had sought to interfere with an official inquiry into sex abuse and/or to interfere in any way with Irish civil law or civil authorities investigating abuse. Relations between Church and State reached a level of contentiousness that would have been unimaginable even just five years earlier, and the subsequent closing of the Irish embassy in Vatican City, whether cost effective or not, marked a watershed sign that Catholic Ireland, a long-standing, exemplary stalwart of deference to Rome, would no longer be so beholden to the imprimatur of the Church.

Currently, the Church is enjoying a moment of high favorability around the world among Catholics and non-Catholics alike as a result of Francis's style and the high expectations for what his papacy might accomplish. It is thus ironic that despite Irish pride in its heritage as the island of saints and scholars, the Irish have been absent from the Vatican supper. It is no coincidence that the reopening of the embassy is occurring in this changed Church context, and it is noteworthy that the decision has been warmly welcomed by Irish bishops and Vatican officials. The re-opening of the Irish embassy is a significant cultural and symbolic act. It is also crucial to re-crafting and maintaining effective institutional ties between Church and State in Ireland as well as in terms of global inter-institutional and transnational relations. Nonetheless, the reaffirmation of these symbolic and institutional ties should not be seen as the restoration of the *status quo ante*. The demise of the Church's institutional authority and moral hegemony in Ireland began in the late 1970s and, though it stalled in the 1980s, subsequently accelerated during Ireland's rapid economic growth and its co-occurrence with the public documentation of the Church's myriad sex abuse scandals.[5] Today, there is no going back to the previously unquestioned place of the Church in Irish society. Rather, a new era of Catholicism and of the Church's role in Irish society is dawning. What that role might be is relatively open-ended.

IRISH SECULARIZATION

Secularization, the declining significance of religion in society, has given rise over the years to many competing definitions. At its core, however, in line with the writings of the classical sociologist Max Weber, secularization refers both to the displacement of religious values and the attenuation of the authority of religious institutions.[6] Thus, in the context of Catholicism, one way in which we can assess secularization is in terms of Catholics' commitment to or enchantment with the sacramental life of the Church. The celebration of the Mass and the Eucharist is an integral dimension of Catholic belief, practice, and community. Weekly Mass attendance is obligatory for Catholics, and over many generations—as far back in Ireland as Penal times—the Mass has been the constant and core marker of Catholic identity. As stated in the *Catechism of the Catholic Church* as well as in numerous papal statements, "the Eucharist is the source and summit" of Catholic life.[7] In Ireland today, however, the Mass is losing its centrality. Although 84 percent of Irish people currently identify as Catholic, far fewer, approximately 43 percent, report weekly Mass attendance. At the end of the 1990s, approximately 62 percent did so. By contrast, as figure 4.1 shows, in the mid-1980s through 1990, 85 percent of Irish adults reported weekly Mass attendance.[8] It should be noted that there is some uncertainty with regard to recent levels of weekly church attendance among Irish Catholics. The ISSP 2008 data indicate that 43 percent attend Mass weekly or more often, whereas the European Values Survey (EVS) conducted in 2009–2010 indicated that it was 52 percent.[9] Nonetheless, whichever data are used, the evidence is clear that there has been a significant downward trend in Mass attendance, with between three- and four-in-ten fewer Irish adults reporting weekly Mass activity over the course of two decades (1990–2008).

We also see clear evidence of secularization when we look to assess the Church's moral authority in individual lives and in Irish public culture. According to the information in appendix 1, the legalization of contraception (1978), the legalization of divorce (1996), the legalization of same-sex civil unions (2011), and the legalization of abortion (2013), all point to the steady erosion over time in the Church's moral authority in determining the content of Irish civil law. Church teachings and the public advocacy of bishops have not been successful in convincing successive Irish electorates, parliamentarians, and Supreme Court justices that the Church's teachings on sexual morality should also be institutionalized in civil law.[10] The shift in Irish atti-

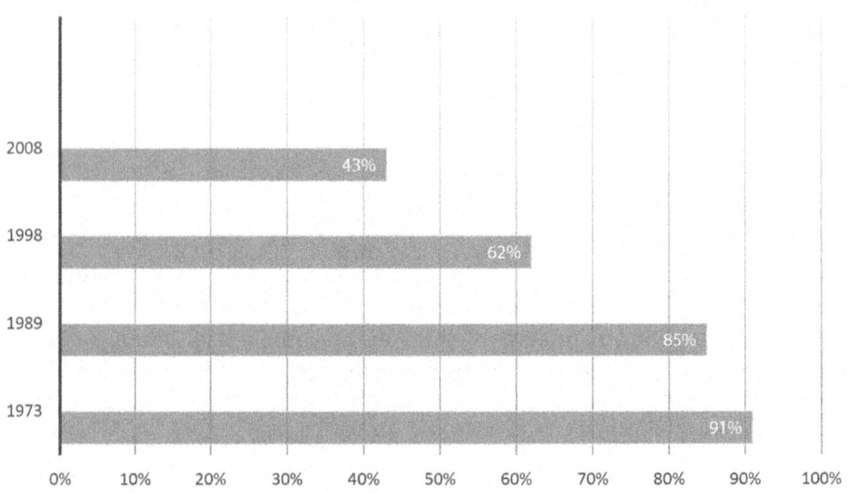

Figure 4.1. Weekly Mass attendance in Ireland, 1973–2008

tudes both reflects, and translates into, changing behavioral patterns.[11] For example, in 2011 the Census recorded 26,913 Catholics who were divorced and remarried, and an additional 64,798 who were divorced. Among the population as a whole, there are 143,000 cohabiting couples, a number representing an increase of 18 percent since 2006. The number of same-sex cohabiting couples increased from 2,100 in 2006 to 4,000 in 2011 (in 1996 the Census recorded only 150 same-sex cohabiting couples). Ireland's fertility rate is still comparatively high relative to other European countries; at 1.96, it is essentially at replacement level, with more than 70,000 births per year, and—what would be a surprise to demographers—it has not slowed as a result of the recession.[12] Three-quarters of all children in Ireland currently live in a traditional family structure, that is, with two married parents. Nonetheless, close to one in five (18 percent) live with a lone parent, and 6 percent with cohabiting parents.[13]

These secularization trends are driven by multiple intersecting forces. They are interrelated with large scale societal changes propelled by economic and social modernization—increased urbanization (e.g., 62 percent of people in Ireland live in urban areas, defined as towns with 1,500 people or more), the greater accessibility of university-level education, the emergence of a financial services economy—and reinforced by the cultural and attitudinal changes that invariably accompany such modernization.[14] They are also related to the institutional practices of the Church itself, such as, perhaps, its ban on women's ordination which, though a complex cultural and theological issue, contravenes western thinking and practices in regard to gender equality. The declining salience of the Church in Irish society is also related to the Church's sex abuse crisis propelled by the behavior of church officials with regard to priests' sex abuse and its cover-up.

Unlike the more gradual pattern of decreased attendance observable in the United States and elsewhere, the relatively short time span in which the centrality of Mass attendance and Church authority declined in Irish society presents an instance of "compressed secularization." The term "compressed modernity" is used by scholars to refer to the rapid economic, social, and cultural changes that occurred in South Korea in the 1980s, changes which transformed the South Korean economy from being a heavily traditionalist and agricultural economy into a major industrial and economic power in contemporary global markets.[15] The remarkably short interval of time in which those changes occurred in South Korea, compared to the far longer, slower, and steadier pace of industrialization that had characterized western economies is distinctive, that is, compressed. In similar fashion, the impetus toward secularization that has occurred in Ireland, mostly within the last twenty to twenty-five years, is more condensed, especially when compared to the same indicators of secularization which have been demonstrating decline for a far longer period—since approximately the 1960s—in most other western European countries, the United States, and Australia.[16]

In the United States, for example, 55 percent of Catholics reported weekly Mass attendance in 1973, a proportion that was down precipitously from 65 percent in 1968, a decrease largely due to Catholics' disaffection with *Humanae Vitae*'s reaffirmation of the ban on artificial contraception.[17] Mass attendance rates basically stabilized in the 1970s such that in the early 1980s, approximately 52 percent of Americans were attending Mass weekly.[18] Since then there has been decline in American Catholics' and Protestants' church attendance habits. It is strikingly noteworthy, however, that since the late 1980s, while the proportion of American Catholics reporting weekly Mass attendance declined by approximately 13 percentage points (from 44 percent in 1987 to 31 percent in 2011), for Irish Catholics it was a much bigger decline: as noted earlier, a decline shown in figure 4.2 from 85 percent in 1990 to 43 percent in 2008 (based on ISSP data).[19]

Even if one instead uses the data from the European Values Survey conducted in 2009–2010, which indicates a higher level of weekly Mass attendance for Irish Catholics at 52 percent, this higher figure still represents a precipitous decline in Mass attendance by as much as a third in two decades (1990–2010).[20] In any event, a lot has happened in Ireland since 2008 and 2009 (when the ISSP and EVS surveys were conducted). It is likely that as a result of the evidence documented by Justice Yvonne Murphy's inquiries (published in 2009 and 2011) into the Church's handling of sex abuse cases, there may have been a further decline in Mass attendance.[21]

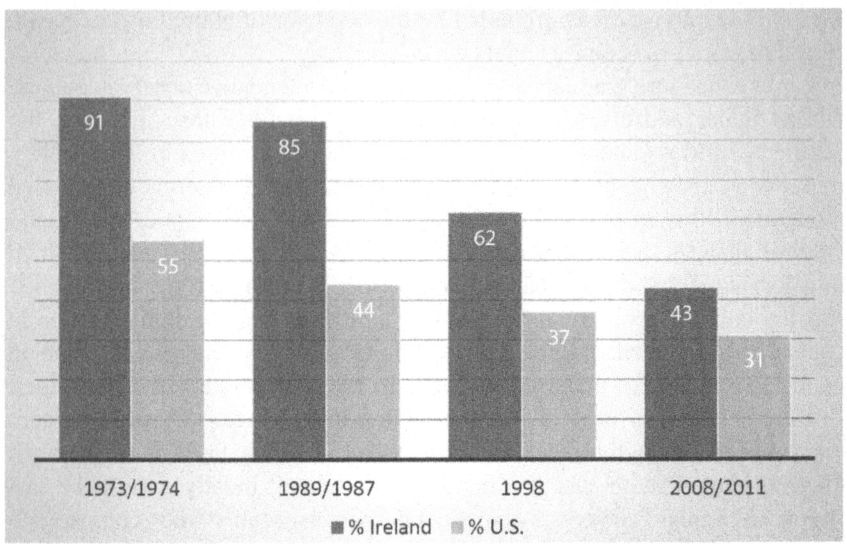

Figure 4.2. Weekly Mass attendance in Ireland and the United States

In addition to declining Mass attendance, there has also been a fairly compressed change in Irish Catholics' attitudes on sexual morality.[22] Irish Catholics are increasingly expressing views that are at odds with Church teachings on sexual morality. For example, in 1998, 29 percent of Irish Catholics said that sexual relations between a man and a woman before marriage are "always wrong." Ten years later, in 2008, 15 percent expressed this view. By contrast, as figure 4.3 shows, American Catholics showed little change on this same question, with 18 percent in 1998 and 17 percent in 2008 saying that premarital sex was always wrong.

The change that has occurred in Ireland therefore is quite noteworthy. Similarly, there was little change in American Catholics' views of same-gender sexual relations during this ten year interval. In 1998, 47 percent, and in 2008, 48 percent, said that same-gender sexual relations were always wrong. Irish Catholics, on the other hand, showed considerable change. Whereas 54 percent said that same-gender sexual relations were always wrong when asked in 1998, according to figure 4.4, only 27 percent expressed this view in 2008. Here again, we see a much more compressed pattern of change in Ireland. The accelerated change in attitudes toward same-gender sexual mores is reinforced by a national survey conducted in April 2014 which found that two-thirds of the Irish electorate, 67 percent, said they would vote in favor of same-sex marriage, an increase from 53 percent in November 2012.[23] Notably, a majority of those who consider

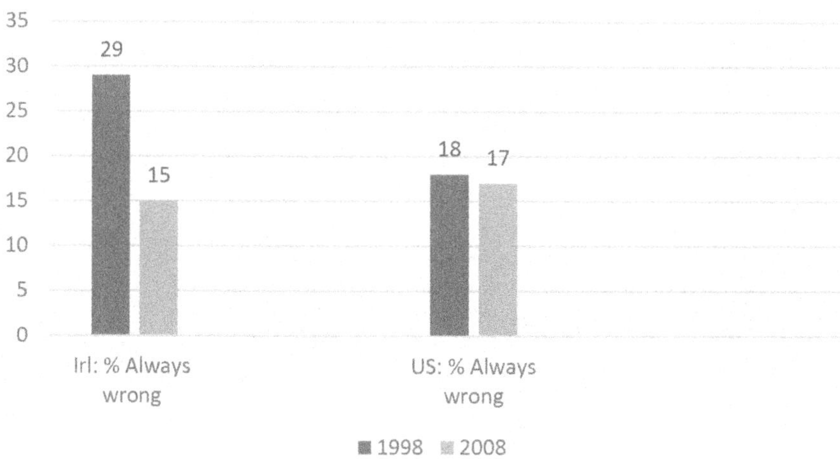

Figure 4.3. Irish and American attitudes toward premarital sex, 1998 and 2008

themselves "very religious," share this view. Additionally, other recent data suggest that large majorities of Irish Catholics increasingly are of the opinion that the church's teachings on sexuality and on divorce and remarriage are irrelevant.[24]

The abortion context in the United States—where abortion was legalized nationwide in 1973 following the Supreme Court *Roe v. Wade* decision—is very different to that in Ireland. Although abortion continues to be a contested and politically charged issue in America, there is actually a great deal of stability in Americans' attitudes toward abortion over the forty years since its legalization.[25] By contrast, there has been a considerable shift in abortion opinion in Ireland in the last fifteen years. In 1998, 40 percent of Irish Catholics said that it was "always wrong" for a woman to have an abortion if there is a strong chance of a serious fetal defect; in 2008, 27 percent expressed this opinion. And, though representing a smaller swing in opinion, whereas 56 percent in 1998 said that abortion is "always wrong" in cases of economic hardship, this was true of 49 percent in 2008, according to data in figure 4.5. Further, in 2013, there was widespread support in Ireland for legislation permitting abortion, with 71 percent supporting the view that abortion should be allowed in cases where a mother's life is in danger, including from the threat of suicide.[26] Again, though the abortion contexts in Ireland and America are very different, as figure 4.5 indicates, Irish public opinion shows greater change over a relatively short period of time than is observed in the United States.

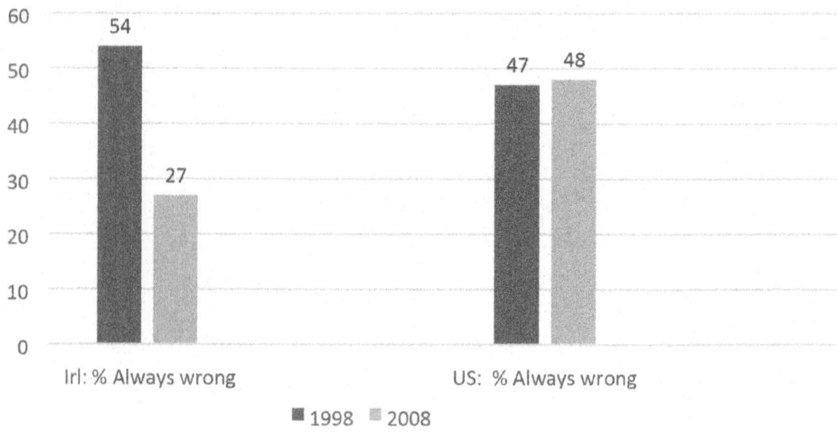

Figure 4.4. Irish and American attitudes toward same-gender sexual relations, 1998 and 2008

THE GENERATIONAL FACTOR IN SECULARIZATION

Irish secularization processes are likely to continue their forward trajectory. Although secularization is not necessarily a straightforward or linear process and can be uneven in how it manifests itself, the generational patterns in the aggregate data highlighted in this chapter suggest that a reversal of the current trends is unlikely. The pattern of decline in weekly Mass attendance in Ireland is likely to continue its downward trajectory because its momentum is driven, in part, by the engine of generational succession. As figure 4.6 illustrates, in Ireland younger cohorts have lower rates of Mass attendance than their older peers. Whereas eight in ten individuals age sixty-five or over attend Mass weekly (79 percent), one-fifth (19 percent) of those in the eighteen to twenty-four age bracket do so. This is a big generation gap.

These differences are not simply an age or life-course effect, that is, that young people in their twenties distance themselves from church but then, like their parents before them, increase their church involvement once they settle down and start families of their own. Rather, as the data show, each new generation shows a notable decline in Mass attendance relative to their proximate peers. Thus, while over two-thirds (69 percent) of those in the fifty-five to sixty-four age bracket attend Mass weekly, this is still 10 percentage points fewer than their age sixty-five plus neighbors. By the same token, middle-aged Irish (ages forty-four to fifty-four) are far less likely than those in their late fifties and sixties to go to Mass on a weekly basis. The consistent pattern of generational decline, therefore, depresses the overall rate of Mass attendance at any given point in time, and, over time, has the clear effect of

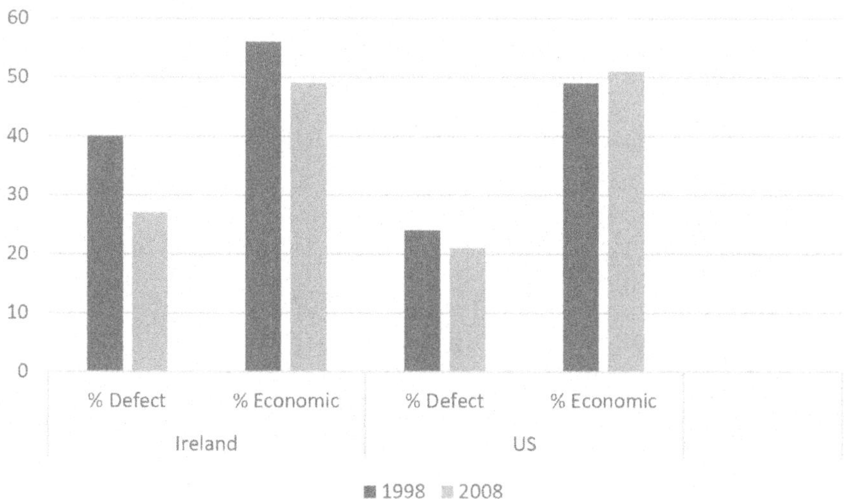

Figure 4.5. Percentages of people in Ireland and the United States who believe that abortion is "always wrong" in specific circumstances, 1998 and 2008

chivvying it along a downward trajectory. This is because the younger generations' lower attendance falls short of the higher attendance pattern of the older generations whom they are replacing. We see a similar generational pattern in the United States. Currently, 24 percent of eighteen- to twenty-nine-year-old Catholics but more than twice as many (56 percent) of those in their seventies attend Mass on a weekly basis.[27]

The significance of generation as a secularizing force is further evident in religious disaffiliation trends. As we see in quite dramatic terms in the United States, there has been a dramatic increase in the proportions reporting no religion. In the early 1970s, seven percent of American adults reported no religious affiliation. By the late 1990s, this figure had doubled, and by 2012, had almost tripled with 20 percent of Americans indicating no religious preference.[28] While the narrative underlying the transformative trend toward disaffiliation is complex, a generational lens helps to illuminate the dynamics of change. Younger age Americans, those between eighteen and twenty-nine in the so-called millennial generation born between 1981 and 1994, are the most likely to be religiously unaffiliated. One-third (34 percent) of this age group compared to one-fifth of those born even only fifteen years ahead of them, and far fewer among older Americans, are unaffiliated.

Similarly, in Ireland, though the numbers are far smaller than in the United States, there has been an increase in the proportion who report "no religion." In 2011, approximately 270,000 people (5.8 percent of Ireland's 4.6 million population), indicated that they had no religion; an additional

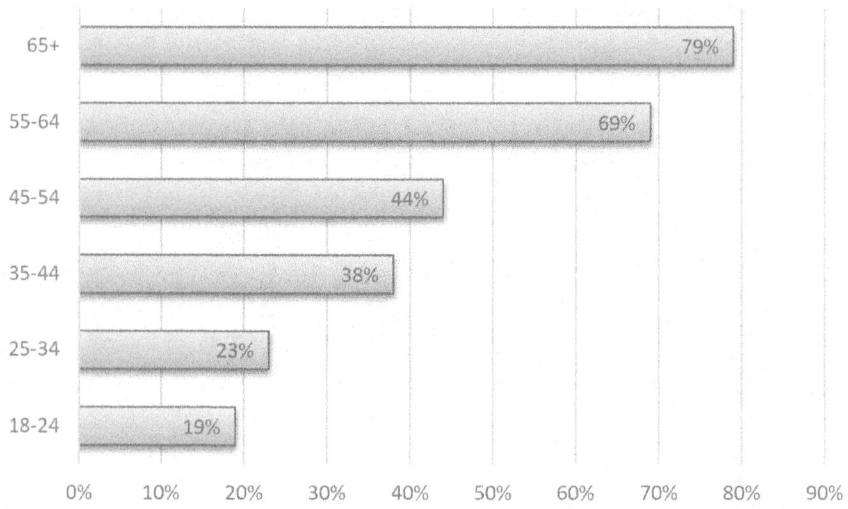

Figure 4.6. Generational differences in weekly Mass attendance in Ireland, 2008–2009

seven thousand people were agnostic or atheist. As figure 4.7 shows, this represents a four-fold increase between 1991 and 2011 in the numbers reporting no religion.

And, paralleling trends in the United States, the largest concentration is found among twenty-five to thirty-four year olds: they comprise 26 percent of the "no religion" group.[29] Thus, in both the United States and Ireland, generational succession is a major social force driving the cultural trend toward religious disaffiliation; older, more religious, generations are being replaced with younger cohorts who are less interested in and committed to institutional religion and the identity it confers.

Similarly, the current cultural momentum in favor of same-sex marriage is driven in both Ireland and the United States by significant support from younger rather than older age cohorts. According to figure 4.8, 80 percent of Irish eighteen to twenty-four year olds compared to 44 percent of those aged sixty-five and over, and 68 percent of American eighteen to twenty-nine year olds compared to 30 percent of those aged sixty-five and over favor same-sex marriage.[30] (The reasons why generation is such a powerful driver of religious and cultural change today are beyond the scope of this chapter.)[31]

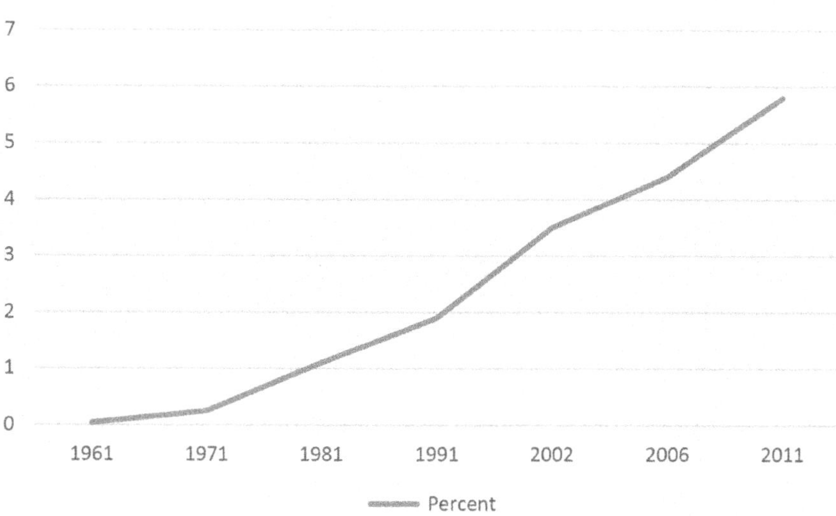

Figure 4.7. Religious disaffiliation in Ireland; percentage with "no religion"

UNEVEN SECULARIZATION AND THE MOVE TOWARD THE POST-SECULAR

Notwithstanding the compelling evidence of Irish secularization, it may nonetheless be premature to declare Ireland a secular society. Secularity is typically somewhat ambiguous as manifested in even some of what tend to be regarded as the most secular of societies—the United Kingdom, for example, where the Queen is also the Head of the Anglican Church, or even France or Denmark. Moreover, compared to almost all other economically developed countries, Ireland is still today a highly religious society. As noted above, eight in ten call themselves Catholic. And on any given Sunday we might expect to see close to one of every two Irish Catholics at Mass, compared to fewer than one of three American Catholics, their most committed Catholic peers (see figure 4.2). Further, the Church still plays a major, though reduced, role in primary and second level education and thus is a central actor in framing socialization values and experiences, and the context of their transmittal and reception.[32] The Catholic imagination, moreover, is hard to repress, and its images, symbols, and paraphernalia (statues, candles, medals, holy pictures, Mass cards) gratefully linger in expected and unexpected places, providing familiarity and comfort amid the flux of change and uncertainty.[33]

Perhaps a fitting sign of the sociological complexity of contemporary Ireland with its tangle of diluted but die-hard Catholic habits and the triumph

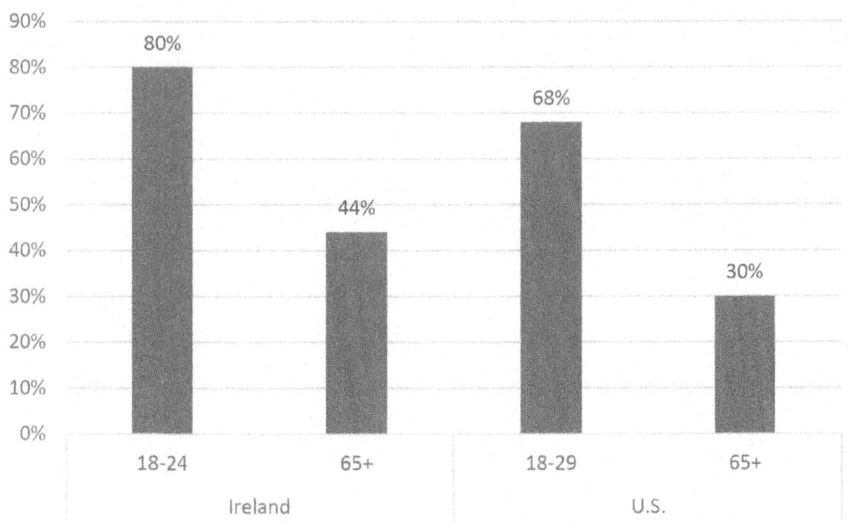

Figure 4.8. Generational differences in Irish and American support for same-sex marriage

of the market is a recent controversy over Mass cards. A Mass card, the religious greeting card one sends to someone to express sympathy on a bereavement, or to convey "get well" wishes, or mark a special birthday or family event (e.g., a wedding, an anniversary, the birth of child), includes the symbolic gift of having a special Mass celebrated for the named receiver's intentions and well-being. Sending a Mass card is a fairly ingrained habit and popular practice in Ireland, at least among the older generation. So commonplace are Mass cards that one can buy a signed card in regular convenience stores rather than speak directly to a priest to request and pay for the Mass. In October 2010, the Irish bishops found it necessary to issue a public statement outlining the proper use and practices surrounding Mass cards. Clarifying both church and civil law on the matter, the bishops noted that: "Having signed or stamped Mass cards for sale to the public in shops and other commercial outlets is a practice that is not approved by the Irish Episcopal Conference . . . because it undermines a correct understanding of the Eucharist."[34]

In Ireland today, therefore, notwithstanding, or perhaps because of, its compressed trajectory of secularization, the secular and the religious frequently entangle in everyday politics, culture, and social routines. This, however, should not be a surprise. There is wide-ranging, cross-national evidence from over the last several decades pointing to the fact that secularization, as is true of societal modernization more generally, is an uneven process. It tends, rather, to present as relatively differentiated and jagged, allowing plenty of spaces for religion and for non-church forms of spirituality to persevere and remain relevant. Industrialization bypassed Irish society such that it transitioned from a largely agricultural to a service and information economy, and more recently with the Celtic Tiger to a high-tech and financial services economy. In parallel manner, we might think of secularization as having bypassed Irish society in the era (1960s–1980s) when it was occurring elsewhere. It then subsequently gave rise to circumstances whereby Ireland is instead transitioning in a relatively rapid interval from a highly religious to what might be called a *post-secular* society. A post-secular society is one in which the hegemony of religion is no longer a controlling social and political force. Secularization has taken hold; yet religion still matters and has public relevance. Importantly, in post-secular as opposed to secular society, the secularistic certainty that religion will disappear amid the forces of modernization is losing ground. Rather, the secularizing society must contend with mainstream religious ideas and ethics.[35]

IRELAND'S POST-SECULAR OPPORTUNITY

Thus in accord with the post-secular frame, the evidence of Irish secularization and the generational and other social forces driving its momentum does not mean that there is no role for the Catholic Church in Ireland. Quite the contrary. In post-secular society, religion continues to have public influence and relevance. As Jurgen Habermas argues, theologically moderate (i.e., non-fundamentalist) religious institutions can articulate the norms and ethical intuitions that can help steer society in a more just and egalitarian direction.[36] He suggests that religious ethics might be drawn on to reorient contemporary society out of the social and economic problems attendant on neo-liberal economic policies, global economic inequality, political indifference, and cultural fragmentation (e.g., due to immigration). Habermas argues, for example, that "The translation of the likeness of the human to the image of the divine into the equal and absolutely respected dignity of all human beings" offers a way of using religious ethics to craft public policies that embody and institutionalize principles of economic and social justice.[37]

The Catholic Church was seen in the 1970s as "the conscience" of Irish society in large part due to its concern for the poor, though the Irish bishops have also been sharply criticized for their failure to engage seriously with matters of Irish economic and social policy and their tendency to ignore issues of economic morality (e.g., tax evasion).[38] Political leaders themselves have at times made recourse to a policy discourse emphasizing the creation of a "just society."[39] Therefore, the articulation of an ethics of justice in the civil sphere would not be unfamiliar to many Irish people. This is a voice that

Church leaders could re-develop and revitalize. There is space for such a discourse because, despite recent economic gains, Ireland must still contend with serious financial issues invariably impacting how public finances are used and how such decisions impact economic and social inequality. Relatedly, the post-Celtic Tiger surge in Irish immigration, the continuing strain of accommodating "non-national" migrants within Ireland, and the economic and social depletion of rural communities creates problems for the quality of the social fabric and the maintenance of social solidarity.[40]

My suggestion that the Church could, or should, develop a public moral voice that is attuned to the present societal realities is not based on the assumption that a society cannot be moral without religion or without, more specifically, Catholicism. From a sociological perspective, however, a vibrant civil society needs institutions that can articulate views that are counter-hegemonic to the dominant material and power interests in society.[41] It would be naïve to think that any institution is devoid of partisan interests, a point underscored by the unapologetically self-interested behavior of the Church over the course of many decades of priests' sex abuse and its cover-up. Nevertheless, those institutions that are relatively more distant from the economic and financial levers of the highly competitive and increasingly globalized marketplace may be better poised to articulate a moral voice that can help to reorient a society to rethink its policies and practices. It does not have to be the Catholic Church—it could perhaps be a not-for-profit organization or an alliance of such groups. In contemporary society, however, when a nation's particular interests are often sacrificed by transnational decision-making bodies (e.g., the EU, the IMF) for the greater capitalistic good of global markets, a robust institution that has both deep national roots and the moral and economic resources of a transnational organization may be better positioned to take on the challenging task of critique that is necessary to help rein in the excesses of neo-liberal economic policies.[42]

The Catholic Church in Ireland has this cultural history and institutional standing. Notwithstanding the Church's ongoing credibility issues stemming from the sex abuse crisis, religious habits and faith intuitions still hold sway for large numbers of Irish people, thus perhaps making them relatively open to the idea of a faith-informed ethical discourse in the public arena. Widespread public disaffection with the government's neo-liberal policies aimed at restructuring Ireland's financial status and exacerbated by new scandals with respect to the management of public finances (e.g., the lavish salaries and fees paid to hospital and Central Remedial Clinic executives, and to Irish Water Board consultants) further dim citizens' confidence in government ministers and political parties. Similarly, the national media, operating in an ever more competitive global and digitalized marketplace, no longer hold the same editorial prestige or influence in public opinion formation that they had, especially in the latter decades of the twentieth century. The Church, on the other hand, has the ethical grounding and the doctrinal imprimatur of a long-standing commitment to social justice, dating back to the late nineteenth century when the first papal encyclical on social justice was issued (*Rerum Novarum*, 1891). The latter focus is gaining renewed momentum largely due to its increased prominence in the statements and lifestyle of Pope Francis, for whom global and local indifference toward the poor is a primary moral concern.

The Church would need to apprehend its renewed moral role, however, as a *contrite* institution, contending as it is with stark evidence of its own moral lapses and a steep decline in its traditional power and cultural significance in Irish society. Given the data I have presented regarding Irish Catholics' liberal views on sexual morality, it would likely enhance the Church's chances of having impact if it were to heed Pope Francis's admonition to Church leaders to mute their obsession with abortion and sexual issues. There is some evidence that the church hierarchy, seizing the opportunity to renew its relevance in Irish society, is addressing themes that mitigate the market-driven ethos of neo-liberal economic and public policies. For example, in anticipation of the publication of the government's annual budget for 2014, the bishops approvingly invoked the argument of an alliance of Catholic social justice groups that "Solidarity must be the defining value of Budget 2014," and reiterated the groups' denouncement of "the devastating and demoralising austerity policies that have characterised annual budgets of recent years." Similarly, prior to the G8 Summit in June 2013, the bishops argued that "against the backdrop of the widespread suffering caused by poverty, inequality and social exclusion, solidarity is needed to rebuild trust, restore relationships and give hope for a real and lasting recovery."[43] These statements, however, though available in the public sphere, are not front and center in political and public dialogue and do not necessarily penetrate the larger Irish consciousness. To help remedy this, the Church could, for example, highlight social and economic inequality in a more systematic way, and do so across the year rather than solely in the context of ritualized political moments (e.g., the annual announcement of the government budget).

ENGAGING, AND SEEING GOD IN, SECULAR CULTURE

More broadly, the opening provided for the Church by the recognition of post-secular society challenges Church leaders to adopt a more differentiated and nuanced view of the secular. Over the last few decades, dating especially to the papacy of John Paul II, Church leaders have become habituated to presenting secularization as, by default, the Church's enemy. This framing may be understandable from the Church's perspective given the secular challenges to the maintenance of the relevance of religion. Nonetheless, it appears to hinder the ability of church leaders to move through and beyond the Church's current legitimation issues. These issues include the restoration of its institutional credibility in the wake of the sex abuse crisis. Additionally, there is the broader fact that large numbers of the laity increasingly perceive the Church and Catholic teaching as irrelevant to or unhelpful in their negotiation of the moral and other dilemmas variously entangled in their everyday lives. At both a macro-political level, and in the local micro-context of pastoral care, a Church that repeatedly denounces secular culture runs the risk of being perceived as lacking the doctrinal and institutional resources to engage productively with contemporary culture and society.

Pope Benedict wrote a widely anticipated special Pastoral Letter to the Catholics of Ireland, in February 2011, in an attempt to restore the stature of the Church in Ireland in the wake of the sex abuse scandals. Surprisingly, in that context, he argued that the "weakening of faith" and the increasingly secularized society in which the Church operates contributed to the Church's sex abuse problem. Benedict lamented that social changes have created a situation wherein "The Church has had to confront new and serious challenges to the faith arising from rapid transformation and secularization of Ireland. . . . Fast paced social change has occurred, often adversely affecting people's traditional adherence to Catholic teaching and values . . . a weakening of faith and the loss of respect for the Church and its teachings."[44]

Secular culture, and economic and social change, have certainly impacted Irish Catholics' Church involvement and deference toward Church teachings. It is not, however, a productive political or pastoral strategy to maintain a defensive posture toward the secular. Such a stance has the effect of presenting the Church as a victim of modernity and of secular culture, when in fact, the Church is itself part and parcel of secular society and is well able to use the gifts of modernity to bolster its own power—whether through the use of mass media, advertising/public relations, political advocacy, legal argument, and so on. It should use these resources because modernity makes these tools and resources available to all individual, collective, and institutional actors. When Church leaders denounce the forces of modernization, it often seems motivated less by a prophetic counter-cultural critique than by a strategic attempt to divert attention from its own institutional failures.

Dublin Archbishop Diarmuid Martin stands out as someone who acknowledges the errors of the Church while also being committed to revitalizing Catholic faith practices and the Church's relevance in Irish society. He offers a somewhat more nuanced view than his co-bishops of the church's relation to secular culture. In a contrite, sober, and wide-ranging assessment of the "future of the Church in Ireland," presented in May 2010, he noted that the "world around us and the culture of Irish life have changed. . . . Irish culture has drifted from being the culture of an enlarged faith community into a heavily secularized culture." He noted, moreover, that secular culture "is at times even . . . a hostile culture." Yet, he also seemed to acknowledge that the Church itself has to change the ways in which it responds to, and acts in, this culture. Thus, rather than presenting a unilateral denunciation of societal change, Archbishop Martin identified ways in which the church itself can/must change and act differently within society; the goals outlined included ways for the church to do a better job evangelizing, communicating the theology informing its moral teachings, and providing high-quality services for the poor.[45] More recently, he has argued that Irish Catholicism needs to find a balance between the "rigorism" of its past incarnation and the "laxism" in current practices.[46] Relatedly, he has also acknowledged the disconnect between church teaching on marriage and the family and the everyday experiences and realities in many Irish people's lives, and the need for the Church to develop pastoral care that responds to these realities.[47]

The Second Vatican Council (1962–1965)—the Church's own institutional self-reflexive assessment of its doctrine and practices—was convened by Pope John XXIII so that the Church would open itself to the modern world and let in some fresh air. Its goal was for the Church to be relevant in contemporary society. As part of that objective, the Council made a commitment to include the professional and everyday lived experiences of a diverse laity in a collaborative reimagining and implementation of a doctrinally reflexive, pastorally effective, and publicly engaged Church.[48] The papacy of Pope Francis renews hope that this commitment will be renewed. In particular, Francis's insistence that "God is to be encountered in the world of today," that "God is in history [and] in [its] processes," provides a refreshing rebuke to those who see contemporary culture, secular culture, as Godless. As Francis has stated:

> God is certainly in the past, because we can see his footprints. And God is also in the future as a promise. But the "concrete" God, so to speak, is today. For this reason, complaining never helps us find God. The complaints of today about how barbaric the world is—these complaints sometimes end up giving birth within the church to desires to establish order in the sense of pure conservation, as a defense. No: God is to be encountered in the world of today.

Francis's statements to date affirm the importance of a vibrant and inclusive Church community, one in which people "walk united with our differences," a community that discerns from experiences rather than a Church that rules by enforcing "a disjointed multitude of doctrines to be imposed insistently." It is auspicious for Catholics everywhere, but especially perhaps for Irish Catholics who have so precipitously lost the anchor of Church, that Pope Francis appears open to wanting to discern new ways for the Church to move forward through rediscovering the relevance of the gospel for Christian living and the crafting of a just society. Thus amidst the consciousness of Church crisis and evidence of declining commitment to and interest in Catholicism, there is the possibility that the Irish Church in this post-secular moment, can seize the opportunity to "be a Church that finds new roads, [and] that is able to step outside of itself" in its engagement with Irish society.[49]

CONCLUSION

Irish society is slowly emerging from a period of great turmoil. Its unprecedented economic growth followed by the imposition of financial austerity, the collective trauma in response to documented revelations of sex abuse by priests and its cover-up by Church officials, and the relatively abrupt breakdown in the cordiality of Church-State relations all imposed a strain on the Irish psyche. Amid societal change and strain, the centrality of Catholicism to Irish habits and the authority of the Church in individual lives and in public culture has diminished quite dramatically. The declining significance of the Church is especially evident in the attitudes and practices of the younger generation whose experiences of Church and society are remarkably different to those of their parents and grandparents. A narrative of decline, however, does not capture the whole story of the current place of the Church in Irish society. Many people still go to Mass on a regular basis and the symbols of Catholicism still carry some weight. The social justice teachings of the Church may have renewed relevance given the rise of economic neoliberalism and its attendant social challenges, challenges exacerbated by the new resurgence in Irish emigration and the depletion of rural communities. Should Church leaders venture to engage the public in a moral discourse on the just society, they would need to collectively do so in a way that appreciates both secular culture and the moral and practical dilemmas that individuals and communities confront in these times.

NOTES

1. See Kieran Allen, "The Political Elite," in *Are the Irish Different*? ed. Tom Inglis (Manchester: Manchester University Press, 2014), 54–64.
2. Figures are for April 2014. See "Economic and Financial Indictors," *The Economist*, June 14–20, 2014, 84.
3. Ireland's Gross Domestic Product (GDP) was at an all-time high in the first quarter of 2007 at 5.5 percent; its all-time low of -3.60 percent occurred in the fourth quarter of 2008. Central Statistics Office, Dublin, accessed June 12, 2014, www.cso.ie.
4. As part of the Irish national media's extensive reporting and analysis of Enda Kenny's speech, an edited version of the speech was printed in the *Irish Independent*, July 21, 2011, 18.
5. Tom Inglis, *Moral Monopoly: Catholic Church in Modern Irish Society* (Dublin: Gill and Macmillan, 1987).
6. Max Weber, *The Protestant Ethic and the Spirit of Capitalism* (New York: Scribner's and Sons, 1958).
7. *Catechism of the Catholic Church* (Dublin: Gill and Macmillan, 1995), par.1341.

8. Author's analysis of the ISSP (International Social Survey Program) data; see also Maire Nic Ghiolla Phadraig, "Religion in Ireland: No Longer an Exception?" *Access Research Knowledge*, Research Update 64, 2009, accessed January 14, 2014, www.ark.ac.uk.

9. Eoin O'Mahony, *Practice and Belief among Catholics in the Republic of Ireland* (Dublin: Irish Catholic Bishops Conference, 2011).

10. Michele Dillon, "The Orphaned Irish: Church and State in Neo-Liberal Irish Society," in *Religion and Regimes: Support, Separation, and Opposition*, ed. Mehran Tamadonfar and Ted Jelen (New York: Lexington Books, 2014), 187–211.

11. See, for example, Peter Lunn and Tony Fahey, *Households and Family Structures in Ireland* (Dublin, Economic and Social Research Institute, 2011).

12. Central Statistics Office, Dublin, accessed March 21, 2014, www.cso.ie.

13. Lunn and Fahey, *Households and Family Structures*.

14. Central Statistics Office, Dublin, accessed March 21, 2014, www.cso.ie.

15. Kyung-Sup Change, "The Second Modern Condition? Compressed Modernity as Internalized Reflexive Modernization," *British Journal of Sociology* 61 (2010): 444-64.

16. On Europe and the United States, see Andrew Greeley, *Religion in Europe at the End of the Second Millennium* (New Brunswick, NJ: Transaction Books, 2003); on Australia, see Robert Dixon, Stephen Reid, and Marilyn Chee, *Mass Attendance in Australia* (Fitzroy, Australia: Australian Catholic Bishops Conference, 2013).

17. Andrew Greeley, *American Catholics since the Council* (Chicago: Thomas More Press, 1985), 53–55.

18. Michael Hout and Andrew Greeley, "The Center Doesn't Hold: Church Attendance in the United States, 1940–1984," *American Sociological Review* 52 (1987): 332.

19. William D'Antonio, Michele Dillon, and Mary Gautier, *American Catholics in Transition* (Lanham, MD: Rowman & Littlefield, 2013).

20. O'Mahony, *Practice and Belief*.

21. A survey conducted in Ireland in 2011 (for the Iona Institute by Amarach Research) found that approximately 30 percent of Catholics had gone to Mass within the past week. I have been unable to track down the sampling procedure used for this survey and hence I don't know how much confidence to have in the reliability of the Iona data.

22. The data presented in this section for 1998 and 2008 come from the ISSP.

23. Poll data are from *The Irish Times* and Ipsos MRBI. See "A Winnable Referendum," *The Irish Times,* April 7, 2014, 15; and Stephen Collins, "Support for Same-Sex Marriage Increasing, Poll Finds" *The Irish Times*, April 7, 2014.

24. See Michael Kelly, "Irish Bishops Decide not to Publish Responses to Synod Questionnaire," *National Catholic Reporter*, March 12, 2014.

25. Michele Dillon, "Asynchrony in Attitudes Toward Abortion and Gay Rights: The Challenge to Values Alignment," *Journal for the Scientific Study of Religion* 53 (2014): 1–16.

26. Stephen Collins, "Over 70% Support X-Case Legislation on Abortion," *The Irish Times*, February 11, 2013.

27. D'Antonio et al., *American Catholics*, 110.

28. See Norval Glenn, "The Trend in 'No Religion' Respondents to U.S. National Surveys, Late 1950s to Early 1980s," *Public Opinion Quarterly* 51 (1987): 292–314; Michael Hout and Claude Fischer, "Why More Americans Have No Religious Preference: Politics and Generations," *American Sociological Review* 67 (2002): 165–90; and The Pew Forum, *"Nones" on the Rise: One-in-Five Adults Have No Religious Affiliation* (Washington, D.C.: Pew Forum on Religion and Public Life, 2012).

29. Irish Census, 2011. Central Statistics Office, Dublin, accessed March 21, 2014, www.cso.ie.

30. The Irish data are from the *The Irish Times* and Ipsos MRBI poll conducted in April 2014; see Collins, "Support for Same-Sex Marriage Increasing." The U.S. data are presented in Dillon, "Asynchrony in Attitudes Toward Abortion and Gay Rights," based on a poll conducted in November 2012 by the Public Religion Research Institute, in Washington, D.C.

31. For an assessment of the role of generation in religious change, see Michele Dillon, "Christian Affiliation and Disaffiliation in the United States: Generational and Cultural Change," in *The Global Handbook of Christianity*, ed. Stephen Dalton (Leiden: Brill, in press).

32. For example, the Catholic Church is patron of approximately 92 percent of all primary schools in the Republic of Ireland.

33. Andrew Greeley, *The Catholic Imagination* (Berkeley: University of California Press, 2000).

34. Irish Episcopal Conference, *Summary of the Church's Position on Mass Offerings*. (Dublin: Irish Catholic Bishops' Conference, 2010).

35. Jurgen Habermas, "Notes on Post-Secular Society," *New Perspectives Quarterly* 25 (2008): 17–29.

36. Habermas, "Notes on Post-Secular Society."

37. Jurgen Habermas, in Virgil Nemoianu, "The Church and the Secular Establishment: A Philosophical Dialog between Joseph Ratzinger and Jurgen Habermas," *Logos* 9 (2006): 17–42. For an assessment of Habermas's construal of post-secular society, see Michele Dillon, "Jurgen Habermas and the Post-Secular Appropriation of Religion: A Sociological Critique," in *Probing the Post-Secular,* ed. Philip Gorski, David Kim, John Torpey, and Jonathan Van Antwerpen (New York: New York University Press/Social Science Research Council, 2012), 249–78.

38. Liam Ryan, "Church and Politics: The Last Twenty-Five Years," *The Furrow* 30 (1979): 3–18. For critiques, see, for example, Michel Peillon, *Contemporary Irish Society* (Dublin: Gill and Macmillan, 1982), 95–99; and ex-Prime Minister and Fine Gael leader Garret FitzGerald, *Reflections on the Irish State* (Dublin: Irish Academic Press, 2003), 145.

39. The Fine Gael party, for example, which was led by the intellectually influential Taoiseach (Prime-Minister) Dr. Garrett Fitzgerald in the 1970s and 1980s, issued proposals for a "Just Society" in the mid-1960s.

40. See, for example, Paul Melia, "Exodus from Rural Areas Revealed," and related articles, in a Special Report in *The Irish Independent*, March 29, 2014, 18–20.

41. Jeffrey Alexander, *The Civil Sphere* (New York: Oxford University Press, 2006).

42. Zygmunt Bauman, *Liquid Modernity* (Cambridge: Polity, 2000).

43. Statements issued by the Irish Episcopal Conference, accessed February 26, 2014, www.catholicbishops.ie.

44. Pope Benedict XVI, *Pastoral Letter of the Holy Father Pope Benedict XVI to the Catholics of Ireland, March 19, 2010*, The Holy See, accessed July 31, 2014, http://www.vatican.va/holy_father/benedict_xvi/letters/2010/documents/hf_ben-xvi_let_20100319-_church-ireland_en.html.

45. Diarmuid Martin, *The Future of the Church in Ireland* (Dublin: Office of the Archdiocese of Dublin, 2010).

46. Diarmuid Martin, *Pope Francis—One Year On* (Dublin: Office of the Archdiocese of Dublin, 2014).

47. Diarmuid Martin, *Fostering Faith in the City Centre* (Dublin: Office of the Archdiocese of Dublin, 2014).

48. See Michele Dillon, *Catholic Identity: Balancing Reason, Faith, and Power* (New York: Cambridge University Press, 1999).

49. "A Big Heart Open to God: The Exclusive Interview with Pope Francis," *America*, September 30, 2013, accessed July 31, 2014, http://americamagazine.org/pope-francis-interview.

Chapter Five

Clerical Burnout and Political Engagement

A Study of Catholic Priests in Ireland

Elizabeth A. Oldmixon and Brian R. Calfano

This chapter discusses the professional stress experienced by Catholic priests in Ireland in the wake of sociological change and the diminished status of the Catholic Church, and the political significance thereof.[1] The Catholic Church in Ireland has undergone tremendous difficulty in recent decades. More than a process of slow secularization as has been observed in the rest of Western Europe, Irish society has experienced a kind of collective cognitive dissonance with respect to the Church. Traditionally the Church represented the hallmark of Irishness. It "occupied a dominant position in Irish life: powerful, authoritarian, and highly prescriptive in its approach to the laity."[2] In the Republic, the Church functioned as the cultural and political hegemon. In the 1990s, however, the Irish people were confronted with a series of Church sexual scandals that cast the moral and pastoral legitimacy of the Church into serious doubt for many. An upshot of this development is that morale among priests has apparently diminished.

The political significance of clergy morale is in its externalities. The political science literature on religion and politics observes that religious contexts, such as parishes and congregations, play an import role socializing individuals and inculcating the faithful with shared religious values, and this likely affects the political values that religious people bring to the public square.[3] In this context, clergy have an important role to play as opinion leaders. Not only do they tend to have the resources commonly associated with potent political efficacy and engagement, such as educational attainment, but also their job in part is to provide moral guidance. The responsibility to provide moral guidance is one that many embrace.[4] And as Smith demonstrates, clergy political attitudes are related to the political attitudes of the people in the pews.[5]

Even in hierarchical traditions, clergy are, in a sense, the "street-level bureaucrats" of the faith.[6] Policies may be established and doctrines discerned at the highest levels of a religious institution, but both are implemented by clergy, and clergy have a certain amount of autonomy to determine what to emphasize. Day to day decisions about whether to preach on poverty or war or culture, for example, are made at the local level. As such, clergy have the capacity, first, to raise the salience of particular issues and values in the minds of churchgoers, and, second, then frame how the churchgoers will think about those issues.[7] This essay considers how professional stress affects this dynamic. In particular, we are interested in whether clergy who experience high levels of professional stress eschew the political arena. After all, clergy political engagement comes with the risk of alienating one's parish and/or one's religious superior.

Our analysis is based on a survey of clergy in the Republic of Ireland and Northern Ireland. The survey was conducted in summer 2011. It is worth noting that just as the survey went in the field, Judge Yvonne Murphy and fellow commissioners released the Cloyne Report, which was conducted at the request of the Irish Government. The report detailed child sexual abuse perpetrated by Catholic priests in the Diocese of Cloyne, poor diocesan child-protection, and the Vatican's alleged duplicitous response. This tension only added to the pressures associated with ministry that priests were already facing as a function of falling vocations.[8] Even in this period of tremendous stress, however, we find the following: Irish clergy report only moderate levels of burnout, burnout that is associated with lower levels of political engagement. Overall, clergy have a reasonably high sense of professional accomplishment.

THE CHURCH IN TRANSITION

Irish clergy have tremendous potential to wield political and social influence. To be sure, Ireland is not especially religiously pluralistic, as table 5.1 demonstrates. In the American context, by contrast, the political significance of clergy is often tied to the pluralistic, competitive religious economy.[9] Catholicism is the majority denomination on the island as a whole and in the Republic. In Northern Ireland, Catholicism is the plurality denomination, but Catholics and Protestants are in rough numerical parity. Even in this different religious economy, there are several reasons to expect that clergy leadership will be important. First, religious and national identities are organically entwined in Ireland.[10] Catholicism and Protestantism came to represent competing national identities in the nineteenth century. After partition in the early

Table 5.1. Religious Affiliations in the Republic of Ireland and Northern Ireland

Religious Family	Percent of Adults in the Republic	Percent of Adults in Northern Ireland
Catholic	84.2	40.8
Church of Ireland	2.8	13.7
Presbyterian Church in Ireland	0.5	19.1
Methodist	0.1	3.0
Muslim	0.7	0.2
Other	11.8	13.1
Unaffiliated	5.9	10.1
Total	100.0	100.0
N	4,588,252	1,810,863

Central Statistics Office, *This is Ireland: Highlights from Census 2011, Part 1* (Government of Ireland, Dublin, Ireland, 2012); Statistics and Research Agency. Northern Ireland Census, 2011. Accessed March 20, 2014: www.ninis2.nisra.gov.uk/public/Theme.aspx?themeNumber =136&themeName=Census%202011.

1920s, the Catholic Church established itself as the dominant social institution in the majority Catholic Free State, holding sway over cultural, social, and political norms.[11] In Northern Ireland, these competing identities came to define communal boundaries and related conflicts.[12] Second, Irish clergy in different denominations often express systematically different attitudes on some political issues. With respect to abortion and the status of women, for example, Catholic priests tend to be more conservative than non-Catholic clergy.[13] This suggests that clergy have the potential to exercise competitive political and social influence. Third, the Irish Church has a deeply ingrained tradition of clericalism, which is the sense that clergy are an elite group to whom tremendous deference should be shown. Ireland did not develop a strong "critical culture" that challenged Church dominance. In this context, "priests and religious assumed the mantle of moral custodians."[14] Given these three points, the political influence of Irish clergy are surprisingly understudied.[15]

The close relationship between religion and national identity has translated into political influence. Churches developed a role in the running of schools, hospitals, and relief agencies, especially the Catholic Church in the Republic, where it "advanc[ed] decidedly Catholic legislation across an array of policy domains, such as the regulation of dance halls, censorship, education, and divorce."[16] The Church's predominance in the south was institutionalized in the 1937 Constitution, which stated that: "The State recognises the special position of the Holy Catholic Apostolic and Roman Catholic Church as the guardian of the Faith professed by the great majority of the citizens." This language was eventually removed, but Finnegan and McCarron argue that this language would have been even more muscular but for the fear of disaffecting Northern Protestants and foreclosing the possibility of a unified Ireland.[17]

The social and political influence of the Catholic Church was so significant that it held a moral monopoly, allowing it to dominate civil society. It "formed a collective orthodoxy . . . which permeated civil society and the interest groups within it" and provided the raw material for culture, informing Irish identity and the norms by which the Irish Catholics would live.[18] Politically, this has meant that the Church historically has not had an oppositional or adversarial relationship with the state. With certain policy domains ceded to the Church, the bishops rarely needing to directly inject themselves in the policy process.[19] As a corollary, Catholic priests have not had to rally the faithful on political issues. The Church dominated policymaking organically. Some have gone so far as to call this arrangement an "unhealthy theocracy."[20]

Resistance to the dominance of Catholic orthodoxy on key issues such as divorce and contraception, however, grew in the 1960s as Ireland modernized. These trends were fomented by a series of sexual scandals that emerged in the 1990s. In 1992, Eamon Casey, Bishop of Galway, was forced to retire when it became known he had fathered a child whom he supported from diocesan funds. Shortly thereafter, RTE released a documentary that revealed a popular priest, the late Fr. Michael Cleary, had a longtime female partner with whom he had fathered two children. Cleary and Casey "were known as stout defenders of Church teaching on priestly celibacy. The contradiction between theological posture and practice . . . shocked the laity . . . and caused scandal, adverse comment, and great hurt."[21] Maher notes that "when revelations began to surface about inappropriate sexual behavior by certain priests and religious, lay people who were old enough to remember the uncompromising advice given to them in the confessional and in homilies were quick to remark the chasm between the public and private domains. The word 'hypocrisy' naturally sprang to mind."[22]

The revelations of the *child* sexual abuse caused the most profound damage to the Church's reputation. The Cloyne Report, referenced earlier, was not the first of its kind. The 2005 Ferns report chronicled abuse in the Diocese of Ferns over forty years. The report found the bishops regarded abuse as a moral failing, rather than a criminal issue, and placed the interests of the accused above those of the victims. The report also criticized the Garda, the Republic's police force, for its weak response to complaints against priests.[23] Between 1983 and 2000, there were forty clerical abuse convictions in the Republic of Ireland and eight in Northern Ireland.[24] Moreover, by the mid-

1990s, the public was learning more and more about the systematic physical and emotional abuse of children in industrial schools and Magdalene institutions. These were political scandals as well as religious scandals, given that much of the abuse was perpetrated in religious institutions sponsored by the state.[25]

All of this came during a long period of social decline for the Catholic Church, and the result is that it had to compete for influence in a way it previously did not.[26] Many Irish people seemed to have lost faith in the institutional Church. According to the 2011 Irish National Election Study, more than 50 percent of the population in the Republic reports having "no" or "not very much confidence" in the Church. For clergy, this means that they are situated in an institution that used to be the arbiter of social prestige and advancement, but is now viewed with increased skepticism. Not surprisingly, priests report suffering from low morale. They share the disgust of the laity over the abuse scandal, and they are alienated from their bishops. In a 2012 survey of Catholic priests conducted by Newstalk's Moncrieff Show, 65 percent report the Vatican handled the sexual abuse cases in Ireland "poorly," 65 percent report "all priests' reputations have been damaged by abuse scandals in the church in recent decades," and only 61 percent report that "church hierarchy understands the work and challenges faced by priests in a modern world."[27] Some report hostility and fear being seen in public, while others report concern over the possibility of false accusations.[28] At least anecdotally, the confluence of these factors seems to put emotional pressure on priests, the full effects of which remain unknown.

PROFESSIONAL STRESS AND BURNOUT

There are clear psychological consequences to the stress associated with professional ministry. Randall notes that while "parish ministry at its best can be wonderfully fulfilling for clergy, it can also be tough and demanding, and there is frequently the lurking danger of burnout."[29] Given the stress faced by clergy due to the changing social context, we suspect this is especially true for clergy in Ireland. Societal changes and sexual scandals may exacerbate stress due to role-conflict, which occurs when individuals face incompatible expectations in their various responsibilities.[30] Clergy are good candidates to experience role-conflict, given that they are nested within congregations that are nested within larger denominations. Both denominational officials and local parishioners can exert significant, countervailing pressures on clergy when it comes to salient denominational issues. This has been partly established with respect to American Catholic priests, and Ryan conjectures that this has contributed to low morale among Catholic priests in Ireland.[31]

We are especially interested in burnout. Burnout is a response to psychological stress "linked with a predisposition to fail, to wear out, or to become exhausted through excessive demands on energy, strength, or resources."[32] Francis et al. consider three different dimensions of burnout: emotional exhaustion, depersonalization, and professional accomplishment. They find evidence of burnout among Catholic priests in Wales and England.[33] Indeed, Catholic priests experience much higher levels of burnout than their Anglican peers. In comparing Catholic and Anglican clergy, Catholic clergy experience higher levels of depersonalization and emotional exhaustion, but higher levels of professional accomplishment.[34]

METHODOLOGY AND ANALYSIS

We investigate clergy burnout using an all island survey of clergy. In early 2011, we compiled a comprehensive list of parish/pastoral clergy in the Republic and Northern Ireland. This list comprised 4,520 individual clergy.[35] We invited 3,530 clergymen and clergywomen—all those for whom we could identify an email address—to participate. We conducted the clergy survey in June and July of 2011, and received 444 useable responses from clergy in Northern Ireland and the Republic, making our response rate 12.6 percent. This is lower than we would have liked. This is conjecture, but perhaps because the researchers are affiliated with non-Irish institutions, clergy were reticent to participate. Also, the all-island nature of our survey may have led to suspicion among some clergy, particularly some in Northern Ireland, who are traditionally more suspicious of involvement with the rest of the island. The concern for external validity is somewhat mitigated by the rough parity between the responses and the invitations, considered by denomination. Forty-eight percent of invitations were sent to Catholics priests, who comprise 49 percent of the sample. Fourteen percent and 15 percent of invitations were sent to Anglicans and Presbyterians, and they comprise 20 percent and 15 percent of the sample, respectively. In any case, we interpret our results with a certain amount of caution.

Textbox 5.1. Institutional Prime Battery

"As a member of the clergy, I have a responsibility to promote the teachings of the Church to my parishioners as these relate to public policies before elections."

"My parish's financial health reflects on my performance as a member of the clergy."

"I am concerned about the financial condition of my parish."

"My bishop encourages me to make political statements."

"I am hesitant to discuss certain aspects of the teachings of the Church and public policy issues during worship service if I anticipate a negative reaction from parishioners."

"I have encountered a negative reaction from parishioners after discussing the teachings of the Church on public policy issues during worship services."

"I would rather discuss the teachings of the Church as it relates to public policy issues with parishioners outside of services than during services."

"The Bible is the inerrant Word of God, both in matters of faith and in historical, geographical, and other secular matters."

"My bishop has reprimanded clergy who have not followed his instructions on how to discuss the religious teachings of the Church relating to public policies with parishioners."

"I am concerned that discussing public policy issues during services will lead to a downturn in parishioner financial giving."

"I encourage the distribution of voter information resources to parishioners, even if they may not be entirely consistent with Church teaching."

Note: These are 11-points Likert questions, with 11 reflecting the highest level of agreement.

The survey asked respondents a battery of political and socio-demographic questions, and it also included a question order experiment. This allows us to raise the salience of a distinct aspect of clergy professional life—the professional network. Our experimental treatment, which we call the *institutional prime*, positioned a battery of institutional questions at the beginning of the instrument. All respondents received the battery of institutional questions. By randomly assigning some respondents to receive the institutional prime, we can test whether raising the salience of one's professional network contributes to professional stress and burnout. The questions included in the institutional prime can be found in textbox 5.1.

We use Francis et al.'s measure of burnout and its three dimensions of emotional exhaustion, depersonalization, and professional accomplishment.[36] In order to assess emotional exhaustion, respondents were asked their level of agreement with the following prompts:

- *I feel burned out from my parish ministry.*
- *I feel fatigued in the morning when I get up and have to face another day in the parish.*

Table 5.2. Burnout Measures

Likert Item	Percent Agreeing or Strongly Agreeing	Mean Catholic	Mean Other
Emotional Exhaustion		5.4	5.4
I feel burned out from my parish ministry.	25.0		
I feel fatigued in the morning when I get up and have to face another day in the parish.	28.2		
Depersonalization		**4.0**	**3.7**
I don't really care what happens to some of my parishioners.	8.1		
I find it really difficult to listen to what some parishioners are really saying to me.	9.3		
Professional Accomplishment		**7.6**	**7.8**
I have accomplished many worthwhile things in my parish ministry.	75.9		
I feel exhilarated after working closely with my parishioners.	72.7		

Bolded means are statistically different at $p<.05$.
Note: These were 5-point items with a 5 reflecting the highest level of agreement.

Both were 5-point Likert items. This means that respondents were asked their level of agreement with the prompts on a 1 to 5 scale. A score of "5" reflected the highest level of agreement. Responses were summed to create a composite measure, with an overall score of 10 indicating the highest level of emotional exhaustion. Table 5.2 indicates that 25 percent report a sense of burnout, while just over 28 percent report feelings of fatigue related to ministry. A comparison of Catholic and non-Catholic clergy does not reveal any appreciable differences on this dimension, as the mean level of emotional exhaustion for both is 5.4.

The depersonalization dimension covers feelings of alienation from one's parishioners. This is measured on the basis of agreement with the following prompts:

- *I don't really care what happens to some of my parishioners.*
- *I find it really difficult to listen to what some parishioners are really saying to me.*

Just over 8 percent of respondents agree with the former, while just over 9 percent agree with the latter. The mean level of depersonalization for Catholic priests is 4, while the mean level for other clergy is 3.7. The difference is substantively small, but statistically significant. Catholic priests on average feel slightly higher levels of depersonalization than their non-Catholic peers. They also express slightly lower levels of professional accomplishment. This is measured on the basis of agreement with the following prompts:

- *I have accomplished many worthwhile things in my parish ministry.*
- *I feel exhilarated after working closely with my parishioners.*

Here again, the differences are slight (7.6 as opposed to 7.8), but statistically significant.

Borrowing from Randall, we use the two negative components of burnout, emotional exhaustion and depersonalization, to create a new composite measure.[37] This new measure basically confirms the previous findings. The overall mean level of burnout score is 9.2 out of a possible 20. Catholics and non-Catholics alike express moderate levels of stress. We also calculated differences comparing clergy in the Republic of Ireland and Northern Ireland. Again, there were no statistically significant differences. We expected Catholics to be more burned out than their peers in ministry, because Protestant clergy have not had to deal with the systemic sexual abuse scandals. This does not appear to be the case, as they too confront a more secular Ireland. Ireland may be less Catholic that it used to be, but it is not more Protestant.[38]

In order to subject these findings to a more rigorous statistical analysis, we model the Composite Burnout scores as a function of the institutional prime, denomination, a concern for parish finances, belief in God, and the perception that one's bishop reprimands clergy who have not followed his instructions about how to discuss the religious teachings of the Church relating to public policies with parishioners. Again, the institutional prime battery of questions can be found in textbox 5.1. Denomination is measured with two indicator variables for Catholic and Presbyterian clergy. All other clergy comprise the base category. Concern for parish finances is measured by the level of agreement with the following prompt:

- *My parish's financial health reflects on my performance as a member of the clergy.*

Belief in God was measured with a question asking respondents to place themselves on a continuum between 0 and 10, where 0 reflects certainty that God does not exist and 10 reflects certainty that God does exist. Bishop reprimands is measured on the basis of agreement with the following prompt:

- *My denomination's leadership (e.g., bishop, District, Council, General Assembly, etc.) has reprimanded clergy who have not followed his/her/its instructions on how to discuss the religious teachings of the church relating to public policies with parishioners.*

Table 5.3. Regression Analysis of Clergy Burnout

Variable	Unstandardized regression coefficients
Catholic	.57 (.27)**
Presbyterian	.63 (.37)*
Institutional battery	1.91 (.25)**
Finances	.07 (.04)*
Belief in God	-.11 (.05)**
Bishop reprimands	.05 (.04)
Age	-.02 (.01)
Constant	.48 (.28)**
N	442
Adj R-squared	.15
F	10.92**

* = p<.10, ** = p<.05, two-tailed tests.
Note: standard errors in parentheses.

Finally, age is measured in years.

The results of the analysis can be found in table 5.3. The coefficients for Catholic and Presbyterian clergy are both significant and positive. This suggests that when we control for other key factors, both experience higher levels of burnout than their peers in other religious traditions, more than half of whom are Anglicans. The institutional prime is also significant. Among clergy for whom the salience of the professional network was raised, levels of burnout are higher by almost 2 points. The sense that parish financial health reflects the performance in ministry is also associated higher levels of burnout. The only variable associated with lower levels of burnout is belief in God. The more certain clergy are of God's existence, the lower their level of burnout. Incidentally, while 75 percent of respondents are absolutely certain that God exists, only 17 percent believe that the financial health of their parish is at least in some part due to their performance as clergy.

As political scientists, our chief concern is whether and how burnout resulting from professional stress might affect the political role that clergy play. Thus, we consider whether burnout and role-conflict affects behaviors related to political engagement. Political engagement is measured on the basis of agreement with the following prompts:

- *I encourage the distribution of voter information resources to parishioners, even if they may not be entirely consistent with Church teaching*;
- *I am hesitant to discuss certain aspects of the teachings of the Church and public policy issues during worship service if I anticipate a negative reaction from parishioners.*

In order to measure role-conflict, we include the Bishop Reprimands variable, and then two additional variables that measure the extent to which one's parishioners and one's bishop influence one's behavior. For the latter two variables, respondents were asked to rank order which "people, groups, things, or activities listed below . . . determine your BEHAVIOR on Church teachings." Friends and family (outside the ministry), parishioners, prayer and reflection, the Bible and church doctrinal writings, and bishop/church superior were among the response options.

The results can be found in table 5.4. When it comes to supporting the distribution of voter information, parish and bishop influence do not emerge as significant. Interestingly, perception that the bishop reprimands clergy is positively related to support for the distribution of voter information that may not be consistent with Church teachings. It could be that the same clergy who might be willing to promote non-orthodox materials are the very clergy who have run afoul of their superiors and been subject to reprimand. With respect to burnout, a sense of professional accomplishment is unrelated to the willingness to distribute voter information. Higher levels of depersonalization

Table 5.4. Regression Analysis of Activism

	Encourages the Distribution of Voter Information	Hesitant to Discuss Public Policy during Worship
Emotional Exhaustion	-.17 (.08)**	.21 (.08)**
Depersonalization	.19 (.11)*	.22 (.11)**
Professional Accomplishment	-.07 (.13)	.04 (.13)
Parish Influence	-.12 (.08)	.13 (.07)*
Bishop Influence	.06 (.07)	.02 (.06)
Bishop Reprimands	.09 (.05)*	.08 (.04)*
Constant	4.2 (1.4)**	1.20 (1.37)
N	444	444
Adj R-squared	.02	.03
F	2.16*	3.13*

* = p<.10, ** = p<.05, two-tailed tests.
Note: standard errors in parentheses.

are positively related to the willingness to distribute voter information, and emotional exhaustion is negatively related to the willingness to distribute voter information. The emotional exhaustion finding makes sense. The more burnt out clergy are on this dimension, the less willing they are to enter the political fray. We are less sure how to make sense of the depersonalization finding. It does seem, however, that the more alienated clergy are from their parishioners, the more willing they are to expose them to heterodox information. When it comes to hesitance to discuss public policy during worship, we find that while professional accomplishment is unrelated to the willingness to discuss public policy during worship, the other components of burnout are positively related to hesitancy. Thus, burnout leads to disengagement. Bishop reprimands and parish influence are also positively related to hesitancy. Here again, this suggests that in addition to burnout, role conflict leads to political disengagement. Clerics do not wish to run afoul of their parishioners or their superiors.

DISCUSSION AND CONCLUSION

This chapter contributes to a literature that investigates the political role of clergy. We find that while Irish Catholic priests are moderately burnt out, they do report reasonably high levels of professional accomplishment. Catholics and Presbyterian clergy are slightly more burnt out than their peers in other denominations, but the differences are slight. The stresses and rewards associated with ministry are felt across denominations. Anglicans, Presbyterians, Methodists, and Catholics alike confront an increasingly secular Ireland, where religion competes for influence over hearts and minds, and where religion is increasingly more of a cultural trope than a sign of creedal fealty. What contributes to this sense of burnout? By far the key factor appears to be institutional concerns. Clergy primed to think about their institutional church and the more bureaucratic elements of their ministry report higher levels of burnout than those who were not primed. This suggests that the stresses associated with ministry do not necessarily come from the more pastoral elements of their job.

Our central concern is with the political implications of clergy burnout. Previous scholarship has demonstrated that Irish Catholic priests are more conservative than their peers in ministry on cultural and gender issues such as the status of abortion and the propriety of working mothers.[39] If burnout diminishes the willingness of priests to engage their congregants on key political issues that are doctrinally important, the Church will lose an important resource. And unfortunately for the Church, this will happen at the very moment when the socio-political status of the Church faces its greatest challenges, and when it most needs its priests—its street-level bureaucrats—to catechize the people. We find that the more exhausted clergy are, and the more alienated they are from their congregates, the more hesitant they are to discuss public policy during worship. A generation ago that might not have mattered, but in 2014 the Church must compete for influence.

It is important not to overstate the level of burnout experienced by Irish clergy, which is lower than we expected given the socio-political context. Even with moderate levels of emotional exhaustion and depersonalization, almost 76 percent of clergy agree that they have accomplished many worthwhile things in parish ministry; nearly 73 percent agree that they feel exhilarated after working closely with parishioners. If one were looking for a reason to be sanguine of the state of clergy morale, these findings provide a strong reason. Clergy may not wish to engage politically, and Catholic priests in particular may be frustrated with the episcopacy, but they find their work as pastors satisfying. An important next step in this research might be to engage in long-form interviews with clergy to further suss out the level of burnout and the implications thereof.

Table 5.5. Appendix: Participant Characteristics

Characteristics	Percentage
Ministry	
Roman Catholic	48.65
Anglican (Church of Ireland)	20.45
Presbyterian	14.41
Other	16.49
Leads Services Weekly or More	72.52
Mean Years Ordained	24.88 (SD=12.40)
Demographics	
Married	41.44
Female	9.91
Mean Age	55.50 (SD=11.45)
Geography	
Northern Ireland	9.48
Congregation SES	Middle Class (modal category, 49.32%)
Urban	56.98
Nationality	
Irish	69.82
UK	23.87
Other	6.31

Calfano, Oldmixon, and Suiter, "Assessing Clergy Attitudes."

NOTES

1. Parts of this chapter are drawn from Brian R. Calfano, Elizabeth A. Oldmixon, and Jane Suiter, "Assessing Clergy Attitudes: Ideology and Institutional Superiors," *Journal of Church and State* (2013), accessed August, 4, 1014, doi:10.1093/jcs/cst028; and Brian R. Calfano, Elizabeth A. Oldmixon, and Jane Suiter, "Who and What Affects the First Estate? An Analysis of Clergy Attitudes on Cultural and Economic Issues," *Politics* (2014), accessed August 4, 2014, doi: 10.1111/1467-9256.12063.

2. Andrew Auge et al., "After the Murphy and Ryan Reports: A Roundtable on the Irish Catholic Church," *New Hibernia Review* 14 (2010): 59.

3. R. Huckfeldt et al., "Alternative Contexts of Political Behavior: Churches, Neighborhoods, and Individuals," *Journal of Politics* 55 (1993): 365–81; C. P. Gilbert, *The Impact of Churches on Political Behavior: An Empirical Study* (Westport: Greenwood Press, 1993); and Kenneth D. Wald et al., "Churches as Political Communities," *American Political Science Review* 82 (1988): 531–48.

4. James L. Guth et al., *The Bully Pulpit: The Politics of Protestant Clergy* (Lawrence: University of Kansas Press, 1997).

5. Gregory Smith, "The Influence of Priests on the Political Attitudes of Roman Catholics," *Journal for the Scientific Study of Religion* 44 (2005): 291–306. See also John P. Bart-

kowski et al., "Faith, Race-Ethnicity, and Public Policy Preferences: Religious Schema and Abortion Attitudes among U.S. Latinos," *Journal for the Scientific Study of Religion* 51 (2012): 343–58; R. Kahari Brown, "Religion, Economic Concerns, and African American Immigration Attitudes," *Review of Religious Research* 52 (2010): 146–58; and Ted Jelen, "Notes for a Theory of Clergy as Political Leaders," in *Christian Clergy in American Politics,* eds. Sue E. S. Crawford and Laura R. Olson, 15–29 (Baltimore: Johns Hopkins University Press, 2000).

6. Michael Lipsky, *Street-Level Bureaucracy: Dilemmas of the Individual in Public Services* (New York: Russell Sage Foundation, 1980).

7. This is not to say that the faithful are passive recipients of clergy guidance. See Paul A. Djupe and Christopher Gilbert, *The Political Influence of Churches* (New York: Cambridge University Press, 2009).

8. Michael Kelly, "Irish Priestly Vocations in Worrying Decline," *The Catholic World Report*, October 30, 2012.

9. Roger Finke and Rodney Stark, *The Churching of America, 1776–2005: Winners and Losers in Our Religious Economy* (New Brunswick, NJ: Rutgers University Press, 2005).

10. Marianne Elliott, *When God Took Sides: Religion and Identity in Ireland—Unfinished History* (Oxford: Oxford University Press, 2009).

11. Michele Dillon, "The Orphaned Irish: Church and State in Neo-Liberal Ireland," in *Religion and Regimes: Support, Separation, and Opposition*, eds. Mehran Tamadonfar and Ted G. Jelen (Lanham: Lexington Books, 2014), 197–211; but see also Diarmaid Ferriter, *Occasions of Sin: Sex and Society in Modern Ireland* (London: Profile Books, 2009).

12. Elliott, *When God Took Sides;* and Claire Mitchell, *Religion, Identity and Politics in Northern Ireland: Boundaries of Belonging and Belief* (Burlington: Ashgate Publishing Company, 2006).

13. Calfano, Oldmixon, and Suiter, "Assessing Clergy Attitudes."

14. Auge et al., "After the Ryan and Murphy Reports," 60 and 62.

15. Although, see, for example, W. D. Birrell, J. E. Greer, and D. J. D. Roche, "The Political and Social Influence of Clergy in Northern Ireland," *Sociological Review* 27 (1979): 491–512; and Patrick Fahy, "Some Political Behaviour Patterns and Attitudes of Roman Catholic Priests in a Rural Part of Northern Ireland," *Economic and Social Review* 1 (1971): 1–24.

16. Calfano, Oldmixon, and Suiter, "Assessing Clergy Attitudes," 4.

17. Richard B. Finnegan and Edward T. McCarron, *Ireland: Historical Echoes, Contemporary Politics* (Boulder, CO: Westview Press, 2000).

18. Tom Inglis, "Irish Civil Society: From Church to Media Domination," in *Religion and Politics: East-West Contrasts from Contemporary Europe,* eds. Tom Inglis, Zdzislaw Mach, and Rafal Mazanek (Dublin: University College Dublin Press, 2000), 50.

19. John H. Whyte, *Church and State in Modern Ireland, 1923–1970* (New York: Barnes & Noble, 1971).

20. Auge et al., "After the Ryan and Murphy Reports," 61.

21. Dermot Keogh, "The Catholic Church in Ireland since the 1950s," in *The Church Confronts Modernity: Catholicism since 1950 in the United States, Ireland, and Quebec*, ed. Leslie Woodcock Tentler (Washington, DC: Catholic University of America Press, 2007), 134.

22. Auge et al., "After the Ryan and Murphy Reports," 62.

23. "Ferns Report Highlights 100 Cases," *RTE,* October 25, 2005, accessed July 24, 2014, http://www.rte.ie/news/2005/1025/68988-ferns/.

24. Keogh, "The Catholic Church in Ireland since the 1950s," 134.

25. For detained discussions of sexuality and the sexual abuse scandal in Ireland, see Ferriter, *Occasions of Sin*; Marie Keenan, *Child Sexual Abuse & the Catholic Church: Power, Gender, and Organizatinal Culture* (Oxford: Oxford University Press, 2012); and Gordon Lynch, *The Sacred in the Modern Word: A Cultural Sociological Approach* (Oxford: Oxford University Press, 2012), chap. 3.

26. Tom Inglis, *Moral Monopoly: The Rise and Fall of the Catholic Church in Modern Ireland* (Dublin: University College Dublin Press, 1998).

27. Additional information and results can be found at Gladys Ganiel, "What Irish Priests Really Think? Moncrieff Show's National Priest Survey 2012," *Gladys Ganiel: Building a Church Without Walls*, March 8, 2012, accessed August 4, 2014, http://www.gladysganiel.com/

irish-catholic-church/what-irish-priests-really-think-moncrieff-shows-national-priest-survey-2012/.

28. Stephen Maguire, "Younger Priests Fear 'Being in Public,'" *Irish Times,* August 5, 2011; Patsy McGarry, "Clergy 'Appalled' by Handling of Abuse," *Irish Times,* August 1, 2011; Ralph Reigel, "Cloyne Parishes to Hold Meetings over Abuse Report," *The Independent*, August 14, 2011; and Kathy Sheridan, "The Fearful Fathers," *The Irish Times*, July 23, 2011.

29. Kelvin J. Randall, "Clergy Burnout: Two Different Measures," *Pastoral Psychology* 62 (2013): 333. See also Leslie J. Francis and Christopher J. F. Rutledge, "Are Rural Clergy in the Church of England under Greater Stress? A Study in Empirical Theology," *Research in the Social Scientific Study of Religion* 11 (2000): 173–91; Leslie J. Francis et al., "Burnout Among Roman Catholic Parochial Clergy in England and Wales: Myth or Reality?" *Review of Religious Research* 46 (2004): 5–19; and Eugene Newman Joseph et al., "The Relationship between Personality, Burnout, and Engagement among Indian Clergy," *International Journal for the Psychology of Religion* 21 (2011): 276–88.

30. J. R. Rizzo, R. J. House, and S. I. Lirtzman, "Role Conflict and Ambiguity in Complex Organizations," *Administrative Science Quarterly* 15 (1970): 150–63.

31. Brian R. Calfano, Elizabeth A. Oldmixon, and Mark Gray, "Strategically Prophetic Priests: An Analysis of Competing Principal Influence on Clergy Political Action," *Review of Religious Research* 56 (2014): 1–21; Aidan Ryan, "Clergy Morale." *The Furrow* 57 (2006).

32. Randall, "Clergy Burnout: Two Different Measures," 334.

33. Francis et al., "Burnout among Roman Catholic Parochial Clergy in England and Wales."

34. Francis and Rutledge, "Are Rural Clergy in the Church of England Under Greater Stress?"; see also L. K. Barnard, and J. F. Curry, "The Relationship of Clergy Burnout to Self-Compassion and Other Personality Dimensions," *Pastoral Psychology* 61 (2012): 49–163; L. Francis, P. Hills, and P. Kaldor, "The Oswald Clergy Burnout Scale: Reliability, Factor Structure and Preliminary Application among Australian Clergy," *Journal of Pastoral Psychology* 57 (2009): 243–52; and Eugene Newman Joseph et al., "The Relationship between Personality, Burnout, and Engagement among Indian Clergy."

35. We are grateful to Gladys Ganiel and Therese Cullen of the Irish School of Ecumenics, Trinity College Dublin, from providing a portion of our data.

36. Francis et al., "Burnout among Roman Catholic Parochial Clergy in England and Wales."

37. Randall, "Clergy Burnout: Two Different Measures."

38. Tom Inglis, *Moral Monopoly*.

39. Calfano, Oldmixon, and Suiter, "Assessing Clergy Attitudes."

Chapter Six

God May Not Need a Passport, but Priests Do

Exploring the Migration Experience of Polish Catholic Priests in Ireland

Agata Piękosz

The arrival of Polish priests in Ireland relates to three key factors of contemporary Irish migration. With the expansion of the European Union in 2004, Polish priests began emigrating to Ireland due to (1) a declining population of vocations in an Ireland ill-equipped to fill the needs of a new bourgeoning immigrant Catholic population; (2) the increased need to serve an ethnic Polish community that was requesting Polish priests; and (3) the formal acknowledgment by the Pontiff in 2006 of the comparative abundance of vocations in Poland, giving many Polish priests the added incentive they needed to apply to leave their country. Pope Benedict, addressing Polish clergy at the Warsaw Cathedral in 2006, stated: "The gift of many vocations, with which God has blessed your Church, must be received in a truly Catholic perspective. Polish priests do not be afraid to leave your secure and familiar world, to go and serve in places where priests are lacking and where your generosity can bear abundant fruit."[1] A few short weeks after the Pontiff's message, a BBC radio documentary referred to Polish priests as "Easy Jet" priests: the modern-day transnational participant in the European Union, zipping about to different parts of Europe, quickly, effortlessly, and for a reasonable price.[2] The BBC reported that Polish priests were emigrating to "fill European gaps" where priests were needed. Polish priests arrived in Ireland overwhelmed by the task of simultaneously tending to their "immigrant flock" and building bridges between diverse communities. In this chapter, I examine the migration experiences, insights, and narratives of Polish

Catholic priests who arrived in Ireland in the years that followed the expansion of the European Union. The central questions of my research are, first, What is the role of the Polish priest in relation to migration? and, second, What is the experience of the priest as an immigrant in the contemporary immigrant-receiving context of Ireland?

Drawing from migration literature on settlement (assimilation/integration) and transnationalism (keeping ties to home), in an attempt to better understand the connection between migration and religion, I explore the limitations of migration scholarship by focusing on the migration experience of religious leadership. Overall, I claim that the priest's experience of migration enriches his understanding of Catholicism as it uproots him. My findings suggest three central, yet overlapping, migration concerns. First, the general mobility of the Polish Catholic priest necessitates a unique balance between his objective institutional role and subjective experience of migration. Second, the task of having to define what "integration" means to an unsettled Polish immigrant population vis-à-vis the emerging integration discourse in Ireland is particularly straining on Polish priests in general. Third, the apparent incompatibilities between the "conservative" approach of Polish Catholic priests and the demoralized state of Irish Catholic affairs can help us better understand the general strengths and weaknesses of global Catholicism.

THEORIES OF MIGRATION AND THE ROLE OF RELIGIOUS LEADERSHIP

The classic conceptualization of assimilation theory assumed that integration was a linear process where immigrants who settle eventually shed their "old" cultural practices and national or political loyalties.[3] The contemporary assimilation thesis focuses on a multi-path process, one that involves integration—be it political, economic, social, and cultural—either into the mainstream society or different segments of the host society. Unlike theories of assimilation, theories of transnationalism do not focus solely on the "receiving context," but also aim to consider the "sending context," exploring how immigrants constantly rework their attachments (physically and ideationally) in multiple sites.[4] Both assimilation and transnational scholars now agree that migration has never been a one-way process toward complete integration into the host society, but more indicative of a two-way reciprocal accommodation, one that requires the examination of multiple layers within diverse social fields.

In traditional immigrant-receiving countries, the immigrant church was seen as a field where ethnic and religious identity could be nourished.[5] "Ethnic parishes" were once thought of as "a buffer zone between ethnic groups."[6] In classic immigrant receiving countries, and among his faithful, the Polish priest prevented the complete assimilation of his flock by instilling a sense of national pride.[7] In the past, "immigrant clergy saw themselves as nurturing Polishness" in immigrant receiving contexts that seemed resistant to diversity and cultural change.[8] Blejwas wrote of Polish Catholic Priests in the United States in 1937: "[Their] role was to counter assimilation, to purposively go against the Americanization and assimilation of the Catholic immigrant at that time."[9] We have since found, however, that while Polish communities were initially maintained in this way, threats of complete assimilation were more ideological than real. As time went on, many Polish immigrants embraced hyphenated identities that contained a unique, diverse, mix of "the old" and "the new."

Yet contemporary European scholars seem to suggest a similarly panicked clerical response to ethnic assimilation/integration in countries that have little experience with new and emerging migration dynamics. What such a response suggests has not been properly addressed. In Scotland, it has been observed by those such as Trzebiatowska that Polish priests seem more concerned with "Polish business" than with forging ties between communities or following the tenets of the global Catholicism, which aims to unite and integrate all Catholics around the world.[10] She writes, "Polish Catholics reinforce their Polishness through the use of native language and ethnic rituals, which in turn creates 'parallel congregations' that moves them further away from integration."[11] Yet we should stop and ask if these reactions are as common as the claim suggests. How integration is defined is a multifaceted process that engages multiple actors and often changes over time. While it is important to question the sense and purpose of the assumed "parallel congregations" in contemporary immigrant receiving countries, we should not forget that the role of ethnic chaplaincies around the world is to provide sacramental and pastoral support for an ethnic community in need of both. The aim of chaplaincies has consistently been centered on the intention of preserving or nourishing different cultural expressions of faith and community. How the chaplaincies are established, received, and subsequently understood, on the other hand, is both historically and contextually specific.

Overall, the extant scholarly migration work, past and present, on the role of the church tends to explore only the religious local or transnational participation of lay immigrants, but it seldom turns its focus to the lives, roles, and work of religious leadership. The idea that "the church" either facilitates integration into the host society or transnational participation (keeping ties to home) overemphasizes the role of "the church" (parallel congregations or otherwise) as the place and space where relationships are created, organized, and established. Current migration research tends to overlook the important and relevant dynamics within and beyond the church related to the multifaceted migration experiences of religious leadership. More often than not, it is the clergy who facilitate and maintain the desire to keep the home and/or host connections alive.[12] Often these connections grow out of and are maintained by the interpersonal ties of non-immigrants, immigrants, and clergy.[13] In Ireland, it is not definitively clear whether Polish priests are interested in nurturing "Polishness" by creating parallel congregations, if they are interested in integrating Polish immigrants into the existing Irish church structure, or both. At this point, it seems that Polish priests are generally more focused on their mobility—"to go and serve in places where priests are lacking and where your generosity can bear abundant fruit."

INTERVIEWING POLISH CATHOLIC PRIESTS IN IRELAND

Polish priests are scattered around different parts of Ireland. For me, their dispersion was an automatic marker of where Polish immigrant communities were situated in Ireland at the time. I interviewed thirteen priests in the summer months of 2011, and then followed-up with interviews the following year.[14] The average age of the Polish priest in Ireland is thirty-seven; they are both diocesan and religious order priests, and most of them did not know each other before leaving Poland.[15] The interviews were conducted in Polish and English, depending on the individual priest's comfort and facility with English at the time of our first interview. All of the priests arrived in Ireland on the basis of short-term contracts; most of them were invited to Ireland only to serve the Polish community. While some had migration experiences outside of Poland and Ireland, for the majority Ireland was the first place they had ever emigrated to.

The interview questions were broken down into three parts. I asked the priests about their personal migration history, their role in immigrant and non-immigrant communities, and their personal reflections on their own migration experience. What emerged were often nuanced insights into the role and experience of being a Polish priest in contemporary Ireland. Most of the interviews lasted more than two hours.

I found the research mutually beneficial; as I gained insights into their lives, I also enriched their understanding of migration. I allowed my research process to be reciprocal by opening up a two-way dialogue about migration. I was aware that for many it was the first time anyone had asked them about their migration experiences. Their rich narratives provided me with a unique migration story to tell, one that is often misunderstood and misidentified in much secular sociological research, particularly in migration studies. All of the transcripts and my findings contain pseudonyms. My findings fall in three main areas.

The Mobility of the Priest

While God may not need a passport, God's workers—that is, priests—require permission from their bishops, letters of appraisal, passports, permits, and citizenship to be able to participate in local parish structures and care for their immigrant flock.[16] Objective institutional and national constraints are closely connected to the priest's personal experiences of migration. While *the migrant priest* is bound by the institutional decrees and philosophies established by the Catholic Church regarding his pastoral role in diverse communities, the priest can, in various ways, negotiate his mobility. Once away from the familiar surroundings of his local parish, the *priest as migrant* becomes an immigrant when he experiences similar (if not the same) processes associated with being an immigrant, such as culture shock, accommodation, acculturation, and integration.[17] These two features of priestly mobility occur simultaneously; it is often difficult to determine which one predominates. The ways in which priests narrate their migration experiences, however, helps unpack this relationship.

Most priests arrived in Ireland on the basis of short-term contracts (two to five years). While some contracts were extended, others were revoked and, as I learned, many Polish priests either returned to Poland or went on to other countries. Fr. Jarek explained being a priest is like " . . . the army, when an order is given, you have to go pack and go!" Yet others, like Fr. Jerzy, also pointed out that many Polish bishops and cardinals were not fond of letting their priests go abroad: "I'm sure they were very proud to have a big number of students and they didn't want to send them anywhere. They just wanted to keep [us] and be happy that they have a big number of priests." Exacerbated by the apparent egoism of the Polish Catholic Church's pride in its large number of vocations, the tensions associated with staying or going had to be negotiated by each individual priest. Fr. Richard's decision to leave, for instance, exposes how closely his own emigration was tied to the emigration of Polish people during the expansion of the European Union:

> I never thought about going abroad [za granicę] for work. But during my first year, and after caroling [during the Christmas season], I realized upon talking to people that 90 percent of them were unemployed, and many of them were young couples. After a few days of visits, I thought to myself "Geeze!" "Why are they sitting in this country?" "It's such a waste of time, they should leave and go where they will have it worthwhile, and where they will succeed, as opposed to sitting around and thinking what they were going to eat the next day." So I started to urge people to "Go!" "You're young!" "To England! To Ireland!" . . . *you know*, those borders were opening up then.

Around the time of the expansion of the European Union, priests like Fr. Richard intuitively understood that Polish emigration would present opportunities that one could not find in Poland at the time. Others, like Fr. Jarek, explained his exit as an overtly strategic one. He wanted to leave Poland, to go to work abroad, even though initially his bishop did not allow it. In negotiating his exit with his bishop, Fr. Jarek made reference to Pope Benedict's message around the time of the expansion of the European Union. He described how several factors came together leading to his exit; in particular, he emphasized the ways in which he was able to use Pope Benedict's message to fulfill his ambitions of leaving Poland "to go anywhere."

> Agata: When you were making the decision to come to Ireland, was it the bishop's decision or did you want to come here on your own . . . to leave Poland?
>
> Fr. Jarek: To be sure, this all depended on a variety of factors. But overall, I wanted to leave Poland to go anywhere. The first time priests starting leaving Poland, with this current wave of emigration, was after Pope Benedict XVI's visit in Warsaw . . . because then he said *strongly* and *concretely* that Polish bishops were to allow Polish priests to work across borders, there where Polish people were . . . after Benedict's visit, all the bishops had to listen to the Pope, so I wrote a letter to my bishop stating that I wanted to leave wherever. And he said . . . "Ok, I agree, under the condition that someone will ask for a Polish priest," so I waited for two years, not knowing where I would end up, but finally a bishop from ______ asked for a Polish priest of my bishop, and that's how I ended up here. Ireland was not my choice, but it was based on a need. In reality, I never prepared myself before coming to Ireland because, on the one hand, I didn't have much time, and, on the other hand, I said "ahh" to myself "it's best not to set up any expectations, but to see how it all looks [when I get there]."

Fr. Richard and Fr. Jarek's experiences highlight some key features of the mobility of the *migrant priest*. First, both were invited to take care of Polish immigrants—without the formal invitation, their hopes and dreams of leaving Poland would not have occurred. Yet being able to use as leverage both the emigration of their Polish faithful and the Pontiff's message, they were able to fit their personal request into the larger framework of the expansion of the European Union at the time. Their actions also coincided with the inability of the Irish clergy to meet the demands of a bourgeoning immigrant Catholic population.

Once in Ireland, the priests began to reflect on their experiences as immigrants (read *priest as migrant*). Fr. Richard, for example, explained that when he first arrived in Ireland he was not entirely certain how he would feel, though he was able to lessen his feelings of anxiety by travelling back home more frequently, and by negotiating his stay in Ireland with the receiving bishop to be able to adjust in Ireland.

> First I came for two years, because I didn't know how I would feel here [in Ireland], and I didn't want a contract for five years, so I suggested two years to the priest bishop, and he agreed that it would be a two year adjustment period. During the first year, I missed Poland terribly. Because it's so close from here to Poland, I went home almost every month, and it added up to almost three months in one year that I was there. I was horribly home sick. But today Poland has passed [faded away] so much! Now when I think about it, so many things irritate me about Poland, I can't understand certain things, why some things take so long, such simple things create such big problems and so on.

Clearly, Fr. Richard's experience in Ireland was not immediately pleasant, but he quite capably minimized his general discomfort. With time, he became more accustomed to Ireland as Poland faded into the background. Although many priests understood Ireland to be a predominantly Catholic country, many were largely unaware of what was waiting for them upon arrival. Most priests tended to adjust in similar ways, and once the acculturation process was set in place, they became more comfortable with the idea that the migration experience was changing their views of the world, as well as practices which had been, until their emigration from Poland, largely informed by their own cultural and national traditions.

While the changes did not occur for every priest in the same way, in general each priest left some room for uncertainty and flexibility. Most were astutely aware that they could not prepare or plan for everything. In large part, they conceived of their struggles as being a part of a "natural" or human experience, eased by the fact that the fundamentals of their socio-religious experience do not change, even though the place and space where they find themselves might. Fr. Jozef explained:

> As I said, every migration is unique, and to be really prepared you'd have to prepare yourself in terms of that immigration. But the *work of a priest*, I think, is *very much the same regardless of where he is in the world*, the substance of human beings doesn't change, *human nature is the same all around the world*, thankfully. So in this regard, we are prepared to work with people, regardless of whether they live in this state or another. But to prepare yourself about one culture or history, you'd have to know which one [you are going to]. The most effective [training] is on the spot, although you could have a small amount before leaving Poland, which a week after leaving Poland the reality [of what you learned] could be a lot different.

In general, as highly skilled priests with extensive training and liturgical insights, they often fell back on the certainty of their Catholic teachings to be able to deal with their experiences. Thus, while the priest clings to the objective rules and regulations that govern his life as a priest, he notices differences in and limitations to his daily practice that have shifted as a result of his change of place. The shift away from familiarity toward uncertainty creates a new subjective awareness, mediated by his relationship with God.[18] Fr. Richard expressed his mobility, and relationship with God, in a unique way when he said that he did not want to be tied to Ireland forever:

> I wouldn't want to become an Irish hostage. I always remind myself, be prepared to leave, to go further, because I'm uncertain where God will send me. For now I have two years here, and what Lord God may give me in the future I don't know, it might be Ireland, I'm thinking of continuing my studies here, so it might be Ireland for the next five years.

In this way, while Fr. Richard accepts that in the future he might end up where God would send him, he also expresses the goals he has in his current place of reception, such as continuing his studies. Thus, while the future is uncertain, the experience of migration provides experiences that are enriching and ultimately beneficial. Some, like Fr. Albin, also seemed to see Ireland as a springboard for his future success. When I asked Fr. Albin whether or not he would like to move back to Poland or go elsewhere, he spiritedly explained that he wanted to go to Rome, and, with more hesitation, said that if he could not do that, he would go back to Poland. "That's how things look at the moment," Fr. Albin explained, "it could be that things don't work out that way . . . so this is really like a '*bus stop*' for me, Ireland is my 'bus stop.'"

In general, many hopes and dreams of being mobile were tied to priestly ambitions, to experience the world as well as gain knowledge and understating that would enrich their pastoral work. The Polish priests in Ireland are younger, are quick to travel for pleasure, have ambitions that are directly tied to their priestly vocation, and possess hopes of moving elsewhere. While the potential to move informs many of their perspectives and decisions, during their tenure in Ireland most hoped to be at least recognized for their role and efforts within and outside the Polish community. Many of these efforts were tied up with trying to understand the continually unstable, emerging interpretations of "integration" in Ireland.

The Meaning of Integration in Ireland

Polish priests in Ireland understood their role primarily with regards to integration. Their role, many expressed, was to "integrate" their Polish faithful into Irish society, and the Irish Church structure, without completely eliminating Polish national festivities or taking away anything from the well-established Polish Catholic tradition. This multifaceted concept of integration, however, generated a significant amount of stress for the priests as its meaning was informed by insights on both sides of the integration debate. While those on the Irish side were anticipating the eventual inclusion of

Polish people into Irish parishes, Polish immigrants remained more comfortable about being undecided about their long-term plans to settle in Ireland.

Fr. Zenek vented that "[f]rom the start . . . *Irish* people have talked about 'integration,' and it's been *their* eleventh commandment." Fr. Richard similarly explained, "When I first arrived every other word uttered by my bishop was 'integration.' I almost had enough of that word, 'integration,' 'integration,' but it's nice, and it's a good direction." Referring to his homily, Fr. Richard said "sometimes I write it and I write let's pray for our 'new home' [and] I wonder if I can even use that word 'dom' (home). Or for our new 'fatherland' . . . I have this feeling that I want to think that way . . . but most [Polish people] think that they are here for the short term." In their unique ways, by being aware of Irish and Polish admissions, Polish Catholic priests attempt to reach a balance between the outwardly incongruent extremes.

What was understood by all of the Polish priests in Ireland, however, was that "parallel congregations," or "ethnic" or "personal" or "linguistic" parishes were discouraged by Irish people and Irish clergy alike.[19] Fr. Richard explained that the main goal of the Irish Church was to "integrate" Polish people into their parishes and guard against the formation of independent ethnic parishes. When I asked him why he would not want to lead his own Polish congregation in a Polish Church (an ethnic/linguistic parish), he assumed that I was suggesting a separate parish structure away from the Irish parishes that the Polish immigrants were already using. Fr. Richard responded: "No, no, no, the Irish Church would not allow for that, to create a new structure with its own framework? No! There is no chance for that. I think they are open to our traditions, like blessing the food, and they watch sympathetically, and Irish pastors bless the food, but to create our own structure then, no, integration is the main goal and it *has to* happen."

Despite the fact that "parallel congregations" in Ireland were discouraged, a contradiction emerged when St. Audeon's Catholic Church was loaned to the Polish community in Dublin. There were two different interpretations of this event. On the one hand, some of the Polish clergy assumed that St. Audeon's served as a central site for Polish community building. On the other hand, a fear emerged that a "Polish ghetto" would form in the neighborhood surrounding the church. While the fear eventually subsided, the confusion about how to integrate Polish immigrants in Ireland continued. Some priests, like Fr. Jarek, began to distance himself from the Polish community at St. Audeon's, and he criticized the Polish Church in Dublin for isolating itself from Irish congregations. Fr. Jarek likened the Polish Church in Dublin to a "mental ghetto," where Polish immigrants were not encouraged to integrate beyond the church walls.

Fr. Jarek, like other Polish priests who went on to actively engage and participate in both the Irish community and among the Polish faithful, explained that integration would eventually occur when Polish people no longer needed him. When I asked Fr. Jarek to tell me what he envisioned for the Polish community in his care, he explained that the integration of his Polish faithful would in large part be connected to his departure:

> Even if I wasn't here the goal is to create a strong Polish group within the boundary of the diocese . . . that is a part of this diocese. I even had this idea that even if I wasn't here, an Irish priest could lead them, and this would be ideal . . . if an Irish priest took them in. But I'm not sure if this is possible for now. Everything takes time, a lot of time.

Fr. Jarek's point, about replacing himself with an Irish priest, reflects an interesting paradox. While Polish immigrants are welcome to integrate into Ireland and Irish churches, the same is not true for Polish priests in Ireland. The general exclusion of Polish priests in the Irish Church, for the long term, is related to the inaccessibility of incardination for Polish Catholic priests, despite their active efforts to be recognized for their pastoral and chaplaincy roles.

The notion of Polish priests leaving Ireland when Polish immigrants eventually "integrate" contradicts multiple realities in present-day Ireland. The first is related to the fact that the number of priests and vocations in Ireland has significantly decreased in the last thirty years. Thus, Polish priests, more than ever, are now needed to fill those vacancies. Second, the idea that Polish priests would eventually go back to Poland is not consistent with the hopes of Polish clergy in Ireland themselves. With one exception, all the priests in my study did not want to go back to Poland to be priests, often stating that the process of migration had changed them, and that they would not know how to be priests in Poland anymore. As Fr. Zenek explains:

> It's very different going somewhere to visit than it is living somewhere for a few years, and seeing what people go through, and the challenges they have. I'll tell you what my professor told me in the seminary. "Zenku! Don't stay too long! Because afterwards the Bishop won't want you back, you don't know what you'll bring [back] with you, what kinds of feelings, and he'll be worried about putting you in a parish somewhere [in Poland]."

These priests are therefore left somewhere in-between acculturating into an Irish way of life and never being able to go "home" again. Fr. Francis explained that although he feels good in Ireland, he does not feel good about seeming disposable in Ireland while also feeling like he could never be able to return to Poland to be a priest. "It's a difficult situation for a priest to be in. Almost like . . . I don't want to compare it to this [*he says quietly*] . . . but . . . almost like refugee status . . . [*he laughs awkwardly*]." The tension of staying or going created a liminal moment defined by openness, ambiguity, and indeterminacy.

Ultimately, the priests stayed in Ireland for undetermined lengths of time, seldom feeling that they were being recognized for their chaplaincy work, with low rates of incardination despite high hopes (in some cases) to be full members of their adopted Irish dioceses. Much of the tensions associated with the Polish priests' permanence and presence in Ireland is related to their experience of being perceived as "conservative," a reality that outlines the ways in which the Polish priest is a foreigner, never able to fully "integrate" into the Irish landscape.

The Conservative Polish Catholic Priest in Ireland

The Polish priests explained their conservatism in two ways. First, they held that most Irish clergy, being more or less jealous of their burgeoning Polish congregations, perceived Polish clergy as conservative because they displayed a superior knowledge of Catholic liturgy and doctrine and, ultimately, a better approach to the Catholic faith. Second, they understood that their approach was seen as more conservative because the quality of Irish Catholicism had declined with increased rates of secularism and liberalism. According to the Polish priests, the Irish Church is waning, along with everything that it includes—priests, parishes, and religious materials. Thus, they took it upon themselves to revive and *enrich* the Irish Catholic Church and its faithful.

All of the Polish priests said that when they went back to Poland they always brought something back. Taking matters into his own hands, to help re-connect the priests to their role in and outside of the parish, Fr. Edek stated that when he goes back to Poland he brings things back for his Irish priests. "I bring back more for the Irish priests, like vestments. They (Irish priests), don't take care of the church, they are old, no one takes care of them . . . everything in Ireland is getting old, and they are not taking care of it, they are not investing in the church." Comparing Poland to Ireland, Fr. Maciek similarly explained that the Polish Catholic Church is extremely "rich in religious materials," which in-turn has benefits for Irish clergy and Polish immigrants alike. As Fr. Maciek explained:

> Well the Polish church is extremely rich, rich with materials for chaplaincies. In Ireland, I often can't find it, although sometimes I can, but in Poland everything is readily available, even in English. In Poland we are extremely well prepared in this regard . . . I also bring back certain things. For example, Oh! In Poland there is a tradition that a child would receive a picture [religious icon] to hang on their wall as a keepsake. Here there are no such icons. Polish parents come to me and say that there are fifteen kids here taking communion in Ireland and they ask me to bring fifteen icons for them, they collect money, and I bring it for them. I do a special mass for them, and hand out the keepsakes. So there continues to be a certain attachment, sentiment to certain

> things, like to rosary or I don't know, some music from Poland, and they come to me and say how lovely it is and I lend it to them. I always bring something back; it's a fact, yes.

After I spoke about how this is an example of transnational ties, Fr. Maciek added, as to emphasize why these things are occurring:

> It's not trade [barter] [*said with a loud laugh*]! Where there are Polish people, from time to time they will say, let's buy something for the church, what shall we buy? Let's buy a chasuble [ornate vestment worn during special celebrations like Easter], I told them, collect the money, I will go! I will buy it and bring it back, and you will nicely offer it during English mass. When they did it everyone was [wniebowzięcie] delighted to high heavens, and all were very happy about it.

Fr. Maciek was committed to the idea that Polish religious materials were of superior quality to anything that he might have found in Ireland. While many of the priests aimed to enrich the Catholic experience through the introduction and use of religious materials, they also aimed to introduce some practices thought to be long forgotten in Ireland. Some, like Fr. Edek, candidly critiqued the Catholic Church in Ireland, stating that confessions in Ireland seemed "a thing of the past." Polish priests, as he explained, are more familiar with people coming for elongated confessions and looking to priests for spiritual guidance. In Ireland, the role of a priest seems less and less important, so much so that priests have also stepped away from their responsibilities. "Sure it's much quicker, and much easier for the priest [to do] the service in fifteen or twenty minutes and go back to their cup of tea, or golfing," Fr. Edek said. He continued: "I don't think priests in Poland have much time during the week for golfing. Priests in Poland teach in the schools, they have different services . . . there is always something to be done." Thus, while most acknowledged that they were seen as "conservative," the priests embraced this label, despite knowing that it did not add to their overall popularity.

Some priests, however, were able to broaden their experiences beyond the differences they observed between the two countries. Most of these experiences were informed by their mobility, experiences they had had in countries other than Ireland or Poland. When I asked Fr. Jarek about his "conservative" label, he observed:

> The Irish Catholic Church has gone a little bit too far in the forward direction. Now, I accept this, but on the other side, I try to uphold the ways in which I was taught in Poland, but if some of them tell me that "we don't do that here, you do that in Poland" I then have a very concrete argument. "No, the way I do things is *not* just the way we do it in Poland, but it's also done like this in Germany, in Italy, in Spain and in many nations," and then the argument that I

> am a conservative falls to the wayside . . . I'm not saying they are worse but if I know that [some things are done certain ways] not only in Poland, since I've traveled a lot and have some experience. . . . I know that in the majority of churches [for example] around the world people kneel, so I kneel. . . . I noticed that there was a group of people [in the Irish church] who didn't kneel [and only bowed their heads] but now kneel, because maybe, they observe the priest, [they observe me]. . . .

Fr. Jarek's experience as a Polish priest and a "seasoned traveler" has given him both cultural and social capital that could be exchanged in Ireland. Although his experiences abroad allow him to make connections between nations, exposing a clear relationship to migration and his Catholic faith, this type of "migration capital" is not necessarily welcomed in the Irish context. By having traveled to other parts of the world, Fr. Jarek makes general observations about the state of Irish Catholicism and can make a direct connection between himself and the changes that he hopes will eventually take place in his presence. Fr. Jarek's insights can be seen in two ways. The first is his attempt at reigniting the Catholic passion for practice that was once seen in Ireland. The second is the emergence of a Polish superiority in Ireland that threatens the dominant, established, and less conservative ways of present day Ireland. Whether or not Irish clergy see Polish priests as helpful or threatening, it is clear that the direct connection between Poland and Ireland has opened up real possibilities for the exchange of insights into the relationship between culture and religion, particularly in light of their shared faith.

CONCLUSION: RELIGIOUS LEADERS AND FUTURE RESEARCH TRAJECTORIES

While my research does not aim to be prescriptive, my conclusions point to the ways in which both migration studies and the Catholic Church could enrich their understanding of migration through an exploration of the migration experiences of priests. My research has uncovered the unique challenges Polish priests face, many of which are associated with the distances they travel to access the Polish immigrants in their care. Their constant mobility affects the ways in which they adjust to their surroundings. Since Poland and Ireland are easily accessible through available modes of transportation, the Polish priest can quickly and efficiently access Poland when and if he feels his isolation in Ireland is a burden too great to bear. While the availability of travel enriches his understanding of the processes associated with migration, the mobility of the priest creates tensions as it uproots him. He does not have the same potential to integrate and connect as he would have in his country of origin, but this outcome has less to do with his hopes and dreams to stay in

Ireland than it does with those who accept and integrate him. Ultimately, the priest falls back on his relationship with God to guide the uncertainties and remains, to various degrees, unattached to his place of residence.

The Polish priest in Ireland is pulled in multiple directions. While some see Ireland as a temporary place to practice English skills and to learn new culturally informed traditions, others wish that they were recognized for their culturally informed efforts in more formal ways. For many, hopes of incardination are clear, particularly since all the priests I interviewed, with one exception, did not want to go back to Poland to be priests. Even though, as Fr. Jozef assumed, "the work of a priest . . . is very much the same regardless of where he is in the world, [and that] the substance of human beings doesn't change, [or that] human nature is the same all around the world," the significance of contextual level factors that pertain to history and culture should not be underestimated.

The relationship between Irish Catholicism and Ireland's contemporary migration history is not being properly addressed. As Fr. Maciek explained, "incardination is like a citizenship" for priests. This citizenship, however, does not come with a formal citizenship test, and many of the decisions made about priests occur behind closed doors, informed by a general inability of the Irish Catholic Church to see potential for long term growth in diversity. Currently, it seems that the Irish Church actively fears the difference its own religious faithful represent. Perhaps the exclusion of Polish clergy is also an active attempt to hold onto the Irish Catholic superiority that once dominated both the secular and religious realms. Although some might claim that the Irish Church has "gone a little bit too far in the forward direction," the inclusion of Polish priests in Ireland has created a moment where two cultures, sharing one faith, can learn from each other and strike a balance between the assumed "conservatism" or "too forward direction" that each represents to the other.

In the end, it should be apparent that the strength of this chapter comes from the choice to study the migrant lives of religious leaders. By *ever so gently* unveiling the objective (*migrant priest*) and subjective (*priest as migrant*) experiences of religious leadership, the aim has been to enrich our general understanding of the relationship between migration and religion. Moving forward, for those interested in the role and migrant lives of religious leaders—priests, rabbis, imams, and so on—I suggest a larger theoretical project that interrogates the simultaneous relationships between "diasporic religion" and "religion in the diaspora" from secular and religious perspectives.[20] While "diasporic religion" takes into account the ways in which religion should connect people of different backgrounds, ethnicities, cultures, and those speaking a diverse range of languages under the tenets of one faith, "religion in the diaspora" exposes the challenges of diversity and faith in the context of reception and in immigrant communities. Ultimately, while one faith community might ascribe to certain norms, objectives, and morals, as my findings illustrate, the practices and understandings of that faith are changed and altered in the receiving culture and immigrant community. These changes require more extensive analyses and warrant more collaborative research.

NOTES

1. Benedict XVI, "Address by the Holy Father, Warsaw Cathedral," May 25, 2006, accessed August 14, 2014, http://www.vatican.va/holy_father/benedict_xvi/speeches/2006/may/documents/hf_ben-xvi_spe_20060525_poland-clergy_en.html.
2. See also Marta Trzebiatowska, "The Advent of the 'Easy Jet Priest': Dilemmas of Polish Catholic Integration in the UK," *Sociology* 44 (2010): 1055.
3. Richard Alba and Victor Nee, "Rethinking Assimilation Theory for a New Era of Immigration," *International Migration Review* 31 (1997): 826-74; Richard Alba, *Remaking the American Mainstream: Assimilation and Contemporary Immigration* (Cambridge, MA: Harvard University Press, 2003); Milton Gordon, *Assimilation in American Life: The Role of Race, Religion and National Origins* (New York: Oxford University Press, 1964); Robert E. Park, "Assimilation, social," in *Encyclopedia of the Social Sciences*, ed. Edwin R. A. Seligman, vol. 2, 281–83. (New York: Macmillan, 1930); and Robert E. Park and Ernest W. Burgess, *Introduction to the Science of Sociology* (Chicago: University of Chicago Press, 1921).
4. Peggy Levitt and Nina Glick Schiller, "Conceptualizing Simultaneity: A Trasnational Social Field Perspective on Society," *International Migration Review* 28 (2004): 1002–39; and Nina Glick Schiller, Ayse Caglar, and Thaddeus Guldbrandsen, "Beyond the Ethnic Lens: Locality, Globality, and Born-Again Incorporation," *American Ethnologist* 33 (2006): 612–33.
5. Mark McGowan and Brian P. Clarke, *Catholics at the 'Gathering Place': Historical Essays on the Archdioceses of Toronto* (Toronto: The Canadian Catholic Historical Association, 1993).
6. Jay P. Dolan, *The Immigrant Church: New York's Irish and German Catholics, 1815–1865* (The John Hopkins University Press: Oxford, 1976), 5
7. Joseph John Parot, *Polish Catholics in Chicago , 1850–1920* (Northern Illinois University Press: Dekalb Illinois, 1981).
8. William Galush, "Both Polish and Catholic: Immigrant Clergy in the American Church," *The Catholic Historical Review* 70 (1984): 412.
9. Stanislaus Blejwas, "A Polish Community in Transition: The Evolution of the Holy Cross Parish, New Britain, Connecticut," *Polish American Studies* 35 (1978): 24.
10. Trzebiatowska, "The Advent of the 'Easy Jet Priest,'" 1064.
11. Ibid., 1069.
12. Cinzia Solari, "Transnational Politics and Settlement Practices: Post-Soviet Immigrant Churches in Rome," *The American Behavioral Scientist* 49 (2006): 1530.
13. Ibid., 1536, 1538, and 1548.
14. For this chapter, I present only the findings from the first round of interviews in Ireland.
15. In my analysis, I do not identify whether the priest is a religious order priest or a diocesan priest, although I am aware that the ways in which they migrate are different—the religious order priest will most often emigrate to a community of priests, while the diocesan priest's emigration is tied to the decisions made by the sending and receiving bishop in each diocese.
16. Peggy Levitt, *God Needs No Passport: Immigrants and the Changing American Religious Landscape* (New York: New Press, 2007).
17. I refrain from using the term "immigrant" (or "the priest as immigrant" or the "immigrant priest") as the term "immigrant" limits my theoretical tool kit. Using the term "migrant" (instead of "immigrant") better exposes the two sides of the migration process—emigration and immigration. It is my claim that the term "immigrant" too often implies that the migrant who

emigrates from his country of origin may eventually settle in the context of reception. Similar to Park's uni-directional focus on assimilation, using the term "immigrant" often assumes that the "immigrant's" experience of migration is associated with the end result as "settlement." Using the terms the "migrant priest" and "the priest as migrant" allows for a better theoretical orientation. In particular, although they may be (to different degrees) analogous with the concept of "immigrant," "cosmopolitan," and "transnational," focusing on the idea of "the migrant" allows for the "potential mobility" of the priest as stranger to be maintained. Georg Simmel, *On Individuality and Social Forms*, ed. Donald N. Levine (Chicago: University of Chicago Press, 1971); and Robert E. Park, "Human Migration and the Marginal Man," *American Journal of Sociology* 33 (1928): 881–93.

18. See Courtney Bender, "How Does God Answer Back?" *Poetics* 36 (2008): 476–92.

19. "Ethnic parishes" are different from (ethnic) "chaplaincies" in that "ethnic" or "linguistic" parishes have *traditionally* been built for and by immigrant faithful functioning as part of, but apart from, the established Catholic diocese. The building of "churches" in Ireland by immigrants is largely seen as inappropriate, as many Irish Catholic churches are largely vacant. Chaplaincies, on the other hand, function as part of the receiving diocese and emerge on the basis of "need." In Ireland, many small chaplaincies initially emerged upon the expansion of the European Union and functioned inside Irish churches under the schedule of Irish clergy to serve Polish immigrants. Many of these chaplaincies were only seen as providing Polish immigrants with mass in their language and thus other efforts went largely unappreciated or unacknowledged. Eventually, most stopped extending their services as many Polish people moved to other parts of Ireland, to different countries in the EU, or back to Poland—multiple emigrations that were initially precipitated by a failing Irish economy.

20. Academic interest in this relationship can be linked to the work of Thomas A. Tweed in *Our Lady of the Exile: Diasporic Religion at a Cuban Catholic Shrine in Miami* (New York: Oxford University Press, 1997), Solari's "Transnational Politics and Settlement Practices," and the collaborative ethnographic and sociological works of Bender, Cadge, Klassen, and Levitt.

Chapter Seven

Theology and History at the 2012 Eucharistic Congress, Dublin

John C. Waldmeir

Although Eucharistic Congresses began as national gatherings in France in the late nineteenth century, they gained notoriety as international events that traveled between countries every four years under Pope Pius X (1903–1914). Pius saw them as ways to promote his wider Papal agenda, which was to encourage Catholics to receive the Eucharist more frequently, and he even brought the 1905 Congress to Rome, where he said Mass for the gathering before issuing *Sacra Tridentina Synodus*, "On Frequent and Daily Reception of Holy Communion." Under one of his successors, Pius XI (1922–1939), the international versions of these Congresses began to attract enormous crowds. In 1926, for example, 500,000 people were reported to have attended Mass at Soldier Field in Chicago at the close of the twenty-eighth International Congress, and in 1932, Dublin welcomed twice that number for a High Mass in Phoenix Park that concluded the thirty-first such gathering.[1]

These Congresses still occur in many countries annually, and every four years the Church asks a city to host an international version. For the fiftieth installment—in 2012—the Church returned to Dublin. Eighty years had elapsed since the previous Congress had overwhelmed the city in 1932, and during the intervening years tremendous changes had taken place. Theologically, the notion that the Church gathered in large numbers in order to demonstrate strength and resolve in its fight to "triumph" over secularism was now largely (though not entirely) absent. Although the week-long 2012 event grew until about 80,000 were reported at the closing Mass in Croke Park, for most of the days attendance was modest. Unlike the celebrations of 1932, when neighborhoods, streets, and houses participated in the struggle against worldliness by decorating familiar spaces with banners, statues of the Virgin, and images of various saints, most Dubliners in 2012 were unaware that any Church meeting was taking place. And those who did know debated whether such a Congress should even occur during a time when the nation was reeling from both economic hardship and spiritual crisis.

Despite these reservations, the 50th International Congress opened and ran for seven days with the theme "Communion with Christ and with One Another." In keeping with standard papal practice, Benedict XVI did not attend but instead sent his representative or "legate," Cardinal Marc Ouellet, to represent him. The Pope did address the crowd at the closing Mass, and though his appearance on an enormous screen in Croke Park was not as inspirational as the voice of Pius XI in 1932 (loudspeakers carried Pius's remarks to those million in attendance at the closing Mass), the Papal address nevertheless carried significant weight.

In his comments, Benedict offered those in attendance an interpretation of the Congress theme that had two important consequences. On the one hand, the remarks developed ideas from previous addresses by his legate, Cardinal Ouellet. When combined with an address given by the Cardinal during a symposium of Church leaders just prior to the Congress, a detailed interpretation of communion as "*communio*" emerged. This was a concept that Benedict began to develop during his days as head of the Congregation for the Doctrine of the Faith, and it provided the theological foundation upon which the words of both the Pope and his legate rested.

On the other hand, the second consequence of Benedict's address was that it cast into sharp relief the differences between the theology behind this approach and the rationale offered by a second theological statement issued specifically for the Congress. Following the guidelines from the Pontifical Committee for Eucharistic Congresses, twelve Irish theologians (and one philosopher) penned a sixty-four page statement titled *Theological and Pastoral Reflections in Preparation for the 50th Eucharistic Congress*, a document subsequently published by Veritas Publishers.[2] Although this text posed no direct challenges to either the Pope or his legate, it did proffer an interpretation of "communion" that constituted an alternative vision for how the Church might understand its relationships both to God and the world. One way to explain the nature of this difference is to note that (1) the approach assumed by Benedict and Cardinal Ouellet and (2) the one taken up by the thirteen Irish thinkers rested on very different understandings of "history."[3] By apprehending the distinctive features of these separate notions, and by relating their respective claims to the setting for the Congress provided by the 2012 Irish Church, listeners could witness a remarkable example of theological influence. In these three statements, theology was not simply the by-product of sociological conditions; rather, it proved to constitute the motive and justification for far-reaching ideological choices about tradition and change.

THE ADDRESSES BY PAPAL LEGATE CARDINAL MARC OUELLET

The most obvious occasion for references to history in all three of these documents is the confluence of anniversaries that each text recognizes. Cardinal Ouellet, Pope Benedict, and the authors of *Theological and Pastoral Reflections* all note that 2012 marks both eighty years since an International Eucharistic Congress was last in Ireland and fifty years since the opening of Vatican II. This double anniversary is even reflected in the theme of the Congress, which, as the Irish theologians point out, "picks up on the notion of communion that was so central to the Council's vision." In each document (and in many others presented at the Congress), Vatican II becomes something of a subtext for the gathering; references to it, in fact, constitute opportunities to interpret the meaning of communion for the Church both in the past and currently.

The address by Cardinal Ouellet provides a remarkably clear example of this confluence. His address purports to offer an "Ecclesiology of Communion," and the Cardinal readily admits that his proposal begins with Vatican II, specifically, with the document *Lumen Gentium*, the Dogmatic Constitution on the Church, which he quotes on the very first page of his remarks.[4] But before he begins his analysis of this Counciliar text, Ouellet poses a question from Pope Benedict that introduces the basis of his historical approach: "Why has the implementation of the Council," the Cardinal asks (quoting the Pontiff), "thus far been so difficult?" The answer Ouellet provides also comes from Benedict: "Well, it all depends on the correct interpretation of the Council or—as we would say today—on its proper hermeneutic, the correct key to its interpretation and application."[5] Through his choice of question and response, Ouellet signals that his theological investigation of ecclesiology and communion will rest upon presuppositions that are essential to a theology of *communio*. Breifly stated, for advocates like Cardinal Ouellet and Pope Benedict, the term *communio* refers to the notion that communities are highly structured and, as such, inherently hierarchical. In the case of the Church, its structure and hierarchy is nothing less than divine, as it was instituted by Jesus of Nazareth. In this vision of *communio*, the Church is maintained through the ongoing presence of the risen Christ, who abides within its institutional framework.

In order for the idea of *communio* to remain relevant, history must be seen not as a realm of change but as the sphere of continuity, and in modern Church memory no undertaking calls to mind issues associated with change and continuity as profoundly as the Second Vatican Council. For this reason, as early as 1985 then Cardinal Joseph Ratzinger, Prefect for the Congregation for the Doctrine of the Faith, found himself insisting that the Council was nothing more than one more example of an enduring tradition. In an interview with Vittorio Messori that eventually was published as *The Ratzinger Report*, the Cardinal insisted that the "schematism of a before and after in the history of the Church" was "wholly unjustified by the documents of Vatican II." There is not a "pre-" or "post-" conciliar Church, the future Pope claimed, but only "one, unique Church that walks the path toward the Lord." To interpret the Council properly is to conclude that "There are no leaps in this history, there are no fractures, and there is no break in continuity. In no wise did the Council intend to introduce a temporal dichotomy in the Church."[6] This position would be presented as policy by 2000 when John Paul II insisted that: "The church has always known the rules for a correct interpretation of the contents of dogma. These rules are woven into the fabric of faith and not outside it. To read the Council as if it marked a break with the past, while in fact it placed itself in the line of the faith of all times, is decidedly unacceptable."[7]

From his opening interpretation of *Lumen Gentium*, Cardinal Ouellet's remarks to his Maynooth audience reveals the influence of this way of thinking about history.[8] For example, when he reads from *Lumen Gentium* that "the Church is in Christ like a sacrament or as a sign and instrument both of a very closely knit union with God and of the unity of the whole human race," the words admit only one conclusion: that "*Lumen Gentium* speaks first and above all of the mystery of the Church and hence of her divine dimension."[9] The analysis that follows in Ouellet's remarks pays strict attention to the "union" of the Church with God; by contrast, virtually nothing is said about the other half of the description in the quotation—the half that refers to the Church as a sign or instrument of "human" unity. If one's ecclesiology values the Church for the ways it embodies an incarnate God within the fluctuations of history, one might be puzzled by Ouellet's omission. However, the Cardinal makes it clear that the Church must be about correcting past interpretations of its communal life—interpretations that "privileged" what he calls "reform within continuity or rupture within the Tradition." Given that aim, the Cardinal's choice makes perfect sense.[10] He must be about advancing the notion of a consistent *communio*.[11]

But as Ouellet's address to this pre-Congress gathering demonstrates, once an argument locates the Church in a realm apart from the vicissitudes of historical reality, it is difficult to identify points where it re-enters to intersect and influence human experience. Ouellet's initial response in his address to that particular problem is to retrieve an earlier and more "concrete" notion of *corpus mysticum* that, he argues, at one time was associated with the ecclesial community.[12] The Cardinal's efforts to identify the source of more "concrete meaning" in the "visible dimension" of historical existence suggests that he will explore another charge from Vatican II, the call in *Gaudium et spes* to "scrutinize the signs of the times."[13] But that is not where Ouellet's remarks take him. Rather than consider, for instance, the growing role of the laity (who constitute a significant portion of the Cardinal's Maynooth audience as well as the overwhelming majority of people who attend the Congress generally), he chooses instead to focus on aspects of the institutional Church that can be traced primarily to roles held tightly by the ordained clergy—more specifically, by bishops. Quoting not *Gaudium et spes* but *Ecclesia de Eucharistia* by Pope John Paul II, Ouellet locates "the visible dimension" of Church unity—its "communion" of the faithful in Christ—in three areas that are, in the eyes of the institutional Church, of limited access to the laity: "the teaching of the Apostles . . . the sacraments and . . . the Church's hierarchical order."[14]

Because "*communio*," is inherently "differentiated"—rife with particularities that obtain their meaning from within a hierarchical system—the distinction between clergy and laity is crucial to any subsequent ecclesiology of communion offered by the Cardinal or Pope Benedict. The role of the priest, for example, is decidedly not "relative" to the "conscious and active participation of the assembly" but instead belongs to a realm that rises above the historical or the everyday.[15] Within this hierarchy, bishops, notes the Cardinal, are people who can serve as bridges between historical reality and transcendent ideals, but only as a result of their authoritative position at the top of the hierarchical chain. Accordingly, the Cardinal discusses bishops primarily in terms of authority and hierarchy, two concepts that, for Ouellet, do not emerge from historical human experience but rather from a union with God that is "magisterial" and "Apostolic." The role is only indirectly related to the people of God. So, for example, according to the Cardinal, bishops are "shepherds" because they have been given "authority over [a] portion" of what he identifies as the "Universal Church"[16]

In Ouellet's argument, references to the longstanding tradition of the Church as both "Universal" and "particular" becomes the final step toward insuring that the Congress theme, "Communion with Christ and with One Another," does not embroil the institution too deeply in worldly affairs. But the means for meeting this objective does not open Ouellet to quite the same criticism that others have levelled against proponents of a similar position, advocates such as Pope Benedict, for example. Typically, the distinction between the "Universal" and "particular" Church leads critics to equate "particular" with "local" and "Universal" with "Rome." This was, for example, one of charges Cardinal Walter Kasper levelled against Benedict in the remarkable exchange they undertook within the pages of *America* magazine.[17] But in this case, Ouellet (and perhaps Benedict as well) means something different by these two terms. In the Cardinal's address, the Universal Church is not equated with Rome but with the sacrament of ordination. For this reason, the role of the Universal ideal to "integrate" the communion of believers falls to "the ordained minister," who models the proper relationship between the Universal and particular Church when he "exercises his liturgical function."[18] In the Cardinal's argument, the terms "Universal" and "particular" Church become metaphors for something like the lives (or "souls") of individual Catholics: those who are ordained are equated with a Universal ideal that, through its "ontological primacy," transcends any worldly order, while those who remain members of the laity are associated with the fluctuations of historical existence.[19]

To deliver this argument in Ireland in 2012 after the release of four major "reports" detailing physical, emotional, and sexual abuse by members of the ordained clergy and women religious is a surprising approach to communion or even *communio*.[20] After all, less than one year earlier, Taoiseach Enda Kenny had captured the attention and attitudes of most Irish Catholics with a speech in the Dail Chamber where he referred to evidence in the Cloyne Report of efforts by the Church to interfere with investigations into charges of abuse, and where he cited the moral "arrogance" of the institution that had failed to respect and obey the "laws . . . rights and responsibilities" of the Republic.[21] Now, eleven months later, the Papal Legate outlines for his largely lay, Irish audience a vision of Church community and communion that privileges a higher unity, even at the expense of those more human bonds at work in the daily life of the Church. His comments about the "multiple structures of participation" established by Vatican II to promote greater participation in decision-making processes within the Church are not just surprising but outright shocking. In them, Ouellet all but dismisses the value of structures such as "pastoral and presbyteral councils," "episcopal conferences," and "parish communities" because they contribute little to an "ecclesiology of communion" and "involve the danger of reducing the Eucharistic celebration to its ethical or social implications."[22] By the end of his address, the Cardinal loses sight of the fact that many who hear or read his words in fact are praying that the Eucharist stimulates within the Church greater attention to the ethical and social consequences of ecclesiastical actions.

In his reluctance to stand before his Irish audience and recognize a more theologically complex relationship between the transcendent ideal of a Universal Church and the historical realities of an institution that lives in particular places and times, the Cardinal does come close to echoing the triumphalism that dominated so many addresses eighty years earlier at the Dublin Congress. Like his predecessors in 1932, who spoke frequently of purity in order to motivate congregations to fight against the world, Cardinal Ouellet too calls upon his listeners to prepare so that they might "confront the challenges of secularized societies."[23] But in the end, even triumphalism is too "concrete" or historical for Benedict's Legate. He does conclude his address by saying that genuine "communion" within the Church is one that involves "an authentic participation in the witness of the Trinity in history."[24] However, by the time listeners or readers reach this point in his remarks, it is clear that the Cardinal has been unable to ground his rhetoric in any shared, human reality. Even his proliferation of metaphors—body, bride, spouse, nuptial love, temple—might satisfy the need for something tangible and historical if they were acknowledged to be metaphors that could address the Irish Catholic environment. At the end of his address, the audience is left only to imagine what it means for "the visible realities of the Church [to be] immersed in the invisible reality of Trinitarian communion."[25] It will be left to another document—based on another understanding of history—to articulate how a historical moment, such as the one providing the context for the 2012 gathering, might open listeners and readers to a deeper sense of divine presence in the experiences of pain, loss, and anger that had grown to define a nation's response to its religious heritage.

THEOLOGICAL AND PASTORAL REFLECTIONS BY IRISH THEOLOGIANS

Although Eucharistic Congresses are organized by Vatican offices, not all documents that are written for a Congress come from Rome. For example, the Pontifical Committee for Eucharistic Congresses issues a set of guidelines or "Statutes," but within them there is a call for the publication of a "working document" meant to be written by representatives of the host nation. Because it is written for an international audience, the document needs to be translated into "main Congress languages," but its purpose is "to promote theological reflection, spiritual renewal, and the good of the particular Church."[26] This statute is the motivation behind the work of the "commission" of twelve Irish theologians and one philosopher who wrote *Theological and Pastoral Reflections in Preparation for the 50th Eucharistic Congress*. Available to Congress participants well before the start of the event, the text surely was on the minds of some who attended Cardinal Ouellet's symposium address, and even the most cursory listeners would have noted the sharp discrepancies between what the Irish theologians wrote and the Legate's words.[27]

The *Reflections* begin with a very different understanding of history, which is demonstrated in their contrasting interpretation of Vatican II. Though the authors do not speak of a "rupture" to describe the break in Church history that they clearly believe has occurred because of the Council, they also do not employ that hermeneutic of continuity the Papal Legate would prefer. Instead, these theologians label the decisions and documents of Vatican II as "reforms" and the Council itself as a "Pentacostal event." Because the Council demonstrates to these authors the actions of God within history, it is possible for them to view the "double anniversary" captured by the 2012 Dublin gathering as its own "*kairos* moment," an event within history "when something special can happen due to God's intervention."[28] Like Cardinal Ouellet, the authors of the *Reflections* do see their task as contributing to the wider conversation surrounding an "ecclesiology of communion"; however, these thirteen Irish writers chose to begin their discussion with the one figure from within the tradition who best represents the importance of evangelizing in the historical moment, St. Paul. For instance, the document opens with words from Paul's first letter to the community at Corinth, where he connects eating the bread and drinking the wine with "discerning" the proper relationship between members of the community. "I hear that when you meet as a church there are divisions among you," writes Paul. The Eucharistic gathering in Corinth, which Paul knows should be an occasion to bring people together, has become an opportunity for some to flaunt what they possess at the expense of others who have little. The *Reflections* describe Paul as a figure who shows no interest in notions of "*communio*" where a hierarchy of roles is played out as part of the liturgical setting. His interest is in those congregational divisions that threaten to grow unless the Corinthians allow the physical actions of sharing bread, wine, and food to help them overcome their inflated self-understandings (I Cor. 11:17–22). Accepting the boldness of Paul's challenge to traditional religious identities, the Irish writers of these *Reflections* make references to a variety of texts, including a remarkable citation attributed to the joint declaration between Roman Catholics and Anglicans issued in 1981 by Anglican-Roman Catholic International Commission and titled simply *The Final Report.*[29] The citation itself testifies to the difficulty of maintaining an argument for "continuity" within Church history, for it is hard to imagine a sharper example of contrast between this Congress and its 1932 predecessor. In 1932, no one could have imagined any document making a similar ecumenical gesture. Not only would such a reference have run counter to the consistent theme of "triumph" that was so forcefully promoted in 1932, it also would have met with the harshest of words from those who conceived of Britain as nothing more than an Anglican oppressor. Nevertheless, what was by all accounts impossible in 1932 becomes a reality in 2012.

Historical contingency is not to be avoided in this vision of communion; rather, it is the starting point for reflection. Barely two pages into their opening discussion of ecclesiology, the authors of the *Reflections* reference events that provide an obvious context for the 2012 Congress, including the North Ireland Peace Process and the nation's recent financial turmoil. Within those first pages the authors also confront the issue that Cardinal Ouellet mentions only once in passing during all three of his lengthy addresses: "It must be recognized . . . at the outset of these theological reflections and pastoral reflections," the authors write, "that today the Catholic Church in Ireland is treading a path of healing, renewal and reparation for the abuse of children and vulnerable young people, particularly by priests and religious."[30] For these twelve theologians and one philosopher, history is not something to be kept at arm's length by the community. Although it is not perfect, neither is it the imperfect, particular expression of what is otherwise transcendent and universal. Through the incarnation, history is already the locus of transcendent meaning; it is where God walks with the Church, and for that reason it is valuable in itself.

To emphasize their point, the authors of the document take their central motif from Luke 24, the story of two disciples (one named Cleopas, the other unnamed) who travel with Jesus on the road to Emmaus. As the authors point out, here Christians discover God and humans moving together along the same road toward the climactic scene, which is the breaking of the bread and the corresponding recognition of Jesus by his fellow travelers. The story presents certain problems for the position taken by the Papal Legate, for it casts the liturgical experience of Jesus breaking bread with his disciples in the context of a journey. The famous quote from *Lumen Gentium*, which describes the Church itself as a "pilgrim," undoubtedly is on the minds of the Irish authors as they complete this section of their *Reflections*. The metaphor, however, is a problem for those interpreters of the Council who, like Cardinal Ouellet or Pope Benedict, want to avoid discussions of the Church as an example of change. As Benedict insisted before he became Pope, the words "pilgrim Church" are valuable primarily for their "'eschatological' import," not their historical description. "The phrase conveys the unity of salvation history which comprises both Israel and the Church in her pilgrim journey," the Pope wrote when he was Cardinal Ratzinger. True, "the phrase expresses the historical nature of the pilgrim Church," but only to highlight the fact that the Church "will not be wholly herself until the paths of time have been traversed and have blossomed in the hands of God."[31]

As the Emmaus story culminates with the breaking of the bread, so the authors of the *Reflections* offer a lengthy analysis of the Mass as a way of grounding their ecclesiology of communion in a shared experience. As they write, they reiterate Cardinal Ouellet's concern for the "universal character" of the Eucharist and of the Church that celebrates it. But in their text, references to "universal character" presume the paramount importance of historical existence. As the document says: "Even when it is celebrated on the humble altar of a country Church, the Eucharist is always in some way celebrated on the altar of the world. It unites heaven and earth. It embraces and permeates all creation."[32] Such a relationship, the authors go on to point out, is not so easily managed under the terminology of a transcendent idealism; "continuity" and "tradition," for instance, always occur within the framework of history and change. For these authors, even the Liturgy of the Word that unfolds during the Mass is "prophetic and disturbing" because of the way it pushes all listeners to change course.[33] As the authors of the *Reflections* remind readers, on the road to Emmaus, Cleopas and his friend are figures who easily could be associated with ecclesial leadership, yet in that story both are reproached by Jesus "for not sufficiently allowing Scripture to nourish their faith"—specifically for not hearing the prophetic voice that speaks from within the text.[34] They are, as Luke's narrator says, "foolish," their eyes "closed" to the very challenges to tradition that operate within history itself. Like those Church leaders who await them back in Jerusalem, they have failed to grasp the very "words that I spoke to you while I was still with you."[35]

In the work of the thirteen Irish thinkers who composed those *Pastoral and Theological Reflections* for the Congress, distinctions between leaders and followers recede into the background; the word "bishop," for instance, never even appears. Perhaps it should. Yet, on the other hand, if the starting point for these *Reflections* truly is "the contemporary Irish setting," why would these writers choose to highlight the very office that has caused the Irish nation so much grief? Moreover, why would they tie any presentation about the communal life of the Church—its *koinonia*—to figures who represent so prominently the hierarchy and its failures? U.S. Catholics have been able to fall back on national claims of a separation of church and state and to rely on a propensity to see problems like sexual abuse exclusively in terms of individual clerical offenders. These options have never been available to Ireland and Irish Catholics. The explicit ties between church and state that Eamon De Valera helped to craft in 1937 as part of the Irish constitution thrust the institutional Church and its representatives (made explicitly "representative" by their own theological claims of "part" and "whole") to the forefront of controversies that have done immense damage to the ecclesial community. Rather than reiterate a rationale for Church hierarchy and offer it as the starting point for an ecclesiology of communion, the authors of the *Reflections* choose instead to begin and end by taking about *koinonia*. For them, this decision marks a choice to locate common ground for all God's creation, for the term "signifies a relation between persons resulting from their participation in one and the same reality." "*Koinonia* with one another," the document goes on to say, "is entailed by our *koinonia* with God in Christ. This," the document concludes, "is the mystery of the Church." It is also perhaps the most powerful justification for risking the theological interpretation of communion that places—as these writers do—greater hope in the vagaries of history.[36]

THE CLOSING MASS AND POPE BENEDICT XVI

Pope Benedict's address to the Congress, delivered via a giant screen in Croke Park, came during the closing Mass on Sunday and also raised the topic of liturgical change. But in advancing a historical thesis similar to

Cardinal Ouellet's, Benedict took greater pains to justify his claims. Like Ouellet and the authors of the *Pastoral and Theological Reflections* before him, the Pope also paralleled the fifty years intervening since Vatican II with the eighty years that had elapsed since the last international Congress in Ireland. And when his topic turned to liturgy, Benedict repeated the Vatican position that had echoed in Rome ever since John Paul II took office, namely, that "At our distance today from the Council Father's expressed desires . . . it is clear that a great deal has been achieved; but it is equally clear that there have been many misunderstandings and irregularities."[37]

Extending the words of his Legate, the Pope continued by explaining what he believed to be at stake in the difference between liturgical renewal properly inspired by the Council and changes that otherwise are merely "misunderstandings and irregularities." For Benedict, the explanation depends upon a metaphor: Vatican II renewed "external forms" so that the faithful could gain greater access to the "inner depth of the mystery" that defines the essence of liturgical practice and experience. At first glance, Benedict's words seem to imply a type of historical change, but the apparent "change" turns out to have been "external" or, more accurately (according to this argument), "superficial." Upon closer inspection, no real alteration occurred, because what really matters is an ideal that lies deeper within the heart of the tradition—and that ideal is constant. Once one accepts the metaphor that posits such a distinction between "external" and "internal" elements, one can follow Benedict to his intended conclusion, namely, that since Vatican II "the revision of liturgical forms has remained at an external level, and 'active participation' has been confused with external activity."[38]

There are a number of theological issues raised by the Pope's proposal, not the least of which is what does one make of the unity between external and internal elements presented to Catholics in the Eucharist itself? But Benedict's distinction also reveals a rationale for the wider claim about the Church and its relationship to historical change more generally. If one accepts that God's presence in the Church—if not the world—operates according to a distinction between external and internal, outer and inner, then a vocabulary emerges to evaluate the things that belong to these two realms. "Internal" things, for example, are always perceived as being "deeper," more spiritual, and therefore closer to God, while "external" things remain less important because of the "superficial" quality implied by the metaphor. As Cardinal Ratzinger said before he became Pope Benedict, the best presentations of a Eucharistic ecclesiology always show how cohesion within the Church "becomes more concrete while remaining totally spiritual, transcendent and eschatological."[39] In stating his preference this way, the Cardinal foreshadowed his thoughts about liturgical change that he came to deliver as Pope Benedict. His words at Croke Park invite listeners to imagine an external realm where alterations to the liturgy have taken place as a result of the

Council's call for "full and active participation."[40] But in addition to this realm, Benedict also has us imagine a second arena that is "internal." This is the place where there is no change, a dimension of Ratzinger's thought that Cardinal Kasper identified as the site of his Platonic ideals, where the Pope seeks only to transcend history in order to make manifest its constancy.

Since at least his 1985 interview with Vittorio Messori, this element of Benedict's thinking has been essential to his broader ecclesiology. For him, this is where the essence of the Church resides. "For a Catholic, the Church is indeed composed of men who organize her external visage. But behind this, the fundamental structures are willed by God himself, and therefore are inviolable. Behind the *human* exterior stands the mystery of a *more than human* reality, in which reformers, sociologists, organizers have no authority whatsoever."[41] In that lengthy 1985 interview, the Cardinal saw no greater problem facing the Church than the reluctance of Catholics to accept this dichotomy. "My impression is that the authentically Catholic meaning of the reality 'Church' is tacitly disappearing, without being expressly rejected. Many no longer believe that what is at issue is a reality willed by the Lord himself."[42] What was disappearing in 1984 even as the Cardinal gave his interview is all but gone by 2012 in Dublin. Among many of the Irish who even bother to note that a Eucharistic Congress is taking place, this description of an "external" organization run "internally" by God does not work; they simply can no longer accept the claim that God is responsible for an institution whose problems are so thoroughly systemic that they touch virtually every aspect of Irish life. The reluctance of advocates like Benedict and Cardinal Ouellet to reconceive their understanding of the Church to account more seriously for the existential realities around them results in positions that, to contemporary Ireland, are at best anachronistic. In fact, when those positions result in actions—like Benedict's 2010 Pastoral Letter that calls for Irish Catholics to "devote their Friday penances, for a period of one year" to the renewal of the Church—the position becomes more than anachronistic; it becomes offensive.[43]

The Pope's lament that a diminished faith has left Catholics unable to see the internal essence of the Church as divinely-instituted may in the end be an ironic insight into a more hopeful Catholic future, both in Ireland and elsewhere. For many Catholics, this unwillingness to accept the Church as an institution of God's will becomes one of the few ways left for the faithful to preserve their beliefs. If those who read with interest the *Reflections* of the thirteen Irish thinkers discover that they no longer can separate an internal "essence" of the Church from its existential roles and historical presence, then perhaps they can bear witness to a community renewed in its commitment to humanity. Contrary to leaders like Benedict, Cardinal Ouellet, and John Paul II, who have insisted on barring change from a theology of *communio*, history continues to place variation, transformation, and revolution at the feet of the hierarchy. Gone is the age of the 1932 Congress, when Catholic leaders could speak like Pius XI about establishing the "Empire of the Church over all nations"—divinely-mandated by a Christ who, as King, repeatedly issued calls to arms.[44] But gone too are the days when Catholicism could motivate stadiums full of followers with an uncritical summons of disembodied ideals like Mary's Immaculate Conception or Jesus's Sacred Heart. For all of us, despite our most gallant efforts, change comes, borne to us in the historical exertions of our very bodies. As the authors of the *Theological and Pastoral Reflections* note, when we make the sign of the cross in prayer, tracing it upon our chests, we don't affirm a unique reality instituted by the Lord, we affirm reality—the history of flesh and blood, including God's. Sometimes within that reality we commune together to change the world, and sometimes we commune together just hoping for change. Despite sincere efforts by Rome to explain why neither should be occurring in Dublin during June, 2012, both did.

NOTES

1. A good survey of the 1932 Congress is Rory O'Dwyer, *The Eucharistic Congress, Dublin 1932* (Gloucestershire: The History Press Ltd, 2009).

2. *The Eucharist: Communion With Christ and One Another: Theological and Pastoral Reflections in Preparation for the 50th International Eucharistic Congress* (Dublin: Veritas, 2011). The authors of the document are anonymous.

3. For all three, history refers to a record of past events as well as the general course of human experience, both material and spiritual.

4. An "ecclesiology of communion" explains how the Church functions as a body with an internal order, sources of authority, and relationships to both God and the world.

5. Cardinal Marc Ouellet, Papal Legate to the 50th International Eucharistic Congress, untitled address (IEC 2012 Theological Symposium, Saint Patrick's College, Maynooth, Ireland, June 6–9, 2012, accessed March 18, 2013, http://www.iec2012.ie/index.jsp?p=108&n=4866), 1. All subsequent references to this address will be to this site.

6. Cardinal Joseph Ratzinger with Vitterio Messori, *The Ratzinger Report, An Exclusive Interview on the State of the Church*, trans. Salvator Attananasio and Graham Harrison (San Francisco: Ignatius Press, 1985), 35. This conclusion about the continuous and unbreakable history of the Council seems to have pushed the Church into some strange positions. For example, in 2005 the Vatican published *The Ecumenical Council Vatican II: A Counterpoint for Its History* by Archbishop Agostino Marchetto, which argues vigorously against the notion that we can properly refer to the Council as an "event." Marchetto follows John Paul II and Ratzinger in his thesis, arguing that the only true legacy of Vatican II is constituted by the documents it produced, and because the documents do not explicitly call for a break in Church tradition, interpreters have no evidence that such a break ever occurred (a point that renders insignificant the fact that a gathering of Church leaders took place). Given the lack of any explicit call for change in the Council texts, Marchetto (like John Paul II and Ratzinger before him) concludes that, in fact, there is no evidence that a historical "event" ever occurred—if by "event" you mean something that interrupts time to create a sense of "before" and "after." Agostino Marchetto, *The Second Vatican Ecumenical Council: A Counterpoint for the History of the Council*, trans. Kenneth Whitehead (Scranton: Scranton University Press, 2009).

7. John Paul II, "The Implementation of Vatican II," reported by Sandro Magister in "Vatican II: The Real Untold Story," accessed March 20013, http://chiesa.espresso.repubblica.it/articolo/34283?eng=y.

8. *Lumen Gentium, Dogmatic Constitution on the Church, promulgated by Pope Paul VI November 26, 1964*, The Holy See, accessed March 19, 2013, http://www.vatican.va/archive/hist_councils/ii_vatican_council/documents/vat-ii_const_19641121_lumen-gentium_en.html.

9. Ouellet, paper delivered IEC 2012 Theological Symposium, 3.

10. There was a time when the term "mystical body" was conceived of in physical terms. But the Cardinal goes on to point out that the conception altered (as opposed to "changed") when the Church responded to Medieval heresies surrounding the belief in God's real presence in the Eucharist. As a result of those responses, the elements of bread and wine became the locus of discussion about concrete evidence of God's presence, and the sacred elements gained the title *corpus verum* or "true body." The term *corpus mysticum* remained connected with the Church but, absent any association with items as tangible as physical bread or wine, the term increasingly assumed more "ethereal" references. "*Mysticum*" tended to conjure up images that encouraged people to think of it "in a purely spiritual sense." Ibid., 4.

11. His words may cohere with the rest of his argument, but they are inconsistent with important themes from *Lumen Gentium*, which takes great pains to argue for essential connections between the Gospel message, the Church, and the wider culture. "There are many ties between the message of salvation and human culture. For God, revealing Himself to His people to the extent of a full manifestation of Himself in His Incarnate Son, has spoken according to the culture proper to each epoch." The document raises issues of education, the arts, economics, technology, and communication—in short, many of the topics that make discussions of the Church as a sign of "human unity" both challenging and uncomfortable. *Lumen Gentium*, pars. 53–62.

12. Ibid., 4.

13. *Gaudium et spes, Pastoral Constitution on the Church in the Modern World, promulgated by Pope Paul VI December 7, 1965*, par. 4, The Holy See, accessed July 31, 2014, http://www.vatican.va/archive/hist_councils/ii_vatican_council/documents/vat-ii_const_19651207-_gaudium-et-spes_en.html.

14. John Paul II, *Ecclesia de Eucharistia*, par. 35. Quoted in Ouellet, paper delivered IEC 2012 Theological Symposium, June 6–9, 2012, 6. For the Cardinal, the Church ultimately is the "bearer of a mysterious divine reality that no image or analogy of this world will adequately express." The Church carries that which transcends this world, and that which transcends the Church also defines it. Ibid., 17.

15. Ibid., 13.

16. Ibid., 9. The thinking behind each of these comments requires Catholics to understand the office of the bishop—and to accept the man himself—as both a part and a whole, that is, as the individual who stands before you but also as the embodiment of something "larger" or more comprehensive. It's true that we see this same logic at work when other public figures take the stage—American Presidents, for example. But even if the United States views its leaders through lenses colored by a long tradition of a civil religion, which places their individual qualities in an almost sacred context, that perception pales next to the far more explicit claims made by the Church on behalf of its ordained leaders. The *Catechism of the Catholic Church* states the position most forcefully, noting "in the beautiful expression of St. Ignatius of Antioch," that "the bishop is *typos tou Patros*: he is like the living image of God the Father." Such an understanding affirms the claims of those in 1932 who would see the individual bishop (and not just his "office") as someone who is able to "represent" the wider Church precisely because he spiritually or ontologically "is" the wider Church. The same understanding seems to provide a rationale for the ease with which Ouellet reduces the dense notion of an ecclesial communion to a series of formal relationships between bishops. The Holy See, *Catechism of the Catholic Church*, par. 1549, accessed March 19, 2013, http://www.usccb.org/beliefs-and-teachings/what-we-believe/catechism/catechism-of-the-catholic-church/epub/index.cfm.

17. In his address, Cardinal Ouellet refers to that exchange, which began with the publication on May 28, 1992, of a letter from then Cardinal Ratzinger's office in the Congregation for the Doctrine of the Faith, "Letter to the Bishops of the Catholic Church on Some Aspects of the Church Understood as Communion." The exchange seemed to culminate in the essays written by both men for *America* magazine. According to Ouellet, the strength of Ratzinger's argument is his insistence on the "ontological primacy" of the universal Church, which refers to a belief

that the purpose of the Church "universal" constitutes an irreducible reality upon which all individual or "particular" churches rest. Without this universal whole, the particular examples are like puzzle pieces that may fit together but nevertheless fail to make a coherent picture. Ouellet dismisses Kasper as someone who just "misunderstands" Ratzinger's argument, though the former seems to have a strong grasp of the details. Kasper's approach, however, is very different. "I reached my position not from abstract reasoning but from pastoral experience," writes Kasper, and, he goes on to maintain, that experience reveals not a unified whole based on a notion of ontological priority but a series of gaps, "emerging and steadily increasing between norms promulgated in Rome for the universal church and the needs and practices of our local church." If one begins with the assertion of an ontologically prior "universal" Church, there can be no such gaps, just misunderstandings of how the particular pieces are supposed to form the picture. But as Kasper points out, that's not how Catholics experience their faith in the early years of the twenty-first century. On a variety of issues that directly influence the lives of Catholics—from "ethical issues, sacramental discipline and ecumenical practices," to the "adamant refusal of Communion to all divorced and remarried persons and the highly restrictive rules for Eucharistic hospitality"—the Church can speak with ontological priority, but that does not mean that individual parishes or parishioners will understand or "comprehend" the big picture, no matter how far back they stand. There simply is too much "history" in the way. Walter Kasper, "On the Church," *America*, April 23, 2001; Joseph Ratzinger, "On the Local and the Universal Church," *America*, November 19, 2001.

18. Ouellet, paper delivered IEC 2012 Theological Symposium, June 6–9, 2012, 14.

19. Ibid., 8.

20. These include the Ferns Report (2005), Ryan Report (2009), Murphy Report (2009) and Cloyne Report (2011).

21. "Taoiseach Enda Kenny: Cloyne Report," YouTube video, 12:13, posted by RTE, July 21 2011, accessed June 7, 2014, http://www.youtube.com/watch?v=mo5MXrqbDeA.

22. Ouellet, paper delivered IEC 2012 Theological Symposium, June 6–9, 2012, 2–3.

23. Ibid., 5.

24. Ibid., 17.

25. Ibid.

26. Pontifical Committee for Eucharistic Congresses, *Statutes, promulgated by Cardinal Bertone, Sec. of State, Vatican City, January 7, 2010*, The Holy See, accessed March 19, 2013, http://www.vatican.va/roman_curia/pont_committees/eucharist-congr/documents/rc_committ-_euchar_doc_20091224_statuto_en.html.

27. *The Eucharist: Communion With Christ and One Another, Theological and Pastoral Reflections in Preparation for the 50th Eucharistic Congress*. This is a remarkably clear and well-organized text that balances theological insight with pastoral concerns, all in the service of addressing the same topic that forms the center of Cardinal Ouellet's symposium address, the "ecclesiology of communion."

28. Ibid., par. 6.

29. Anglican-Roman Catholic International Commission, *The Final Report, Windsor, September 1981* (London/Cincinnati: SPCK/Forward Movement Publications, 1982), 11–16.

30. Ibid. par. 6.

31. Cardinal Joseph Ratzinger, "The Ecclesiology of Vatican II," opening address at the Pastoral Congress of the Diocese of Avila, Italy (September 15, 2001). *L'Osservatore Romano, Weekly Edition in English*, January 23, 2002, 5 accessed March 19, 2013, http://www.ewtn.com/library/curia/cdfeccv2.htm.

32. *Theological and Pastoral Reflections in Preparation for the 50th Eucharistic Congress*, par. 24.

33. Ibid., par. 35.

34. Ibid., par. 65.

35. Luke 24:44. In this context, Cardinal Ouellet's long rehearsal in his address about how bishops exercise their "episcopal authority," each one "over the portion he has been given" and all as "vicars of Christ, but in dependence on the head of the college of bishops, the pope," seems very much beside the point. Ouellet may well have had the Vatican II document *Christus Dominus* in mind when he delivered his lengthy rationale for hierarchy as integral to his vision

of "communion"; after all, that earlier text underscores the office of bishop for the consistency it represents: "in the episcopal order," the document states, "the apostolic body continues without a break. Together with its head, the Roman pontiff, and never without this head it exists as the subject of supreme, plenary power over the universal Church." But if the Cardinal finds in these words support for his emphasis upon continuity and permanence, he must look past other portions of the same text that emphasize how "bishops should present Christian doctrine in a manner adapted to the needs of the times, that is to say, in a manner that will respond to the difficulties and questions by which people are especially burdened and troubled." Because, as the document goes on to insist, "it is the mission of the Church to converse with the human society in which it lives," it remains "especially the duty of bishops to seek out men and both request and promote dialogue with them." Although Ouellet makes plain his desire to advance an understanding of the bishop as part of a large and unbroken system of authority, he is silent about whether the bishop's vocation should include (let alone emerge from) his commitment to historical awareness, his sense of adaptability, or his willingness to enter into a dialogue with other members of the body of Christ. See: Ouellet, paper delivered IEC 2012 Theological Symposium, June 6–9, 2012, 9–10 and *Christus Dominus, Decree Concerning the Pastoral Office of Bishops in the Church, promulgated by Pope Paul VI October 28, 1965*, especially chap. 1, "The Relationships of Bishops to the Universal Church," The Holy See, accessed July 20, 2014, http://www.vatican.va/archive/hist_councils/ii_vatican_council/documents/vat-ii_decree_19651028_christus-dominus_en.html.

36. *Theological and Pastoral Reflections in Preparation for the 50th Eucharistic Congress*, par. 14.

37. Benedict XVI, "Message to the 2012 Eucharistic Congress, June 17, 2012," accessed March 19, 2013, http://www.iec2012.ie/index.jsp?p=108&n=144&a=2412.

38. Ibid.

39. Ratzinger, "The Ecclesiology of Vatican II."

40. *Sacrosanctum concilium, Constitution on the Sacred Liturgy, promulgated by His Holiness Pope Paul VI December 4, 1963*, par. 14, The Holy See, accessed July August 1, 2014, http://www.vatican.va/archive/hist_councils/ii_vatican_council/documents/vat-ii_const_19631204_sacrosanctum-concilium_en.html.

41. Ratzinger and Messori, *The Ratzinger Report*, 46.

42. Ibid., 45.

43. And Cardinal Ouellet's decision in his address to call for an understanding of (infant) baptism as a "nuptial bath" is almost incomprehensible given the need for his audience to recover from the horrors of clergy sexual abuse of children. Ouellet, paper delivered IEC 2012 Theological Symposium, June 6–9, 2012, 12.

44. *Quas Primas, Encyclical of Pope Pius XI on the Feast of Christ the King, 1925*, par. 24, The Holy See, accessed July 31, 2014, http://www.vatican.va/holy_father/pius_xi/encyclicals/documents/hf_p-xi_enc_11121925_quas-primas_en.html.

Chapter Eight

Lost in Translation

William Donohue and the Recent Controversies of the Catholic Church in Ireland

Matthew J. O'Brien

On May 30, 2009, listeners to Matt Cooper's radio show "The Last Word" on the Irish network RTE were treated to a remarkable encounter. The main feature of that show, billed as a debate over the Ryan Report on clerical abuse in Ireland, pitted Dr. William A. Donohue, leader of the American Catholic League for Religious and Civil Rights, and Colm O'Gorman, a prominent Irish activist on behalf of his fellow victims of clerical abuse. For Irish listeners, Donohue's brash style, littered with American (or more precisely New York) idioms, might have been strikingly reminiscent of the archetypical "American Uncle"—a particular type of return visitor whose speaking style was marked by braggadocio and outspoken polemics. On the other hand, for the American audience there was a different distinction. Those familiar with Donohue's louder than life public person would have been surprised to hear how O'Gorman (and eventually Cooper) deftly parried Donohue's charges, leaving him swinging like an exhausted prizefighter.[1] As they critiqued both the substance and the style of Donohue's reading of the Ryan report, the Irish host and O'Gorman underscored the transatlantic differences between the respective debates on clerical abuse in Ireland and the United States.

Part of this was stylistic, as Donohue engaged in some particularly American debating tendencies. Foremost among these is his tendency to try to control the terms of the debate by shifting what academics call "the Overton window," that is, the acceptable range of popular opinion. Known in the sporting world as "working the refs," the practice tries to sway public opinion through frequent, loud protests about alleged transgressions by opponents: hence Catholic League campaigns against B-list pop stars like Joan Osbourne (whose otherwise anodyne song, "One of Us," speculated about an anthropomorphized notion of the divine).[2] Another practice, Donohue's rapid-response talking style, was also out of place: well-suited to the emergent 24-7 cable news networks, but less appreciated in the more deliberative style that marked discussions in Donohue's ethnic homeland.

But there was also a deeper problem with Donohue's underwhelming performance on RTE radio: his unconvincing response to O'Gorman's assertion about the Irish hierarchy's admissions seemed to indicate that Donohue had done little of the preparatory work that usually enables him to effectively read his adversaries, or at least his audience. In fact, Donohue's often-overlooked underlying strength has been his canny advance work, which offers better awareness of any chance to knock opponents off their stride. Thus, while he clearly relishes the prospect of on-camera confrontation, a number of Donohue's past and present opponents attest to his considerable off-stage charms, welcoming interview requests, engaging in green room chatter before shows, and even proudly maintaining friendships with prominent members of institutions that he rhetorically vilifies.[3] For one such figure, Norman Siegel of New York Civil Liberties Union, Donohue is "a bright, well-read individual" whose forthright manner has helped established him as a likeable character.[4] Donohue does not so much manufacture his "outrage" as much as he channels it, driven to unusual lengths by the wider perception that the Catholic Church is being slandered.

The relative parts played by Donohue's bluster and presumption can be better understood by comparing his public career, and specifically his transatlantic performance in Ireland, with a mid-twentieth century Irish-American Catholic figure, Father Edward Lodge Curran. In a forty-year career that spanned the middle decades of the twentieth century, Curran shared with Donohue several important attributes, from their Brooklyn-oriented upbringing, to their forceful leadership, to their louder than life rhetorical styles. Both men would be involved in the same electoral project as well: establishing the conservative credentials of American Catholics on the right side of the U.S. ideological spectrum. But the contrasting results of each man's respective engagements in Irish affairs speak not only to personal differences, but also to the superpower presumptions that have insinuated themselves into some varieties of Irish-Catholic conservatism during the second half of the twentieth century. Their comparison also shows how the perception of Irish Catholicism by Irish Catholics in the United States has shifted over time.

BROOKLYN AND THE IRISH

Neighborhood roots have always played a central role in Irish Catholic history in the United States. With the exception of South Boston, there were few urban areas in the United States that could compete with Brooklyn for its deep association with Irish-American ethnicity. Located across the Hudson River from its more glamorous neighbor, Manhattan, the borough of Brooklyn included a number of prominently Irish-American sections such as Bay Ridge and Windsor Terrace, as well as its own version of the Tammany Hall political machine. Irish-American writers also abounded there, from Jimmy Cannon to Pete Hamill, and it produced the most prominent Catholic newspaper in the country in the mid-twentieth century: the Archdiocese of Brooklyn's weekly, the *Tablet*.

Edward Lodge Curran remained true to these roots during his half-century long public career, balancing regional and national endeavors with a fierce commitment the borough that would persist with his tenure as president of the Brooklyn Pastors' Association during the late 1960s. Curran's muscular oratory and journalism reflected his Brooklyn roots, whether in his frequent contributions to the (Brooklyn) *Tablet*, the (New York) *Gaelic American*, or even his stump speeches during the 1930s, which would earn him the title "the Coughlin of the East."

Born into a middle-class household, Curran came of age during the apogee of Irish influence in Brooklyn, and he scrupulously maintained his connections with his neighborhood at the same time as he pursued scholarly distinctions. Curran attended St. John's College (now St. John's University) in nearby Queens and graduated in 1918, after which he traveled to Catholic University in Washington, DC, and earned his bachelor's degree in Sacred Theology. After his ordination there, he returned to Brooklyn and took up a teaching post in the diocesan seminary, Cathedral College. At the same time, the young Fr. Curran accumulated a number of impressive degrees, traveling up to Manhattan to obtain a master's degree in History at Columbia University, followed by studies in the Bronx at Fordham University, where he earned the doctorate in History that would result in the distinguished byline of "Dr. Edward Lodge Curran, Ph.D." that would appear on his columns (and printed announcements of his speaking appearances). Shortly thereafter, he enrolled in St. Lawrence Law School in Brooklyn and took his degree in 1933, before passing the New York State bar exam the following year. By the mid-1930s, Curran attained impressive scholarly credentials within a community where college degrees were scarce, decades before the passage of the GI Bill.

At the same time as he traveled throughout the boroughs of New York City, Curran's pastoral career remained firmly moored within the Brooklyn Catholic community. Curran's parish assignments included a one-year assignment to St. Martin of Tours in Brooklyn, a subsequent stay at his family's parish, St. Stephen's, and nearly a decade as a Dean at Cathedral College helping to educate priests for the Brooklyn Archdiocese. Curran's writing career also began during this period with two Brooklyn institutions: the *Tablet* and the International Catholic Truth Society (I.C.T.S.), which had been formed in 1900 to provide information that would refute nativist accusations about Catholics in the United States. By the time his work with the ICTS began to appear, that organization boasted a self-reported readership of 436,000. By 1932 Curran had been named president of the organization, and he had branched out into ethnic commentary with a regular column ("Along the Way") in the New York Irish weekly the *Gaelic American* as well as the *Tablet*.

Growing up among many postwar Brooklyn expatriates in the Long Island suburbs, that borough also seemed to play an important role for William Donohue. Young William attended a Catholic grammar school and a Catholic high school in nearby Queens.[5] After college, Donohue served a four-year hitch in the U.S. Air Force, and then he returned to New York City to teach while he pursued a graduate degree at New York University. In an evocative contribution to a recent volume of essays titled *Catholics in New York*, Donohue described sending out applications to fifty-nine parochial schools in Manhattan, Queens, and the Bronx, before landing a position at St. Lucy's school in Spanish Harlem, where the self-described "big Irishman" would leave an indelible impression among his African-American and Puerto Rican students.[6]

In 1977 Donohue left New York to take a position teaching sociology at LaRoche College, just north of Pittsburgh, and received his PhD from New York University in 1980. His first book, *The Politics of the American Civil Liberties Union*, was published in 1985 and helped earn him admirers among conservatives, eventually garnering him an adjunct post as a Bradley Resident Scholar at the Heritage Foundation, an influential conservative think tank that had enjoyed growing influence during the Reagan Administration. In 1993, Donohue's career would complete the circle with his return to New York City, where he secured an appointment as the Director of the Catholic League for Civil and Religious Liberties. Donohue's capacity as a "joiner" would bring a slew of interlocking connections to the Catholic League, with his membership in organizations ranging from the Catholic Social Workers Association, the Ancient Order of Hibernians, the Catholic War Veterans, and the Jewish Action Alliance. In any case, it was soon clear from comments about out-of-town predecessors and rivals that he continues to see New York City as the center of the public relations world.

Like Curran, his New York roots have also influenced Donohue's speaking style. His on-air manner is marked by tough-guy New York phrases, assertions about the purported elitism of his opponents, references to the "reality" that provides the basis for his own argument, and other confrontational tactics. While seemingly designed to distract or intimidate his more genteel adversaries, such practices also remind listeners of Donohue's bona fides as an authentic New Yorker, if not a Brooklynite. As his friend Norman Siegel of the ACLU would remark, Donohue modeled himself on the television character Archie Bunker from the 1970s series *All in the Family*, whose reactionary pronouncements might occasionally seem ridiculous but nonetheless authentic.

New York City also played an important role in Dr. Donohue's early leadership of the Catholic League, both directly and indirectly. In 1993, the League's board of directors turned to Donohue after it "foundered" in the wake of the death of its creator, Fr. Virgil Blum, S.J., a Jesuit priest and professor at Marquette University. Donohue quickly centralized operations of the previously grassroots-directed organization, moving the Catholic League's headquarters from the suburbs of Philadelphia, later explaining to an interviewer "you just don't put a national office in Bala Cynwyd, Pennsylvania."[7] Around the same time, Donohue curtailed Catholic League operations outside New York, closing down several regional branches (including the original headquarters in Milwaukee, as well as those in Los Angeles and Boston) and transforming other branches (such as that in Philadelphia) from paid positions to volunteer operations.[8] These moves raised the hackles of some long-time regulars, but Donohue was ready with rhetoric that cast the resistors as apologists for a dysfunctional and discredited past.[9]

These dramatic operational changes coincided with an intense redefinition of the Catholic League's mission. In an issue of the *Catalyst*, the Catholic League's monthly publication, months after his appointment, Donohue announced his intention to jettison some of the league's earlier campaigns on issues such as state aid to Catholic schools in order to concentrate on "the unprecedented assault on the Church to discredit it and marginalize its impact." Anti-Catholicism took on a more nefarious appearance now, not just as a vague prejudice but also as an assault on "the last bastion of traditional moral authority in our society." From the League's new high-rise offices in Manhattan, Donohue would reach out to the suburbs, announcing "Catholic parents cannot continue to complain over cocktails on a Saturday evening about how bad the culture is."[10]

DEALING WITH (IN?) DIVISION: CURRAN AND DONOHUE'S EARLY CAREERS

After Fr. Curran established his regional credentials as the president of the ICTU and became the best-known contributor to the Brooklyn *Tablet* and the *Gaelic America*, he emerged on the national stage as the champion of Irish-

American anti-communism during the mid-1930s, when Depression-era desperation seemed ready to summon a period of political tribulation. The Great Depression hit American Catholics particularly hard, in part because of their disproportionate reliance on the now-decimated public-sector rolls in major Eastern cities, as well as their concentration in other troubled sectors such as manufacturing and heavy industry. Compounding this domestic trauma was the international threat of communism, which according to Curran, reached its Bolshevik tentacles into the United States from its headquarters in Moscow. The Brooklyn priest would denounce the Nazi regime not long after its installation in Germany, but for the most part he would devote his energies to sounding the alarm about communist attacks on the Church in Mexico and Spain, frustrated by the seemingly indifferent American State Department and Roosevelt administration.[11] Curran was willing to reach out to anti-communists of other faiths, as expressed in the introduction to his 1937 publication, *Facts about Communism*, but it was clear that he viewed the cause through an apocalyptic lens as a Catholic battle against evil.

During the mid-1930s, Curran's increasingly bellicose rhetoric lead to a fellowship with an even more prominent Catholic clerical firebrand, Fr. Charles Coughlin, known for his nationally syndicated weekly radio program that drew up to 30 million listeners at its peak. Even as Coughlin's political fortunes began to fade after an ill-fated foray into presidential politics in 1935, the so-called "Radio Priest" continued to draw hundreds of thousands of followers among East Cost ethnics, and Coughlin's columns regularly appeared alongside Curran's pieces in the Brooklyn *Tablet*. Curran's regional significance, recognized by the nickname "the Coughlin of the East," led to trips to Boston and even a speaking appearance as far away as Cincinnati. Even at this point, Curran balanced his growing national stature with local activities, simultaneously publishing front-page columns in the Coughlinite weekly *Social Justice* while defending the thuggish members of the Christian Front movement in Brooklyn, whose *modus operandi* was to instigate violence by sending anti-Semitic soapbox orators into Jewish neighborhoods.

In early 1941, the ignominious fall of Fr. Coughlin and the concurrent indictment of several Christian Front members led to a retreat from the spotlight for Curran, but only in the short term. In fact, even the Japanese attack on Pearl Harbor, which single-handedly shut down the 800,000-member America First movement along with other isolationist groups, could not silence the Brooklyn priest. Within a few months of the American entry into the war, Curran soon resumed his provocations, venturing to Boston in February 1942 to complain loudly to a South Boston audience about the Allies' strategic emphasis on the North Atlantic. Nor did Curran cease supporting his friend Coughlin, sending a public telegram to him on the birthday of the discredited priest, which was also published in the *Gaelic-American*. Two years later, Curran would mark the same occasion with a public declaration that "We shall beg God to hasten the day when once again his voice may ring out over the airwaves to protect our church, our country, our priesthood, and our fellow citizens." Finally, Curran stubbornly maintained his support of the Christian Front despite their clear identification with America's wartime enemies.

As the Second World War gave way to the Cold War, Curran's dubious association with Coughlin gave way to a redoubled opposition to communism, as well as a persistent distrust of "internationalism" (i.e., diplomatic engagements) in general, and the Anglo-American alliance in particular. Curran would make use of his law degree to mount a challenge to the United Nations in the courts of New York State, and he helped spread the right-wing interpretation of Allied negotiations at Tehran and Yalta as an abandonment of Eastern Europe. The Anti-Defamation League of B'nai B'rith noted that Curran had abstained from "clear anti-semitism" in their 1947 annual report, but it also mentioned his continued association with Christian Front members at an event celebrating Coughlin's birthday, especially in his call for a force that would be needed to counter the "Jewish front." Although such talk became less defensible with the horrifying revelations of the Holocaust, Curran still appeared regularly as a featured speaker at communion breakfasts, Independence Day celebrations, and other public gatherings.

In contrast, William Donohue has generally steered clear of anti-Semitism. Although his public pronouncements have included a few high-profile incidents, such as his obtuse repetition of the old complaint that Hollywood is run by "secular Jews," even these instances have left his Jewish compatriots (of whom there are a considerable number) shaking their heads but still willing to defend his character. In fact, Donohue's leadership at the Catholic League seemingly followed a William F. Buckley-type disavowal of anti-semitism, with positive reviews of philosemitic works in the *Catalyst* that drew the ire of some of the Catholic League's former conspiracy-minded members.[12] Donohue's identification between the Catholic League and the Anti-Defamation League has also drawn a number of prominent supporters from right-leaning Jewish commentators, who have couched their disappointment with his gaffes in a larger appreciation of his fair-minded attitudes toward Jewish Americans.[13] Donohue also characterized the Anti-Defamation League of B'nai B'rith as a "natural analog" for the remade Catholic League when describing his plans for the organization soon after his appointment.

Although Donohue's remarks about Jews garnered the most attention, he reserved his most spirited criticism for his fellow co-religionists, many of whom he saw as insufficiently zealous in their defense of the institutional Church. This trend emerged in the earliest days of his tenure at the Catholic League, when he sought to increase the League's membership. In an early manifesto titled *A True Fighter for the Faith*, published a year after his appointment as president, Donohue flatly declared, "I think that Catholics haven't done enough for themselves. Let me be explicit: I don't mean the clergy." This call to action meant new measures, breaking with the aforementioned tendency to "complain over cocktails on a Saturday evening about how bad the culture is," as he admonished readers to "not be so timid about getting involved with other people." Donohue instructed Catholics to challenge local leadership as well: "Find out what people are being brought into your local church for outside guest speakers. Find out what your local Catholic college or university is doing, it might be a real eye-opener." At the heart of this activism was indignation, since "it means, first of all, getting angry" (although Donohue would also warn against overreaction).[14] Five years into his administration, Donohue looked back on his tenure at the Catholic League and remained convinced that Catholic apathy remained a serious problem, telling readers that that "the troops—meaning the faithful—have gotten fat and lazy," with a complacency that renders them "psychologically disabled."[15] Despite his rallying calls, American Catholics are "preoccupied with Sunday-morning soccer games and the need to be liked," demonstrating "their contemptible tolerance for anti-Catholicism."[16]

In the meantime, Donohue's leadership brought the Catholic League to a new level of prominence, transforming it from a decentralized grassroots interest group into a major political player on the national stage. With regular high-profile campaigns, Donohue helped increase the number of Catholic League members from 20,000 in 1993 to a self-estimated 350,000 by the end of the decade (his figure coming from multiplying the number of donating households by 1.5 to include spouses or other family members). The League's financial resources also grew at a similar rate, with the organization's annual budget increasing from approximately $800,000 to $2.7 million a year in 1999.[17] From the organization's headquarters on the twentieth floor of the Terrence Cardinal Cooke Building on the central east side of Manhattan, Donohue astutely adopted new tactics in the mid-1990s, with targeted direct mail appeals and a demanding regimen of public appearances that made him a ubiquitous presence in the new 24-7 cable news cycle. Despite the purported righteousness of his cause, Donohue demonstrated little hesitation about where he appears, taking out full-page ads in the *New York Times* (a paper he asserted must employ "bigots or idiots") and appearing on the talk show hosted by one of his rhetorical targets, Phil Donohue. In fact, Donohue has been quite open about this approach, explaining in one interview that he instructs his staff not to turn down interview requests, no matter the source, and relaying to a New York Times writer that he "wants results and wants them fast."[18]

Like Curran's anti-communist rhetoric, Donohue's rise to leadership has also been marked by hyperbolic language, although his chosen foe of secularism lacks the tangible villainy of the Soviet Union during the middle of the twentieth century. This might explain his relatively narrow base of appeal within the tens of millions of Americans who define themselves as Catholic. Nevertheless, the Catholic League has also mimicked the public spectacle of Catholic predecessors like Curran. As part of a Catholic League protest against a controversial art exhibit at the Brooklyn Museum, for example, League members dispensed vomit bags to patrons, and campaigns against purportedly anti-Catholic movies never fail to draw crowds of protesters (many of whom seem far outside demographic range of the films' intended audience). Directing it all, of course, is Donohue, whose attempts to inspire supporters include elevating art exhibits or R-rated films to the status of an existential threat to the Catholic Church, as exemplified in his characterization of a life-size statue of Jesus, made entirely of chocolate, as "one of the worst assaults on Christian sensibilities ever."[19]

DEALING WITH DISSIDENTS

After they established themselves in the vanguard of their respective movements, both Curran and Donohue reacted to any contrary argument from their co-religionists with withering responses. In the later years of the Second World War and afterwards, Curran threw his support behind General Douglas MacArthur, announcing that "God, again in His providence, has given us another military savior, a Christian gentleman in heart and soul, a worthy successor of George Washington."[20] After General MacArthur's star faded, Curran (like many other Irish Americans of the time) turned to Wisconsin Senator Joseph McCarthy as his champion. Curran vociferously defended McCarthy with pronouncements that the controversial red-baiter "would have been welcomed as a member of the Continental Congress," along with distributing thousands of "Save McCarthy" petitions through his parish in 1954 and publicly defending the senator from the pulpit.[21] Not surprisingly, then, when in 1954, Chicago Auxiliary Bishop Bernard Sheil voiced his reservations over McCarthy's campaign, Curran angrily defended McCarthy at a communion breakfast as "that great American, that great Marine and great Catholic," and impugning Bishop Sheil with the assertion that the senator from Wisconsin was "a controversial figure *only* in the minds of Communists and fellow travelers that he has on the run." Not only did Sheil offer only "glittering, or rather frittering generalities without one concretely proved charge, but his criticisms were unsubstantiated and uncharitable attacks." According to Curran, this was nothing short of sacrilege, as he described McCarthy as a Christ-like figure who "laid down his life" for "our beloved country and our beloved Church against the forces of atheistic communism forever."[22]

Donohue too has not been shy about openly insulting other Catholics who have questioned the wisdom of his campaigns against otherwise forgettable targets such as pop singer Joan Osbourne and others. Not long after taking over the Catholic League, Donohue characterized his fellow Catholic rivals as the "stupid, nerdy, angel-faced morons you see on TV." After he became more settled in his position, Donohue also adopted an approach similar to Curran's newspaper columns, impugning his opponents with arguments based on notions of masculinity and pugnaciousness. At the end of a long, critical review of Kerry Kennedy's book *Being Catholic*, Donohue concluded by noting that the collection of essays was "loaded with [feminists]." Donohue called for them to leave the Church, since "that would be the manly thing to do," before adding mockingly "but manliness is not one of their notable virtues."[23] In a similar fashion, Donohue derided the *National Catholic Reporter*, perhaps the pre-eminent Catholic newspaper in the country, for a lack of toughness which he attributed to the paper's roots in Kansas City (rather than on the East Coast).[24]

But, as with Curran, Donohue reserves a special caustic disdain for Irish-American adversaries. Part of Donohue's antipathy is predictable, especially in the case of several American controversialists of Irish descent such as Bill Maher, Kathy Griffin and Rosie O'Donnell. Even here, though, Donohue's denunciations add the charge of ethnic betrayal to their alleged crimes. For instance, when Rosie O'Donnell denounced the alleged patriarchy of the Catholic Church during an interview with longtime talk show host (and fellow liberal) Phil Donohue, the president of the Catholic League found it not only objectionable but also ethnically disqualifying: "Well, you know, there is something about two aging and embittered Irish Catholics that is so, well, you know, embarrassing. . . . It's a shame that this close to St. Patrick's Day two *deracinated* [author's emphasis] Irish Catholics should find the need to vent on national television."[25] Irish-American columnists Jimmy Breslin and Maureen Dowd have come in for special censure as well, and when Charles J. O'Byrne, a former Jesuit, aired his dissent in an interview with *Playboy* magazine, Donohue declared "There's nothing worse than an embittered Irish Catholic who is at war with the Church."[26] In a similar manner, when the Irish-American MSNBC host Chris Matthews grilled Bishop Tobin of Providence, Donohue charged that Matthews's background was an aggravating condition: "No non-Catholic would ever treat a bishop this way. But too many liberal Catholics, especially Irish Catholics, think they are exempt from the same standards of civility that apply to others."[27] Frank McCourt also seems to have struck a particular nerve of Donohue's, with an attack on the *New York Times* tribute to McCourt (a day after his death) in which he criticized McCourt as a writer who "made any number of insulting remarks about Catholicism, all to the applause of his sophomoric fans."[28]

Nor do Donohue's fellow Irish-American conservatives get a free pass, as when he labeled Fox News host Bill O'Reilly one of those "Irish Catholics [who] have let their Irish get the best of them" in the wake of O'Reilly's angry comments about the malfeasance of Church leaders during the pedophilia scandal. Overall, though, Donohue's condescension toward his Irish-American rivals on the right differs from his attempts to delegitimize the ethnic standing of his opponents on the left.

In part, the increased frequency and intensity of Donohue's intramural criticism of Irish Catholics speaks to the story of Irish-American acculturation over the course of the mid- and late-twentieth century. When Edward Lodge Curran took over the ICTS, the organization was most obviously directed at providing a defense against proximate nativists such as the Ku Klux Klan, which enjoyed a resurgence during the 1920s, as evidenced by the infamous "Klanbake" at the 1924 Democratic National Convention. But there were other issues as well, most notably assimilation. ICTS pamphlets in the 1920s warned against interfaith marriages, and Curran's first postwar publications started by summoning the straw man of complete denominational relativism in his identification of American Catholicism.[29]

Seventy years later, the Catholic League has been more concerned about the threat posed by Catholic accommodationists rather than Protestant nativists. In his appearance in front of a predominantly evangelical Protestant audience during the "Justice Sunday" rallies against liberal judges in 2005, Donohue began by telling his audience that "If I had a choice between a room of Ted Kennedy Irish-Catholics like myself and people like you I'll take you any day."[30] In a similar fashion, the leader of the Catholic League has been strikingly generous in his ecumenical outreach to conservative Protestants, declaring that President "Bush is focused on matters Catholic in a way that John Kennedy never was."[31] To some extent this identification with Protestant conservatives is not much different than Curran's willingness to reach out to non-Catholic anti-communists—both instances of outreach came as part of larger causes (anti-communism and anti-secularism, respectively). But by the end of the 1990s, the Catholic League seemed to have shifted from admonishing apathetic American Catholics to castigating Irish-American Catholic liberals: the enemy was now from within.

While Donohue seems to draw from Curran's over-the-top Cold War rhetoric, the irony is that his accession to the head of the Catholic League did not take place until after the fall of the Soviet Union. This absence resulted in a programmatic problem for the new-look Catholic League. There is little doubt that Donohue's willingness (even eagerness) to fight offending celebrities in the film, television, and popular music world(s) has been effective in filling the Catholic League coffers. Still, Donohue's prospects for ecumenical success are much more limited. Curran's cold-war zealotry generated at least a grudging acknowledgment from non-Catholics on the right, if only through the Brooklyn priest's willingness to take up the vanguard of ideological anti-communism and the burnished anti-communist credentials of the postwar wave of Irish-Catholic politicians at the national level. Notwithstanding Donohue's appearance during "Justice Sunday," the recent coalition between southern evangelicals and conservative Catholics stops far short of taking up Catholic apologia.

ATTITUDES TOWARD IRELAND AND IRISH CATHOLICISM

This notion of proving ideological *bona fides* by denouncing fellow Irish Catholics helps to explain what might be the most striking rhetorical difference between Edward Lodge Curran and William Donohue: their respective attitudes about Ireland itself. For the earlier figure, Ireland remained almost sacrosanct, troubled only by problems that could still be attributed to British misrule. By Donohue's time, however, decades of independence in the Republic of Ireland (and the emergent Celtic Tiger prosperity) rendered such familiar postcolonial themes obsolete, prompting him to fall back on his standard *modus operandi*, full-bore denunciation and dismissal, as the basis of his transatlantic relationship with the land by which he has chosen to identify himself ethnically.

Curran's direct involvement with Ireland came through the postwar campaign against Irish partition during the late 1940s and early 1950s. In the years following the Second World War, Curran continued to publish his column "By the Way" in the (New York) *Gaelic American*, even as that paper failed in its attempt to revive the shrill Anglophobic isolationism of the interwar period. Seemingly unscarred from his Coughlinite association on a local level, Curran remained prominently linked with the Irish-American nationalist community in New York City, serving as a chaplain in the Ancient Order of Hibernians, the chairman of the National Hibernian Anti-Partition Committee, and even making at least two trips to Ireland during the early 1950s in the waning years of the American postwar anti-partitionist movement.

Curran's Irish appearances carried a much different tone than his bellicose speeches in the United States. In sharp contrast to Curran's bomb-throwing rhetoric in front of American audiences, the (generally sympathetic) Irish press found the Brooklyn priest to be almost mild-mannered and cooperative. Putting aside the iconoclastic fervor that directed him toward MacArthur and McCarthy, Curran's April 1952 visit involved appearances with members of both the Dublin and Stormont parliaments, including two Northern Irish M.P.s (both nationalist, of course) with whom he shared a stage at a Dublin rally, neither of whom adhered to the abstentionist position taken by Sinn Fein.[32] Curran's address at an annual Ancient Order of Hibernians dinner in Dundalk, as chair of the Anti-Partitionist Committee of the American A.O.H., was similarly unassuming and even deferential. According to a description that appeared in the *Irish Independent* newspaper under the headline, "U.S. Support in Unity Plan Promised," Curran's paraphrased remarks acknowledged that "the method by which the question of partition would be settled must be decided by Ireland's own leaders, but it would have the full support of the Irish in America"—a veritable "blank check" to a gathering that included deputies from the Dail, senators from the Seanad Eireann, and the chair of the Irish Tourist Board.[33]

Curran's second visit the following year featured the same tone. The *Ulster Herald* praised him as "a distinguished Irish-American priest" and also noted the "cool and calm reason" that he summoned for the anti-partitionist cause.[34] Curran was also generous in his acclamation of Irish rural life, telling a correspondent that "tremendous progress had been made in the field of economic development and social services."[35] In the last appearance of this tour, Curran actually passed along A.O.H. donations to two Irish organizations: the Anti-Partitionist Association in Dublin and the Anti-Partition League of Belfast.[36]

In some ways, Donohue's antagonism is predictable in a political sense, given his attitudes about ethnic assimilation within the American Catholic Church, and toward recent Irish immigrants to the United States. As he began to consolidate his power within the Catholic League, Donohue took aim at ethnic divisions as a cause of Catholic complacency, surprisingly adopting an anti-hyphenate opposition to ethnic pluralism. Donohue attributed part of the reason why "too many [faithful Catholics] have become disinterested and lacking in initiative" to the lack of a "Catholic collective identity" similar to those found among "blacks and Jews." Ethnic allegiance, which "precedes the hyphen . . . ultimately keeps them distinct," and weakens his envisioned Church militant in comparison to black and Jewish advocates.[37]

But perhaps the most striking aspect of the difference between Curran and Donohue is the way that Donohue remains relatively unconnected to Ireland, despite his conscious self-identification as Irish (usually linked to pugnacity or drinking). When *Irish Voice* columnist Mike Farragher drew the ire of the Catholic League with a tongue-in-cheek column filled with flippant, if not sacrilegious, suggestions, Donohue jumped from criticizing the author or even the paper (which started in 1987 as an alternative to the older and more established *Irish Echo*) to issuing a wholesale indictment of contemporary Ireland. His *Catalyst* column asserted that "far too many Irishmen have divorced themselves from their religion, making possible—if not inevitable—a sick tolerance of those who are intolerant of Catholicism," which Donohue compared to the tumult visited upon American institutions during the 1960s.[38]

More recently, contemporary Ireland has returned as a topic in Donohue's writing, but once again more as a canvas upon which he can project his tableau rather than a place with its own history (which you might expect Donohue to share, at least nominally). The Catholic League's allusions to Ireland now center on two particularly dispiriting scandals from the mid- and late-twentieth century: the Magdalene Homes for unwed mothers and the clerical abuse scandal. In each case, Donohue has been quick to assert that media has overblown the significance of the state-issued McAleese and Ryan Reports, and characterized some of those individuals who have come forth as malcontents and "gold-diggers."

In fact, it was this eagerness to offer an aggressive apologia for the Irish Church that would lead to a strange but telling exchange toward the end of Donohue's appearance on Matt Cooper's "Last Word" program. When told that his line of reasoning was in fact much more aggressive than even the stance of the Irish hierarchy itself, Donohue seemed to acknowledge as much, explaining that he was called into service because the Irish church had been "cowed by the media." This argument comes naturally from the mission taken up by the Catholic League upon Donohue's ascension to power, when he warned that perceived instances of anti-Catholicism would result in that organization's "springing into action." Such a mission, in many ways, is similar to that taken by Curran in the transatlantic nationalist energies that he invested in the expatriate campaign against partition during the late 1940s and early 1950s. But Donohue's approach went even further, with direct attempts to discredit particular Irish figures, whether they be Colm O'Gorman or Taoiseach Enda Kenny.[39] It would take little energy, creativity, or background research to attempt to portray either figure as marginal or out of touch with mainstream Irish opinion, perhaps by asserting the existence of a Nixonian "silent majority" of Irish Catholics who might agree with Donohue's attribution of clerical abuse to homosexuality. In fact, it should surprise no one that such groundwork already exists, with native Irish analogs to the American group, including a conservative group known for its opposition to same-sex marriage that shares the name "the Catholic League." However, as far as can be ascertained from Irish and American newspaper records, there is little contact between the two organizations, and indeed Donohue seems less interested in visiting Ireland than his Irish-American foes—the "deracinated" politicians who would venture across the Atlantic if only to make a token gesture that might win them a few ethnic votes. Instead, with headlines in the *Catalyst* like "Ireland Lies About the Holy See," the stance of the American Catholic League seems to be that the Land of St. Patrick has been lost to the apostates, and should be jettisoned before it can serve as fodder for attacks on the American Catholic Church.[40]

In the end, Donohue's debate with Colm O'Gorman revealed a problem that was deeper than an ill-conceived rhetorical approach for the president of the Catholic League. Donohue's conception of Irish ethnicity is not necessarily inauthentic or fabricated, as seen through the comparison to his predecessor Fr. Edward Lodge Curran. But it is glaringly incomplete. Donohue's on-stage, ill-mannered triumphalism is not just ill-suited to the more restrained style of the Irish media, but also reminiscent of the very type of imperialist politics that Curran condemned during his visits in Ireland. The last half-century has brought many changes to Ireland, with an economic rollercoaster ride, new cultural self-interpretations, and even diplomatic shows of pique, but through it all Irish identity has retained something that Curran understood and Donohue ignored: a postcolonial distaste for outsiders, even those of diasporic stock, who arrive at their conclusions before their planes touch down in Ireland. As the readjustment of the Irish Catholic Church continues, with all its roiling debates, contemporary American evangelists (including those of the Catholic variety) would be well-served to remain mindful of the reception that greeted their Protestant counterparts of the nineteenth century.

NOTES

1. The audio recording of the show on YouTube would draw more than 87,000 replays and 735 comments as of July 2014. "Bill Donohue defends child abuse," YouTube video, 8:34, posted by encliticcopula, May 30, 2009, accessed July 11, 2014, https://www.youtube.com/watch?v=dKLlxAgMO-w.
2. "Grammy Nominee Joan Osborne 'Relishes' Controversy," *The Catalyst*, April 12, 1996, accessed July 11, 2014, http://www.catholicleague.org/grammy-nominee-joan-osborne-relishes-controversy/. Subsequent quotations from *The Catalyst*, the Catholic League's monthly publication, are also taken from its online site: http://www.catholicleague.org/category/catalyst/.
3. According to film director Kevin Smith, whose film *Dogma*, became the subject of a Catholic League boycott campaign, Donohue even approached him after the controversy had died down and suggested that they meet up for a beer. Patrick Goldstein, "A Film is Condemned, Sight Unseen, Yet Again," *Los Angeles Times*, August 12, 2003, accessed July 7, 2014, http://articles.latimes.com/2003/aug/12/entertainment/et-gold12/2.
4. Larry McShane, "Revival of the Catholic League," *The Bismarck Tribune*, May 21, 1998; Winnie Hu, "An Outspoken Church Defender," *New York Times*, November 2, 1999.
5. William Donohue, "Does the New York Times Employ Idiots or Bigots?" *The Catalyst*, May 11, 1994; Thomas J. Herron, "Answered Prayers: Bill Donohue's Catholic League Whacks *Culture Wars*," *Culture Wars*, October 2004, accessed July 10, 2014, http://www.culturewars.com/2004/CatholicLeague.html.
6. William Donohue, "Spanish Harlem Welcomes an Irishman," in *Catholics in New York: Society, Culture, and Politics 1808–1946*, ed. Terry Golway (New York: Fordham University Press, 2008), 177.
7. William R. Macklin, "A Religious Watchdog Bares Teeth at Disney: Catholic League's William Donohue Fights Slurs with Pit Bull Tenacity," *Philadelphia Inquirer*, March 28, 1995.
8. Ibid.
9. Herron, "Answered Prayers."
10. Hu, "An Outspoken Church Defender"; Loretta G. Seyer, "Interview with Catholic League President William A Donohue," *Catholic Twin Circle*, January 9, 1994.
11. Edward Lodge Curran, *The Blood Myth, Story of Nazi Germany* (Brooklyn, New York: International Catholic Truth Society, 1935).
12. Herron, "Answered Prayers." For more on Jewish supporters of Donohue, including prominent figures such as Irving Kristol and Louis Horowitz, see "Letter to the Editor," *Commonweal*, July 18, 1997, 2.
13. Hu, "An Outspoken Church Defender"; Seyer, "Interview."
14. "A True Fighter for the Faith," *The Catalyst*, March 12, 1994.
15. William Donohue, "The Catholic Mind," *The Catalyst*, January/February 1999.
16. Ibid.

17. McShane, "Revival"; Jacob Bernstein, "Bill Donohue: The Catholic League's Attack Dog," *WWD*, February 2, 2007, 17.
18. Hu, "An Outspoken Church Defender."
19. "This Week They Said," *Irish Times* [Dublin], May 31, 2007, 16.
20. Rev. Edward Lodge Curran, "Address by Rev. Edward Lodge Curran, Ph.D. before Citizens U.S.A. Committee, Chicago, Illinois, February 22, 1944," archived at *The Pennsylvania Crier*, accessed July 11, 2014, http://www.pennsylvaniacrier.com/filemgmt_data/files/Address%20by%20Rev%20Edward%20Lodge%20Curran%20PhD.pdf.
21. "Mac Would Have Been Welcome as a Colonial Leader—Father Curran," *Brooklyn Daily Eagle*, July 6, 1954; "Father Curran Gives Mac Petition Drive Boost at His Church," *Brooklyn Daily Eagle*, November 22, 1954.
22. "Bishop Criticized for Attack on McCarthy," *Franklin* (PA) *News-Herald*, April 12, 1954.
23. "Kerry Kennedy Catholics," *The Catalyst*, November 2008.
24. Tim Cavanaugh, "E Pluribus Umbrage: The Long, Happy Life of America's Anti-Defamation Industry," *Reason*, December 2002, 24. Donohue's quotation read: "We're not located in Kansas City. New York is a rough town. The people I debate are smart, quick, and tough. I'm not some pious little bluenose, backwoods kid."
25. "Phil Donohue and Rosie O'Donnell on Display," *The Catalyst,* April 2003.
26. "Playboy Unearths Bobblehead Ex-Priest," *The Catalyst,* September 2002; "Irish-Catholic Pundits Take Aim at Catholicism," *The Catalyst,* March 2002.
27. William Donohue, "Chris Matthews Insults Bishop Tobin," *Catholic League News Releases*, November 24, 2009.
28. "New York Times Features McCourt Insult," *The Catalyst*, July 2009.
29. George Bampfield, *Mixed Marriages: Showing Why the Church Does Not Like Them* (Brooklyn, New York: International Catholic Truth Society, n.d.); Edward Francis Garesché, *Dialogue on Mixed Marriage* (Brooklyn, New York: International Catholic Truth Society, 1932); Fr. Edward Lodge Curran, *We Catholics* (Brooklyn, New York: International Catholic Truth Society, 1946).
30. Mike Doughney, "Justice Sunday—Transcripts, Video, Audio," *Daily Kos*, April 25, 2005, accessed July 10, 2014, http://www.dailykos.com/story/2005/04/25/109317/-Justice-Sunday-Transcripts-Video-Audio.
31. William Donohue, "Is Bush Catholic?" *The Catalyst*, July/August 2001.
32. "Anti-Partition Meeting," *Irish Press*, April 19, 1952.
33. "U.S. Support in Unity Plan Promised," *Irish Independent*, April 23, 1953, 8.
34. "Well-Known American Worker in Ireland's Cause: Visit of the Very Rev. Dr. E. Lodge Curran," *Ulster Herald*, October 17 1953, 5.
35. Ibid.
36. "U.S. Congressmen's Views on Partition," *Irish Independent*, October 23, 1953, 9. This gesture seemed especially significant given the long-running dispute over the tug-of-war between Eamon de Valera and American Irish nationalists over the bonds sold in the name of the Irish Republic during the 1920s.
37. "Catholic League Members Rally to the Cause," *The Catalyst*, October 1994.
38. "Still the Irish Voice," *The Catalyst*, June 2000.
39. "Ireland Lies about the Holy See," *The Catalyst*, October 2011.
40. Ibid.

Chapter Nine

Irish Missionaries in Literature and Life

From Evangelists of Irish Catholicism to Catalysts of its Transformation

Andrew J. Auge

In his famous lecture "A Catholic Modernity," the philosopher Charles Taylor proposed an interesting analogy. He used the sixteenth century Jesuit Matteo Ricci's mission to China as model for the late twentieth century Catholic Church's engagement with modernity. Just as Ricci had to determine which aspects of the Catholic faith were essential and which could be adjusted to accommodate a radically foreign culture, so too, Taylor suggests, contemporary Catholicism must engage in a similar assessment if it is to survive in the strange new world of modernity.[1] I would suggest that in an inverted manner Taylor's analogy is being enacted in contemporary Ireland. There Irish missionaries returned from the service in the Third World have engaged for the last several decades in a parsing of Catholicism akin to Matteo Ricci's, offering glimpses of the transformations necessary to allow the Catholic Church to survive in the seemingly inhospitable terrain of twenty-first century Ireland. To appreciate the value of these missionaries' ideas, we need to understand their provenance, for the shift in the Irish missionary movement from a posture of cultural ascendency to a more deferential awareness of the value of ulterior perspectives presages a potential reorientation of Irish Catholicism as a whole. The inadequacy of the prior understanding of the missionary's role as well as the challenges and promise involved in its transformation become more apparent when we examine the most significant representations of Catholic missionaries in Irish literature: Fr. Terry Keenan in Seamus Heaney's "Station Island" and Fr. Jack Mundy in Brian Friel's

Dancing at Lughnasa. Lastly, we will briefly consider how the pastoral and theological adaptations that two real-life counterparts of these fictional characters gleaned from their missionary experiences epitomize the potentially prophetic role of returned missionaries in Ireland.

It is often noted the roots of Irish Catholicism's missionary movement reach back to the golden age of Irish monasticism when saints such as Colum Kille and Columbanus and many others brought the light of Christ to a Europe shrouded in darkness. But throughout most of the next millennium, the Irish Catholic Church, especially during its relentless colonial persecution, was less an agent than the object of missionary evangelization. With the flood of emigration from Ireland in the nineteenth century, Irish priests and nuns relocated to foreign lands to serve these emigrant populations. But it was not until the twentieth century that Irish Catholicism re-engaged in its mission to evangelize non-Christian populations throughout the world. In the first several decades of the twentieth century, figures such as Fr. Joseph Shanahan (later bishop) and Fr. Edward Galvin established Irish Catholic missions in Nigeria and China. In a remarkable flurry of activity, a series of Irish missionary orders were established: in 1916, St. Columban's Foreign Mission Society, popularly known as the Columbans; in 1922, the Missionary Sisters of St. Columba; in 1924, the Sisters of the Holy Rosary; in 1932, St. Patrick's Missionary Society, known as the Kiltegan Fathers; in 1937, the Medical Missionaries of Mary.[2]

This burgeoning Irish missionary movement was rooted in the traditional Catholic imperative to evangelize—that is, to spread the good news of Christ throughout the entire world. Yet other, less spiritual forces contributed significantly to the creation and rapid expansion of Irish Catholic missionary orders. On the material side, the demographic realities of late nineteenth and early twentieth-century Ireland resulted in a surplus of Irish priests and nuns and, thus, an impetus to establish new geographical arenas in which they could cultivate their vocations.[3] Added to this was the ideology of Irish nationalism and the desire to solidify a political and cultural identity for Ireland distinct from that of Great Britain.[4] While, as Edmund Hogan notes, it was a historical coincidence that Fr. Galvin's establishment of the Maynooth Mission to China (later known as St. Columban's Foreign Mission Society) occurred just six months after the Easter Rising, it would be a mistake to regard the creation of an indigenous Irish Catholic missionary movement as immune to the patriotic fervor of this period. Hogan concludes that "the effect of the Rising was to make Catholics more receptive to the missionary movement. In its aftermath there was indeed a 'smouldering emotionalism' abroad in the land, there was much talk of sacrifice, especially among the young. There is no doubt that the Maynooth Mission and the other missionary agencies drew advantage from such sentiment."[5] When Ireland gained partial independence from Great Britain, its global missionary movement contributed to the nascent nation's assertions of cultural parity with its former colonial master. While Great Britain possessed a vast, albeit increasingly tenuous, material empire, the spiritual counterpart being launched by Irish missionaries was envisioned as equal or even superior to it.[6] As a commentator in the journal *Student Missionary* noted in 1931: "Ireland has not a square inch of territory abroad, yet her spiritual empire is limited only by the bounds of the earth."[7]

While the modern Irish missionary movement was not a direct tentacle of a larger colonializing process, as was the case with virtually all its European counterparts, it was nonetheless entangled with the ideology of Western imperialism. As Fiona Bateman notes, Irish Catholic missionary organizations repeatedly "utilized several key tropes and strategies of nineteenth century British imperial discourse," including most prominently assertions of "the superiority of Western Culture" and backwardness of native peoples.[8] This imperialist posture is exemplified in the writings of one of the most important of the Irish missionaries, Fr. Joseph Shanahan, priest and later bishop from the Holy Ghost Fathers. It was Shanahan who at the outset of the twentieth century inaugurated the Irish Catholic missionary presence in Nigeria, which was to become the crown jewel of the Irish missionary movement. Writing in 1905 to the Vatican, Shanahan requested money for two mission stations to be established "right in the heart of the land of fetish-worshippers, baby-killers, and cannibals."[9]

Such cultural chauvinism typified the Irish missionary movement throughout most of the twentieth century. Fr. Donal Dorr, a member of St. Patrick's Society of Missionaries and consultant to the Irish Missionary Union, has described the template for missionary activity during this time period as being based on "the crusader model": "unbelievers were to be converted, to be 'conquered for Christ' through spiritual weapons. The church was to be 'planted' in the 'pagan lands.' And the people there were also to be helped by being introduced to the real or imagined 'benefits' of Westernisation."[10] A brief glance at one of the magazines produced by the Irish missionary orders to publicize their achievements, recruit new members, and raise funds confirms the pervasiveness of this spiritual imperialism. For instance, in an issue of the journal of St. Columban's Foreign Mission Society, *Far East,* from 1950, the period when the Irish missionary movement was at its apex, one encounters a fundraising letter from the head of the Society, the Rev. Dr. Michael O'Dwyer. The letter indicates that the Columbans have been granted access by the Vatican to new mission territories in Japan, where as O'Dwyer puts it, there are "8,000,000 souls, all practically pagan."[11] Here as elsewhere, the primary measure of the missionary endeavor's success is cast in terms of the number of pagans to be "conquered for Christ." An article published a year later in *Far East* by a Columban missionary, Fr. Lawrence McMahon, reveals the tactics employed in such spiritual conquests. Assigned to a remote area of northern Burma, McMahon describes how he exacted the deathbed conversion of a tribal elder, *Panlum Dingla,* who had reverted from his recently acquired Catholicism back to his aboriginal animistic beliefs. As Fr. McMahon puts it,

> In spite of his perversion the *Panlum Dingla* was a likeable old fellow . . . he never failed to beg for medicine for his many complaints, real and imaginary. But I never turned him down and tried to lend a sympathetic ear to his long litany of complaints. . . . Furthermore, I took the ailments of *Panlum Dingla* as an illustration of what he could expect hereafter should he die outside the Church. "Listen, old man . . . this suffering is nothing compared to the pain of hell fire which will surely be your lot for all eternity unless you repent. Why don't you make a good confession and return to the Church?"[12]

Far from unique, the posture of cultural superiority evinced by Fr. McMahon here was replicated in reports from *African Missionary*, *The Word*, and other organs of the Irish missionary orders from this time period. This deeply-embedded sense of imperial prerogative and obligation was tempered by an often equally profound sense of compassion and by the good works in education and health care that served as the primary "vehicles of evangelization."[13] But even there the taint of a chauvinistic paternalism remained.

Throughout the fifties and sixties, however, this basis for the prevailing "crusader model" of the missionary enterprise steadily eroded. The success of decolonizing nationalist movements in many of the regions where Irish missionaries worked decimated the ideological basis as well as the material apparatus of Western imperialism. On a spiritual level, the declaration in Vatican II's *Lumen Gentium* that salvation was possible for those who practiced religions other than Christianity seemingly undermined the primary justification of the missionary orders.[14] As a result, even though the Irish missionary movement reached its pinnacle in numbers in the mid to late nineteen sixties, with 7,085 Irish priests, sisters, and brothers working as missionaries in Third World countries, a group equivalent in size to the Republic of Ireland's national police force, there were signs of a looming crisis of purpose.[15]

Over the next decade, the dilemma facing missionary orders was exacerbated by a steady decline in missionary vocations as well as increasing skepticism regarding the role of the institutional Church in Irish society. These growing concerns eventually led to the convening of a National Mission Congress in April 1979 in which over 400 missionaries from Ireland and elsewhere gathered at Knock to discuss the future of the missionary movement. The editor of *A New Missionary Era,* the volume of papers collected from this gathering, Fr. Padraig Flanagan from St. Patrick's Society of Missionaries, summarized the purpose of the Congress:

> Missionaries felt that the time had come to recognize the fact that mission today was significantly different from that of years past; that the time had come for a new evaluation, a new study of the elements of mission. Even the essential message itself was being questioned: the means and methods of communicating it—in a sense, the whole reason d'etre of missions could no longer be taken for granted.[16]

While this convocation did not seek or generate an univocal agreement on the future of the Irish missionary movement, there was a consensus of sorts on the need for greater integration of the foreign missions and the home church in Ireland. One vision of what form that collaboration should take was put forth in Pope John Paul II's speech to missionaries and other clergy at Maynooth, which although it occurred six months after the National Mission Congress, was quoted at length in the introduction to *A New Missionary Era* written by Bishop Dominic Conway, the Episcopal Representative on the National Mission Council. After briefly surveying Irish Catholicism's long history of missionary activity, the Pontiff called for "a spirit of partnership [to] grow between the home dioceses and the home religious congregations in the total mission of the Church, until each local diocesan church and each religious congregation and community is fully seen to be 'missionary of its very nature,' entering into the eager missionary movement of the universal Church." He went on to praise the formation of "a National Missionary Centre, which will both serve as a focus for missionary renewal by missionaries themselves and foster the missionary awareness of the clergy, religious and faithful of the Irish Church . . . [and] contribute to a great upsurge of missionary fervor and a new wave of missionary vocations from this great motherland of faith which is Ireland."[17] For Pope John Paul II, the agenda undergirding the closer integration of Irish foreign missionaries and the home church was the re-evangelization of an Irish society whose faith was being eroded by the rising tide of secularism. The enhanced presence of these returned missionaries in Ireland, in the Pope's conception, would result in a revitalization of the status quo rather than a transformation of Irish Catholicism.

A more challenging notion of the role of returning missionaries appears in the lecture delivered at the National Missionary Convention by Fr. Enda McDonagh, one of Ireland's most preeminent theologians. McDonagh's remarks reflect a radical shift in the conception of missionary activity, a move from the idea of "mission as *evangelization*" to that of "mission as *dialogue*."[18] The profound nature of this conceptual change is delineated by the Irish missionary Donal Dorr:

> The very notion of mission as dialogue is a direct challenge to an assumption that was sometimes made in the past that the successful missionary is one who to [sic] gets many converts and builds up the institutional church. . . . By

> starting with the notion that dialogue is integral to mission we take account of the fact that the Spirit is at work in the people being evangelized as well as in the evangelizers; and we acknowledge that there is a two-way exchange of gifts, between missionaries and the people among whom they work.[19]

In his comments, Fr. McDonagh bluntly elucidates the implications of this transformation in the missionary's role, stating that missionaries are no longer just agents of conversion but are themselves "converted" to "the culture of the others" whom they serve.[20] Missionary work in this new formulation involves a reciprocal cultural exchange, so when missionaries return home, they do so with a more expansive vision of their faith. The challenge, McDonagh suggests, is for the Catholic Church in Ireland to "be open" to "integrating" the new ideas and perspectives of these returned missionaries.[21]

To get a deeper understanding of the transformation in the missionaries' role as well as of the challenges associated with their re-integration into their home communities, we can turn to the two most significant literary representations of Irish missionaries, both of which appeared in the decade following the National Missionary Convention at Knock. Given the sheer number of Irish Catholic missionaries, their extensive networks of family and friends, and their effective use of mass media to publicize their achievements, it is surprising that they appear so sparingly in Irish literature. That absence renders the few portraits of missionaries that do exist all the more revealing.

One of the most significant is the Nobel Prize-winning poet Seamus Heaney's unsparing treatment, in his 1984 poetic sequence "Station Island," of his childhood neighbor Terry Keenan, whose tenure as a missionary in the Philippines was cut short by his death from malaria. Based upon the penitential pilgrimage to Lough Derg in Donegal, the site of Station Island, Heaney's poem conducts an appraisal of his childhood faith and its lingering presence in his consciousness. The *modus operandi* for this process of reevaluation is a series of Dantesque encounters between the poet-pilgrim and various specters who emerge from the recesses of personal and cultural memory. Of these, the prematurely dead Terry Keenan occupies a seminal position since more than any of the other ghosts he epitomizes the "self-afflicting compulsions" that according to Heaney lie at the heart of Irish Catholicism.[22]

In Canto IV of "Station Island," Keenan's specter recounts to the poet how his renunciation of the secular world for the sake of saving pagans mired in ignorance and sin eventuated in nothing but loss, how the talents and energy that he offered up as a missionary in the tropics were squandered, how he "rotted like a pear" and "sweated masses."[23] Heaney evokes a familiar image of the Irish Catholic missionary here, presenting the priest performing his most important duty—the saying of the Mass—in an exotic and inhospitable tropical setting. This sense of a stereotype being evoked is even more blatant in the early drafts of this canto where Keenan is cast as a figure straight out of a missionary journal.[24] And the traces of the spiritual imperialism that, as we have seen, pervaded that journal and those of other missionary orders are manifested here as well—most notably, in the missionary priest raising of the chalice stenciled with the Latin tag, *In hoc signo.* Usually translated as "in this sign you shall conquer," the expression allegedly first appeared on the Emperor Constantine's battle standard and is represented by its acronym *IHS,* letters that frequently were engraved on chalices.[25] Heaney's citation of this Latin rubric evokes the "crusader" model of the missionary enterprise.

Throughout this canto Heaney deconstructs the ethos of spiritually ennobling self-sacrifice that served as the linchpin not just for this traditional model of the missions but for Irish Catholicism as a whole. The deflating pun about "sweating masses" in the passage quoted above casts both the Eucharistic sacrifice as well as the missionary's personal immolation as a kind of fruitless dissipation. The problem, Heaney suggests in the poem's later half, is that the sacrifice of the modern-day missionaries, like that of the actual medieval crusaders, was driven more by a latent desire to reinforce tribal solidarity than by any purported higher ideals. Addressing Keenan's ghost, the poet declares how the missionary priest and his heroic sacrifice served to validate the faith of his beleaguered Catholic community in Northern Ireland.[26] A prose gloss written during the drafting of this canto crystalizes Heaney's nuanced critique of the missionary vocation, noting the nobility of Keenan's selfless sacrifice while seeing it as constricted by a narrow chauvinism.[27]

Just over five years after Heaney employed Terry Keenan in "Station Island" to expose the futility of the traditional missionary vocation, a richer and more proleptic image of the missionary appeared on stage at the Abbey Theatre in Dublin. Fr. Jack Mundy of Brian Friel's *Dancing at Lughnasa* (1990) is the most significant literary representation of an Irish Catholic Missionary. A memory play, *Dancing at Lughnasa* is set in 1936 near the fictional village of Ballybeg in County Donegal and narrated from the later perspective of a man recalling his childhood. At its heart is the Mundy family consisting of the five unmarried adult sisters and the youngest one's illegitimate son, Michael, who serves as the play's narrator. The plot is set in motion by the return of the sisters' older brother, Fr. Jack, to Ballybeg after many years as a missionary in Africa, working at a leper colony in Uganda among the Ryangans, a fictionalized African ethnic group. Friel based the Mundy sisters partly upon his maternal aunts and the character of Fr. Jack upon his uncle Fr. Barney (Bernard Joseph) MacLoone, who was in fact a missionary at a leper colony in Nyenga in Uganda and who, ill from malaria, eventually returned home to be nursed by his sisters for several years before dying in 1950.[28]

Fr. Barney's obituary in *The Derry Journal*, which Friel collected and employed in his construction of Fr. Jack, presents him as the epitome of the missionary ideal, the "Wee Donegal Priest" who "with Damien-like courage and fortitude . . . ministered to the spiritual and temporal needs of the afflicted people he loved with such an overpowering love." The obituary concludes by proclaiming that "in the epic annals of missionary labours the story of the young Donegal man who gave up a business career to follow in the saintly footsteps of Father Damien will have a treasured place."[29] Friel transported many of the details of Fr. Barney's missionary career into that of the fictional Fr. Jack, who like his real-life model not only serves as a minister to the lepers but also as a chaplain for the British Army in Uganda during World War I and who similarly returned home to be nursed by his sisters. But Friel introduced a crucial difference into his fictional character. Whereas Fr. MacLoone died in good standing with the Catholic Church, that is not the case with Fr. Jack. Soon after Fr. Jack appears in *Dancing at Lughnasa*, it becomes apparent that rather than converting the Ryangans to Catholicism, he has been converted to their primal animistic religion and has been sent home because of his having "gone native." Whether knowingly or not, Friel constructs Fr. Jack as a liminal figure who reflects the cultural transition from the traditional notion of the missionary as an evangelizing crusader to the more contemporary version of this figure as a partner in a cross-cultural dialogue.

In his drafting of the play, Friel repeatedly vacillated between envisioning Fr. Jack as a victim of senility and regarding him as catalyst for change, as someone who has discovered through his missionary experience a deeper and more liberating religious sensibility.[30] Both of these elements appear in the final version of this character, but that later dimension is muted in ways that bear further attention. *Dancing at Lughnasa* is set on the cusp of the creation of the Constitution of 1937, during the period when the Catholic Church was consolidating its political and social power in the Republic of Ireland. Friel was wary about the play being taken over, as so many works of Irish literature had been, by a critique of this clerical authoritarianism. Indeed, at one point in his manuscript notes, he insists that the play must resist focusing on Irish Catholicism. But only a week or so later, he questions that directive and credits Fr. Jack's conversion to an inclusive paganism with having a transformative effect on the religious attitudes of the Mundy family.[31] That goal, however, is only partially realized in the final version of the play.

To the extent that Fr. Jack provides a counter to the moral rigorism and emotional austerity of Irish Catholicism, it is through his descriptions of Ryangan culture. With their more fluid familial structure in which polygamy is practiced and children born out of wedlock are welcomed by the whole community, the Ryangans are spared the stultifying celibacy and stigmatization imposed upon the Mundy sisters in Ballybeg. Moreover, their sacred ceremonies possess an organic unity and vitality absent from the monotonous Catholic rituals of twentieth century Ireland. Fr. Jack's account early in Act 2 of how the Ryangans dance ecstatically for days in celebration of the harvest culminates with his proclamation that "the Ryangans are a remarkable people: there is no distinction between the religious and the secular in their culture."[32] This evocation of the potency of primal religions in which the physical and spiritual, mundane and transcendent, are seamlessly interwoven in a ritual dance infuses the play's motif of dancing with a heightened significance, casting a sacral aura over its most memorable scene: the Mundy sisters' impromptu frenzied dance to the ceili music on the wireless in the middle of Act 1. But if Fr. Jack's importation of traditional African religious principles is transformative—as Friel had originally planned—it is not so within the world of the play, but only in the retrospective consciousness of the narrator, Michael. His final speech, which concludes the play, blends his memories of this period with a conception of the primal power of dancing: "a wordless ceremony" that puts one "in touch with some otherness."[33]

Like the enfeebled Fr. Jack himself, the traditional animistic religion of the Ryangans does not possess any real potency in the present-day action of the play. It points not toward future possibilities but more toward a superannuated past—specifically, the archaic Celtic rituals and ceremonies, such as the harvest festival of Lughnasa, of which only corrupted vestiges remain. As such, the missionary's gleaning of primal religious truths serves primarily in *Dancing at Lughnasa* as a talisman of a lost spiritual world rather than a catalyst for the transformation of contemporary Irish Catholicism. Through the parish priest's ostracism of Fr. Jack and his attendant sequestration, Friel evokes an insular Irish Catholic Church closed off from the leavening influences of its global missionary outposts. In the thirties, when its influence was pervasive and its power largely unquestioned, the institutional church in Ireland regarded itself as a fount of spiritual wisdom in no need of refreshment from distant springs. The same could not be said for the desiccated version of Catholicism that by the time of *Dancing at Lughnasa's* performance in 1990 had suffered a steady depletion of its moral and spiritual significance.

In *Dancing at Lughnasa* the fictional returned missionary Fr. Jack is relegated to the margins and left to pursue what his sister Kate refers to as "his own distinctive spiritual search" in isolation.[34] That has not been the case with many of Fr. Jack's real-life counterparts. Many of those Catholic missionaries upon their return to Ireland have brought the knowledge and practices garnered through their missionary endeavors to bear upon the problems of the Irish Catholic Church, as well as Irish society as a whole. As the missionary priest Donal Dorr notes, these returned missionaries are uniquely qualified to be agents of transformation: having "worked as missionaries in radically different cultures and in the midst of peoples with a very different religious outlook," they were compelled "to develop a pioneering mentality and approach . . . to adopt a new *attitude* to the people" they worked with and "even a new *vision* of the church."[35] The "freedom of spirit" that they cultivated through their exchanges with non-Christian people makes them less susceptible to the prevailing "legalistic, moralistic, clericalist" mode of Irish Catholicism.[36] In the manner forecast by Fr. Enda McDonagh's comments at the National Missionary Congress in 1979, these returned missionaries, having been converted to some degree by their missionary experience, have worked to integrate the fruits of that conversion into their home church.

Of course, not all missionaries become agents of change nor is it only those priests and nuns who have served in foreign missions who have formulated more dynamic and inclusive versions of Irish Catholicism. Yet as Donal Dorr's comments above indicate, the culture shock involved in missionary work provides a unique opportunity for a creative re-envisioning of the status quo. Among the many examples of such new visions of the church evoked by contemporary Irish Catholic missionaries, we will focus on two, one of which involves a pastoral transformation exemplified and endorsed in an understated manner, the other a more overt expansion of Catholic theology.

Fr. Michael Kane is a member of the missionary order of the Holy Ghost Father, or the Spiritans as they are popularly known. From 1970–1979 he served as a missionary in Brazil, primarily in the remote rural interior of the state of San Paulo. As he notes in an interview conducted in 2011 for *Irish Life and Lore*, it was an exciting time for the Catholic Church in South America.[37] The 1968 Conference of Latin American bishops at Medellin, Colombia, had inaugurated a new movement known as liberation theology and generated new forms of pastoral ministry, most notably base Christian communities. These sought to empower the poor and disenfranchised by using scriptural reflection to illuminate and direct their own social struggles and by bringing these lay people into leadership roles as ministers and catechists. Having been trained in the old modality of missionary work, in which, as he puts it, "we had the truth and we were going out to convert people," Fr. Kane found himself engaged in the formation of these base Christian communities. There he discovered a new model of authority, one that emanated from the people rather than being imposed from the top down. For nine years, he worked to generate and maintain these basic communities, as he refers to them. When he returned to Ireland in the 1980's, he sought to cultivate something similar for the inner city poor of Dublin, creating a retreat center near Navan in the rural environment of County Meath, where young single mothers and their own mothers could leave the squalor of their urban housing projects and engage in spiritual reflection and community building. Through his pastoral work there and elsewhere, Fr. Kane has striven quietly (as he put it) to cultivate a model of church that differs from the prevailing one of rules, regulations, and strict hierarchy. In response to a question about the future of Irish Catholicism from interviewer Maurice O'Keefe, Fr. Kane extrapolates from his experience with base communities in Brazil, where people were trained for various ministries with the notion that "the leaders of [these] communities would assume leadership of the church." The way forward for the Catholic Church in Ireland, he goes on to say, lies not in "people going into seminaries and coming out priests," but rather in ordaining those in these grassroots base communities "who show leadership, show faith, who are willing to serve."

While Fr. Kane's missionary work with base Christian communities in Brazil led him to envision a less hierarchical and more democratic pastoral structure for the Irish Catholic Church, Fr. Sean McDonagh's experience as a Columban missionary in the Philippines resulted in a radical reorientation of traditional Catholic theology. In stark contrast to Terry Keenan in Heaney's "Station Island," McDonagh's tenure in the tropics was not a fruitless exercise in self-sacrifice, although it did involve close brushes with death. The range of McDonagh's activities during the fifteen year period in the 1970s and 1980s was remarkable. As he recounts in his 2010 interview with *Irish Lore and Life*, he worked with poor tenant shareholders to get titles for their land, taught in a university in a predominantly Muslim area where he cultivated a Christian—Muslim dialogue, and trained, as Fr. Kane did, lay people to take on ministerial and catechetical positions.[38] But it was the time Fr. McDonagh spent with the T'boli, a tribal people inhabiting the remote mountainous rainforests on the island of Mindanao, that triggered the most significant transformation in the Irish missionary. Some of his work with the T'boli involved basic human development, which ultimately helped them to reduce infant mortality from fifty percent to ten percent. But much of his energy was directed toward aiding the T'boli in their struggle against the multinational logging companies that were destroying the forest this tribal people had inhabited for centuries, a dangerous endeavor that led to McDonagh's being placed on a death list. A professionally trained anthropologist, McDonagh noticed how the myths and cultural practices of the T'boli reflected their intimate spiritual connection to the trees of the forest and the earth that nourished them.

That awareness precipitated what Fr. McDonagh refers to in a chapter title from one of his recent books as a "conversion in the T'boli Hills."[39] Prior to his experience there, he had paid little attention to the natural world and had internalized the prevailing conception of Christianity as being about humans.[40] That changed utterly after his experience of working with the T'boli. After his return to Ireland in the early 1990's, Fr. McDonagh expanded upon the work of his mentor, the American Passionist priest Thomas Berry, and developed a scripturally-based theology of creation that rectified the anthropocentric bias of traditional Catholicism. In his many books and lectures, he has called attention to the environmental crisis facing the world, spotlighting both global issues such as species extinction and climate change, as well as the more localized problem of loss of Irish bogs and wetlands. In his role as justice and peace coordinator for the Columbans, he has worked to expose the unfair burden of international debt imposed upon Third World countries and its role in their ongoing environmental exploitation. The prophetic fervor with which he has approached these tasks springs from a radically refashioned Catholic theology in which the mystical body of Christ includes the whole of creation. In shifting the focus away from narrow issues of sexual morality that have so long preoccupied Catholic theological discourse in Ireland to these global concerns that jeopardize the future of the Earth, this Columban missionary has staked out a pathway for Irish Catholicism to regain its social relevance.

The notion put forth at the Knock conference in 1979 that missionaries might be themselves evangelized remains, even three decades later, unsettling for some Irish Catholics. Fr. Sean McDonagh's acknowledgment of his indebtedness to the animistic beliefs of tribal peoples, in contrast to Fr. Jack's similar admission in *Dancing at Lughnasa*, does not result in ostracism. But it has elicited some resistance. In the course of McDonagh's account of his work with the T'boli, the interviewer Maurice O'Keefe refers to the missionary's task of saving souls, to which Fr. McDonagh replies by indicating that his "brief" as a missionary was not to save souls but rather to spread the Christian message of peace and justice, and to understand and learn from those whom he served.[41] O'Keefe's apparent concern over McDonagh's deviation from the missionary's traditional role was more forcefully expressed by Rev. Dr. Vincent Twomey, a priest of the Divine Word Missionaries and former student and biographer of Benedict XVI. In a 2009 letter to the *Irish Catholic*, Twomey chastised missionaries such as McDonagh for neglecting the centrality of evangelization in the missionary endeavor.[42] Such reactions are somewhat understandable. It is always easier to be the dispenser of saving truths than the recipient of them. But now more than ever, it would behoove the Catholic Church in Ireland to open itself to the wisdom that her returned missionaries have brought back home with them.

NOTES

1. Charles Taylor, *Dilemmas and Connections: Selected Essays* (Cambridge, MA: Harvard University Press, 2011), 169.
2. Edmund Hogan, *The Irish Missionary Movement: A Historical Survey 1830–1980* (Dublin: Gill & Macmillan, 1990), 94.
3. Joe Humphreys, *God's Entrepreneurs: How Irish Missionaries Tried to Change the World* (Dublin: New Island, 2010), 58.
4. Fiona Bateman, "Ireland's Spiritual Empire: Territory and Landscape in Irish Catholic Missionary Discourse," in *Empires of Religion*, ed. Hilary Carey (London: Palgrave Macmillan, 2008), 268.
5. Hogan, *The Irish Missionary Movement*, 95–96.

6. Bateman, "Ireland's Spiritual Empire," 268–269.
7. J. P. Mullen quoted in Bateman, "Ireland's Spiritual Empire," 268.
8. Ibid., 269.
9. See Fiona Bateman, "Ireland and the Nigeria-Biafra War: Local Connections to a Distant Conflict," *New Hibernia Review* 16 (2012): 49–50.
10. Donal Dorr, *Mission in Today's World,* (Maryknoll, NY: Orbis Books, 2000), 186–187.
11. Rev. Dr. Michael O'Dwyer, "Letter," *Far East* XXXIII, No. 3 (1950).
12. Rev. Lawrence McMahon, "The Panlum Dingla," *Far East* XXXIV, No. 4 (1951), 5–6.
13. Dorr, *Mission in Today's World,* 224.
14. Ibid., 81.
15. Humphreys, *God's Entrepreneurs,* 155.
16. Rev. Padraig Flanagan, S.P.S., preface to *A New Missionary Era*, ed. Rev. Padraig Flanagan, S.P.S. (Dublin: Irish Missionary Union, 1979), 7–8.
17. Quoted in Rev. Dominic Conway, introduction to *A New Missionary Era* (Dublin: Irish Missionary Union, 1979), 11–12.
18. Dorr, *Mission in Today's World,* 16.
19. Ibid., 16.
20. Rev. Enda McDonagh, "Conversion and Mission," in *A New Missionary Era,* 32.
21. Ibid., 30.
22. Seamus Heaney, "Pilgrim's Journey," *Poetry Society Bulletin* 123 (Winter 1984); quoted in Michael Parker, *Seamus Heaney: The Making of a Poet* (Iowa City: University of Iowa Press, 1993), 183.
23. Seamus Heaney, *Station Island* (London: Faber and Faber, 1984), 69–70.
24. Seamus Heaney, MS 49, 493/57, Seamus Heaney Literary Papers, National Library of Ireland.
25. Maurice Hassett, "Labarum (Chi-Rho)," *The Catholic Encyclopedia*, Vol. 8 (New York: Robert Appleton Company, 1910), accessed July 15, 2014, http://www.newadvent.org/cathen/08717c.htm.
26. Heaney, *Station Island,* 70.
27. Heaney, MS 49, 493/57, Literary Papers.
28. Anthony Roche, *Brian Friel: Theatre and Politics* (London: Palgrave Macmillan, 2011), 169–70.
29. *The Derry Journal*, July 10, 1950, MS L 41, Brian Friel Papers, National Library of Ireland.
30. Friel, Holograph Notes, May 23, 1989. MS 37, 104/1, Papers.
31. Friel, Holograph Notes, May 21, 1989. MS 37, 104/1, Papers.
32. Brian Friel, *Plays Two* (London: Faber & Faber, 1999), 74.
33. Ibid., 107–108.
34. Ibid., 92.
35. Dorr, *Mission in Today's World,* 218.
36. Ibid., 275.
37. Fr. Michael Kane, CSSp, interview by Maurice O'Keefe, 2011, Kimmage, Dublin, CDIMU 01-52, IMU Missionary Stories Project, *Irish Life and Lore: An Oral History Archive of Irish Voices.* Unless otherwise indicated, subsequent comments from and information concerning Fr. Kane come from this interview.
38. Fr. Sean McDonagh, SSP, interview by Maurice O'Keefe, 2010, Dalgan Park, CDIMU 01-5, IMU Missionary Stories Project, *Irish Life and Lore: An Oral History Archive of Irish Voices.* Unless otherwise indicated, subsequent comments from and information concerning Fr. McDonagh come from this interview.
39. Sean McDonagh, SSP, *The Death of Life: The Horror of Extinction* (Dublin: Columba Press, 2004), 16.
40. Ibid., 11–12.
41. McDonagh, interview.
42. Humphreys, *God's Entrepreneurs,* 200–201.

Chapter Ten

Contemplative Strands in Irish Identity

Bernadette Flanagan

In "The Second Coming," the Anglo-Irish poet William Butler Yeats draws on the mystical consciousness of the artist to sense that the end of public conflicts—which had taken place in Ireland during the 1916 Rising and subsequent Civil War—marked not only the passing of a time of bitter attack and destruction, but also the end of one form of shared social perception and the birth of a new consciousness.[1] Many social commentators since Yeats have grappled with interpreting that which is moving deep within the soul of Irish society in the twentieth and twenty-first century reconfigurations of identity. Below I will focus on the identification of some interpretative frameworks that I believe are helpful in naming the underlying dynamics that hint at the emergence of a contemplative turn in Irish Catholic identity. The interpretative frameworks that I assemble draw on the work of Michel de Certeau. Robert Orsi, Karl Jaspers, and Lieven Bove.

INTERPRETATIVE FRAMEWORKS

Some of the most everyday experiences can reveal to us how our, often unexamined, interpretative frameworks shape new realities that we encounter. One example that comes to mind from my experience is a time I spent researching with a community that was a new expression of urban monasticism in France. When I joined the community for some shared meals, my framework for the structure of a meal was of no assistance in working out how I should order my food choices. Some days just one plate circulated, and I needed to take a portion which would be the full allocation for that day. On other occasions, a succession of three or four plates passed around at ten minute intervals, in which case the portion taken from any individual plate could be much smaller. I am now much more alert to the diversity of forms that a meal can take in different countries and seek out more information on this subject when my work involves sharing food in non-familiar settings. I am alert to the limitations of the framework of an Irish meal for sharing food in different cultural settings.

Given the novelty of the current spiritual landscape in Ireland, an adequate repertoire of interpretative frameworks is essential to isolate its central features from diverse epiphenomena. My first source of assistance in such discernment is the work of Michel de Certeau (1925–1986). De Certeau, a French polymath, brought the disciplines of history, philosophy, theology, psychoanalysis, politics, cultural theory, and linguistics into creative dialogue so as to develop strategies to assist in "the quest to discern in our earthly, fallen language the now inaudible Word of God."[2] While his Jesuit identity receded over the course of his writings, his Ignatian attunement to God present in all things remained a guiding principle in his writings.

One particular interest of de Certeau's may be useful in reflecting on Catholicism in Ireland today. He observed how the sixteenth- and seventeenth-century flowering of mysticism in Europe took place within the context of a "shattered Christendom." He also noticed the fact that mystics of this era often arose from disdained social groups such as Jews who had converted to Christianity (we remember Teresa of Avila) or from communities ravaged by war and hardship (we remember Ignatius of Loyola); in other words mystics did not arise within the settings where they might have been expected to appear.[3] In this context also, a turn to mysticism within the society did not point to the rise of private, individualized forms of coping within a fractured religious context, but rather indicated the new social practice of religious identity.

For de Certeau, a contemplative turn in society displays in a vivid manner engagement with Christ's empty tomb. Quoting Matthew 28:6–7 ("He is not here . . . he is going ahead of you to Galilee"), de Certeau points out that "After the collapse of certainty, the mystic embraces the elusivity of Christ's presence."[4] In this way, he notes, Mary Magdalene is "the eponymous figure of the modern mystic."[5] Concomitantly, we are reminded by de Certeau that a contemplative turn in society is a recurrent manifestation of ruptured Christian discipleship. In seeking a framework to read what is happening in contemporary Irish Catholicism, de Certeau's writings act as a reminder of the need to begin with those who sense the loss most deeply, those who are engaging in new journeys in search of the one whom they have lost; those who turn to contemplative/mystical designations to name their current engagement with Catholicism.

In this context the rise of three contemplative movements are significant. First, the John Main/Lawrence Freeman's Christian Meditation movement in Ireland is one of fifty-eight branches in different countries around the world.

This World Community for Christian Meditation was formed in 1991 to continue the thirty-year-long work of the Benedictine monk, John Main. The community is now directed by Laurence Freeman, a student of John Main, a Benedictine monk of the Olivetan Congregation, and an English man whose mother was born on the West End of Bere Island (County Cork) in 1916 but emigrated to London at the age of eighteen. While the WCCM International Centre and Meditation Retreat Centre are in London, it is thriving in Ireland and has an outreach to more than 20,000 school children through its *Mediatio* initiative, led by the former school principal Noel Keating, as well as an outreach to the medical profession through a year-long, sixty CPD credit program in the Royal College of Physicians, led by consultant haematologist Dr. Barry White.

The second contemplative movement that is thriving in Ireland is the Thomas Keating Centering Prayer gatherings, known as Contemplative Outreach Ireland. In this case, Ireland is one of the forty-seven national branches spread around the world. Contemplative Outreach has its roots in the early 1970s dream of three monks living at St. Joseph's Abbey in Spencer, Massachusetts. Inspired by Vatican II's universal call to holiness, these monks sought to develop a method of Christian contemplative prayer that would be accessible to laypeople. With no idea that their wish would eventually result in an international organization, Fathers Thomas Keating, William Meninger, and Basil Pennington began by trial and error to develop an easily taught prayer method. Contemplative Outreach came to Ireland in 1994 through members of St. Aidan's Monastery (Ferns, County Wexford) who had visited Thomas Keating. St. Aidan's Monastery is home to a French adoration community on an old monastic site.

The third contemplative movement that is thriving in Ireland is that of the Vietnamese Buddhist Monk, Thich Nhat Hanh, which is promoted through the title "Living in the Present Moment." In this case, Ireland is one of forty national branches. Thich Nhat Hanh's influence in Ireland has been greatly enhanced by the regular columns on his teachings by Tony Bates, a clinical psychologist and the founding director of Headstrong—the National Centre for Youth Mental Health. Tony Bates has been spending retreat time at Thich Nhat Hanh's French Plum Village monastery since 2004, and his popular health columns in the *Irish Times* newspaper have also included accounts of time spent in the vicinity of Thomas Merton's monastery in Kentucky. Thich Nhat Hanh's influence was particularly evident during his 2013 visit, when he filled a 2,000-seat convention center in Dublin and then delivered a five day retreat to 700 people in Killarney.

Overall then, as appendix 2 shows, of the seventy-eight countries involved in these three contemplative movements, Ireland belongs to a group of twenty-two countries that have followers of all three.[6] There are also many other contemplative teachers who visit Ireland who do not have a national network, but who consistently draw large crowds of attendees: the Augustinian writer Martin Laird; the Jesuit Roshi Robert Kennedy; and the Indian teachers Korko Moses SJ, Ama Samy SJ, Br. Martin from the Benedictine Ashram in Shantivanam, and Sr. Ishipriya RSCJ. All of these new approaches will require further study to discern more comprehensively what may be the shape and form of the Irish soul today.

If we leave aside de Certeau's attentiveness to mystical awakening on the margins, we may turn then to another notable group of scholars who have been in the forefront of providing critical frameworks for reading everyday spiritual practice and popular piety as a window on a society's soul. These theorists include the North American triad of Nancy Annerman, Meredith McGuire, and Robert Orsi.[7] These three scholars have collectively developed a new way of understanding religion within a society. Rather than studying the practice of religion as it is defined by a religious organization (for example, Catholicism as it is defined by the Catholic Church), they draw attention to the lived expression of a religion in people's everyday lives. In this group, the scholar Robert Orsi is well known for his insightful analyses of the manner in which religious idioms are inherited, remembered, and reformulated, all in ways that are not primarily concerned with the re-presenting of a tradition but rather with reinventing it in the context of new circumstances. In approaching what these scholars would call "lived religion," Orsi advocates an ethnographic orientation, since such a methodology is committed to reflecting on the intricacies of the otherwise messy, on-the-ground religious practices that illuminate the living presence of a religious tradition within society.

In his research, Orsi has helpfully highlighted that the sort of devotions that people have practiced—and still do at places such as the shrine of the Madonna on 115th Street in East Harlem, New York, one of sites of lived religious practice that he has researched—have "occupied the absolutely lowest rungs of normative modern hierarchies of religion" in the academy.[8] Similarly, in Catholicism since Vatican II, devotional practices have had an ambiguous place in the accounts of cultural religious identity. In Ireland, the visit of John Paul II in 1979 is often perceived as the end of mass public display of devotion. Yet in my own research of lived religion in Dublin's inner-city—a form of religious practice frequently associated with the apotheosis of religious decline in Ireland—I found significant attachment to traditional devotions.[9] It is often the case that these continued devotional practices have not been picked up by positivist research methods, as such methods have tended to focus on measurable phenomena such as attendance at Sunday Mass. The skewed findings that positivist approaches can generate become clear when it is remembered that many traditional devotions often have their key celebrations on weekdays, such as Tuesday for St. Anthony and Saturday for St. Rita of Cascia, rather than on Sundays. The most recent evidence of the vitality of lived religion was the October 2013 tour of the relics of St. Anthony of Padua around the Republic of Ireland: Dublin, Wexford, Cork, Limerick, Galway, and back to Dublin. This tour drew huge crowds with up to 30,000 venerating the relics in some sites, and yet the media coverage tended to focus exclusively on the itinerary of the trip.

When "lived religion" has unique, inscrutable indigenous features—such as holy wells and pilgrim routes—it may occupy an even lower rung on the ladder of academic interest. In Ireland, this cultural bias sometimes results in the invisibility of lived spirituality in any public discussion of the current religious landscape. Indeed, a brief survey of the research taking place in the only department for the study of religion (rather than theology) in Ireland at this time, University College Cork, confirms the lacuna regarding indigenous religious phenomena. The listed research interests of faculty include Eastern Orthodoxy, *Adivasis* across central India from Rajasthan to Gujarat, and Dhammaloka, an Irish Buddhist monk in Burma. In this context, it is ironic that the huge revival of devotion centred on Ireland's abundant collection of holy wells and pilgrimage routes receives no attention.

To more adequately reflect on the reality of Catholicism in Ireland today, the investigative frameworks referred to above—those focused on cultural expression and lived-religion—may be complemented by an evolutionary model of inquiry. The German psychiatrist and philosopher Karl Jaspers (1883–1969) laid the foundations for this perspective, which was later developed by Robert Bellah and Ewert Cousins.[10] These scholars have argued for the periodisation of spiritual consciousness into three key phases: "pre-axial," "first axial," and "second axial" eras. In the 1940s, Karl Jaspers chose the term "axial" to refer to a key shift in human consciousness. The shift is associated with the first millennium B.C.E. when the major religions—Hinduism Buddhism, Judaism, and ultimately Christianity—were established.[11] Jaspers has noted that while "[t]hese paths are widely divergent in their conviction and dogma . . . common to all of them is man's [sic] reaching out beyond himself by growing aware of himself within the whole of Being and the fact that he can tread them only as an individual on his own."[12] Thus for Jaspers, an earlier collective, tribal consciousness gave way to individualized, personal appropriation of the transcendent dimension of reality.

Scholars such as Cousins and Bellah have argued that an equally radical shift in spiritual consciousness is happening in contemporary decades. Its depth and breadth of impact is so comprehensive that it has been viewed as the dawn of a Second Axial Period. Some of the salient features of this era include: a) engaging classical spiritual traditions in order to meet contemporary challenges such as the intensification of poverty, on-going social injustice and expanding ecological destruction; b) developing inter-spiritual gatherings to cultivate deeper respect for the wisdom of all the great religious teachers of the First Axial Period; and c) exploring the mystery of Christ from the perspective of participation in the divine ground of human consciousness. The Camaldolese monk of Big Sur, Bruno Barnhart, has referred to this last feature as "putting on the mind of Christ" or a wisdom Christology.[13]

Some of the features of the second axial turn are evident in contemporary spiritual classics such as Thomas Merton's *Conjectures of a Guilty Bystander:*

> In Louisville, at the corner of Fourth and Walnut, in the center of the shopping district, I was suddenly overwhelmed with the realization that I loved all those people, that they were mine and I theirs, that we could not be alien to one another even though we were total strangers. It was like waking from a dream of separateness, of spurious self-isolation in a special world, the world of renunciation and supposed holiness. The whole illusion of a separate holy existence is a dream. Not that I question the reality of my vocation, or of my monastic life: but the conception of "separation from the world" that we have in the monastery too easily presents itself as a complete illusion.[14]

This emerging consciousness was effectively captured in Ireland by the international author John O'Donohue, who sadly died an untimely death on January 4, 2008.[15] Since O'Donohue's death, the contemplative turn in Ireland has been articulated by Rev Mark Patrick Hederman OSB, Abbot of Ireland's only male Benedictine community at Glenstal, County Limerick. Hederman has named the new growth in spiritual consciousness "an underground cathedral." His proposal is that, at this time, the Holy Spirit is unearthing an underground cathedral in Ireland which is replacing the pretentious, over-elaborate Irish Catholic architecture of the twentieth century. An underground cathedral is a metaphor which describes alternative places and spaces of worship—the Mass rock, the holy well, the monastic ruin.[16] In this context, Glenstal has set as its mission the establishment a spiritual center which will offer initiation into a way of life that aligns the whole person—body, mind, and spirit—with the universe as a whole, which includes those who are in it as well as the Three Persons of the Trinity who have invited all to share in their life.[17] Taking its cue from the enlivening influence of social reform prompted by tenth-century monasticism at Cluny, Glenstal aims to provide many people with an atmosphere that allows them to breathe spiritually in the manner described by T. S. Eliot in "Little Gidding," where he invokes prayer that does not seek verification or instruction but instead seeks to intersect with "the timeless moment."[18]

Visitor records at Glenstal indicate that those seeking to live in alertness to the "timeless moments" of existence now measure up to two hundred visitors per day. These come to find a still point in the rapidly changing Irish landscape, and they include many psychotherapists/counsellors, creative writers and artists, as well as retreat groups and overseas pilgrims.[19]

SECULARIZATION, POST MODERNITY, AND DE-TRADITIONALIZATION

In their Irish context, both the impact of St. Anthony's traveling relics and the visitor records at Glensal Abbey must be interpreted against a background of rapid and fundamental change. Their influences occur within a landscape that has been transformed to its core by globalisation, growing multiculturalism, and the fallout from Catholic Church sexual abuse scandals. The impact of the latter in every corner in Ireland cannot be overestimated as a recent experience revealed to me. I was queuing in my local post-office on a Friday morning, the day when pensioners collect their weekly state pension. A queue of ten to twelve pensioners had gathered, and we were waiting for the de-activation of the safe code. The man at the top of the queue read out the heading from the recent UN human rights committee report that carried a scathing evaluation of the Vatican's handling of sex abuse by priests. Almost every person in the queue contributed a comment on their own disillusionment and un-heard hurt. Those who had attended schools run by religious were particularly upset about harsh regimes they had experienced. In a typically Irish manner, one woman commented "and those nuns call themselves Brides of Christ; I say God Help Jesus!"

That juxtaposition suggests the complexities of studying Catholicism in this setting. It is true that the Republic of Ireland has one of the highest rates of affiliation to the Catholic Church in Western Europe. In the 2011 census, out of a population of 4.2 million, 84 percent identified themselves as Roman Catholic.[20] However these figures conceal various sub-identities within Catholicism. Tom Inglis, following the classification of sociologist Jay Demerath III who distinguished between orthodox and cultural Jews, asserts that much self-identification with Catholicism in Ireland is cultural.[21] In practice this means that people have little personal commitment to the institutional realities of the Catholic Church, but that they are not actively seeking to create, for example, nationally recognised public holidays that are alternatives to those of the Catholic Church for Christmas and Easter, or alternative rituals for life transitions such as births, marriages, and deaths.

Alongside cultural Catholicism, there is also the growing phenomenon of blended Catholic identity, such as Buddhism blended with Catholicism in daily practice. According to the 2011 census, the population of Buddhists in Ireland is 8,703, making it the fourth-largest religion in the Republic after Christianity, Islam and Hinduism. However, the census does not provide for dual or blended identity. The search for training and education in spiritual/ contemplative practices leads many inquirers to Buddhist centers in Ireland, listed in appendix 3. One of the longest-established (1986) of these centres is Dzogchen Beara, a Tibetan Buddhist Retreat venue in west Cork under the spiritual guidance of Sogyal Rinpoche, author of *The Tibetan Book of Living and Dying.*[22] This center is also the sole training center for Spiritual Care Programme in Ireland. The training programs offered seek "to demonstrate practical ways in which the compassion and wisdom of the Buddhist teachings can be of benefit to those facing illness or death and also to their families and medical caregivers."[23] As part of the commitments of this center to raising awareness about the importance of spiritual care, they organised the 2009 Compassion and Presence International Conference in Killarney, which was attended by over 500 people. No equivalent conferences have been organised by Catholic groups despite the long history of indigenous groups such as the Sisters of Mercy and Religious Sisters of Charity in the provision of healthcare, including palliative care.

In the above discussion, then, I am reflecting on a "contemplative turn" in Irish society which extends into such areas as accompanying the dying. During such a significant life experience as serious illness, some Irish people seek more support than a formulized blessing: they look for training which teaches contemplative methods that enable participants to develop qualities of compassionate caregiving for those at vulnerable points on life's journeys. This is not a New Age, self-indulgent quest then, but rather one of spiritual solidarity with those wanting presence and authenticity as they approach the end of life. Regarding some kindred phenomena associated with New Age—reiki, homeopathy, past life regression, soul retrieval, and so on—I am in general agreement with Steve Bruce, who views these as extension of the surgery, therapy room, gym, or beauty salon, rather than spiritual practices.[24] However, while I am in agreement that two key characteristics of Bruce's secular framework—that is, the declining importance of a religion such as Catholicism in Ireland for the operation of social institutions such as hospitals or schools, and the decline in the social standing of religious figures in Ireland in events such as the People of the Year Awards—I am not convinced that there is an equivalent decline in the extent to which people engage in spiritual practices or conduct their lives in a manner informed by spiritual beliefs.[25] In line with distinctions made by the American sociologist Robert Wuthnow, there is in Ireland a growing difference between the traditional *spirituality of dwelling,* which emphasized the return to the stable, unchanging location of encounter with God in church or temple, and a new, nomadic *spirituality of seeking* where "individuals search for sacred moments that reinforce their conviction that the divine exists," even if, as Wuthnow points out, "these moments are fleeting."[26]

In Ireland, this seeking has recently taken a distinctive form, one borrowed from the native ancient Christian heritage of walking the Tóchar, an ancient pilgrim route. The retrieval of this practice has attracted large cohorts of diverse people who are not against religion per se, as in a purely secularized society, but who know that the ancient forms of Christianity in Ireland have something to offer today's new journey. On one single day in July

2013—the last Sunday in July's annual climb of one of Ireland's most holy mountains, Croagh Patrick—as many as 12,000 people took part in the pilgrim walk, which starts before dawn. Interviews by media broadcasters with a sample of these climbers reveal that they recognize that contemporary Ireland has its faults, stretching from the rampant greed that culminated in the Celtic Tiger and the subsequent economic collapse to the overwhelming revelations of abuse, neglect and exploitation in industrial schools and Magdalene laundries. Nevertheless, those interviewed indicated that they were prepared to begin (and to persevere in) a quest for the divine presence, however fleeting.

The recent success of Darach MacDonald's book, *Tóchar: Walking Ireland's Ancient Pilgrim Paths*, witnesses further to the prominence of the spirituality of seeking at this time, as does the development of the first National Pilgrim Paths Day on Holy Saturday 2014.[27] Pilgrimage has been defined as "an attentive journey to a place of spiritual significance" and the practice is almost as old as recorded history. In Ireland, the pilgrim journey (Tóchar) has strong historical resonances with early Christian scholars taking pilgrimages between sites of learning such as Clonmacnoise and Kildare, or medieval penitents journeying to Lough Derg, Holycross, and Glendalough, while still others expressed the yearnings of the pilgrims' inner longings by visiting Skellig Michael or climbing Croagh Patrick. Despite this long tradition of Irish pilgrimage, there has been, until recently, relatively little footfall on Ireland's ancient pilgrim paths. In this context, Ireland's first National Pilgrim Paths Day was aimed at networking a growing interest in these pilgrim routes today. Whereas the new expressions of the spiritual quest in some countries are privatized and even consumerist, it seems that in Ireland the communal dimension of a contemplative turn is much in evidence. The theoretical framework of Lieven Bove seems particularly apt in providing captions for naming this current in-between state of Catholicism in Ireland. He has suggested that the category of "de-traditionalization," in combination with the category "pluralization," offers a conceptual map for the current religious landscape in Ireland.[28] Geographic as well as cyber mobility now means that the prevalence of inter-spiritual influence has greatly accelerated. Catholicism in Ireland has not, at a grassroots level, been replaced by secularity, but rather a plurality of traditions that are drawn on by believers in the face of life's grand challenges. The distinguished Irish philosopher Richard Kearney has called this condition "ana-theism," a moment of creative "not knowing" that represents a break with former sureties and is an invitation to forge new meanings from the most ancient of wisdoms. Kearney suggests that ana-theism is a breakthrough moment that lies at the heart of every great religious journey, a choice between hospitality and hostility to the strange place to which the paths of life lead. The figures whom Kearney chooses to illustrate the transformative power of the choice of hospitality—Dorothy

Day, Jean Vanier, and Mahatma Gandhi—all represent the deep integration of spirituality and the practices of daily life that the walking movement within contemporary Irish spirituality carries.

I believe that there is a strong apophatic quality in the narratives of spiritual identity which are being constructed in this time of change. Neither the president of Ireland nor the prime minister (Taoiseach) mentioned God or Christ in their Christmas addresses in 2013, in sharp contrast to the Christmas addresses of political leaders in Germany, the UK, and the United States. This choice perhaps enunciates our national endeavor to find a God language adequate to the changed landscape in which the Irish Catholic identity is now located. As the contemporary mystic Bernadette Roberts has suggested: "This journey then, is nothing more, yet nothing less than a period of acclimating to a new way of seeing, a time of transition and revelation as it gradually comes upon 'that' which remains when there is no self." As Roberts emphasizes, this "is not a journey for those who expect love and bliss, rather, it is for the hardy who have been tried by fire." Within a whirlwind of profound change, the contemplative strands of Irish spirituality and religion seem prepared to travel toward what Roberts can only describe as "a tough, immovable trust in 'that' which lies beyond the known, beyond the self, beyond union and even beyond love and trust itself."[29]

NOTES

1. Versions of this poem are available in *The Dial* (Chicago), November 1920; *The Nation* (London), November 6, 1920; William Butler Yeats, *Michael Robartes and the Dancer* (Dundrum: Cuala, 1921); and William Butler Yeats, *Later Poems* (London: Macmillan, 1922).

2. Michel de Certeau, "Mystic Speech" in *The Certeau Reader*, ed. Graham Ward (Oxford: Blackwell, 2000), 194.

3. Ibid., 193.

4. Michel de Certeau, "The Weakness of Believing," in *The Certeau Reader*, 234.

5. Michel de Certeau, *The Mystic Fable: The Sixteenth and Seventeenth Centuries* (Chicago: University of Chicago Press, 1998), 81.

6. Ireland is among the 28 percent of countries who have branches of all three contemplative movements.

7. Nancy Annerman, *Everyday Religion: Observing Modern Religious Lives* (Oxford: Oxford University Press, 2006); Meredith McGuire, *Lived Religion: Faith and Practice in Everyday Life* (Oxford: Oxford University Press, 2008); Robert A. Orsi, *The Madonna of 115th Street: Faith and Community in Italian Harlem, 1880-1950*, 3rd rev. ed. (New Haven: Yale University Press, 2010); Robert A. Orsi, *Thank You St. Jude: Women's Devotion to the Patron Saint of Hopeless Causes* (New Haven: Yale University Press, 1996); and Robert A. Orsi, *Between Heaven and Earth: The Religious Worlds People Make and the Scholars who Study Them* (Princeton, NJ: Princeton University Press, 2007).

8. Robert .A. Orsi, *The Madonna of 115th Street*, xv. The New York practice that Orsi refers to is that of Catholics presenting a wax baby to a statute of Mary, which is viewed as a real presence of Mary in the community, in order to request reproductive assistance.

9. Bernadette Flanagan, *The Spirit of the City: Voices from Dublin's Liberties* (Dublin: Veritas, 1999).

10. Karl Jaspers, *The Origin and Goal of History* (New Haven: Yale University Press, 1953); Robert N. Bellah and Hans Joas, eds., *The Axial Age and Its Consequences* (Cambridge:

Belknap Press of Harvard University Press, 2012); and Ewert H. Cousins, *Christ of the 21st Century* (Brisbane: Element, 1992).

11. Ewert Cousins, *Christ in the Twenty-First Century* (Rockport: Element Books, 1992).

12. Jaspers, *The Origin and Goal of History*, 4.

13. Bruno Barnhart, *The Future of Wisdom: Toward a Rebirth of Sapiential Christianity* (New York: Bloomsbury Academic, 2007).

14. Thomas Merton, *Conjectures of a Guilty Bystander* (New York: Image Books, 1989), 156. The intersection of Fourth and Walnut Streets is now Fourth and Muhammad Ali Boulevard. A previous version of this experience was recorded by Merton in his private journal on March 19, 1958, the day after his fateful visit to Louisville and the seventeenth anniversary of his taking the vows of the Trappist order.

15. John O'Donohue, *Anam Ċara: Spiritual Wisdom from the Celtic World* (New York: HarperCollins, 1998).

16. Mark Patrick Hederman, *Underground Cathedrals* (Dublin: Columba Press, 2010).

17. For more information about Glenstal Abbey, see their website at http://www.glenstal.org.

18. T. S. Eliot, "Little Gidding," in *The Oxford Book of American Poetry*, ed. David Lehman (New York: Oxford University Press, 2006), 369–72. "Little Gidding" is named after a seventeenth-century Anglican monastery renowned for its devotion.

19. See "Mark Patrick Hederman in Conversation with Shirley Ward," *Inside Out* 62 (Autumn 2010), accessed August 1, 2014, http://iahip.org/inside-out/issue-62-autumn-2010.

20. By population the membership of the following groups is Roman Catholic: 3,861,000; Church of Ireland: 129,000; Muslim: 49,200; Orthodox: 45,200; Other Christian: 41,299; Presbyterian: 24,600; Apostolic or Pentecostal: 14,000; No religion: 269,000; Not stated: 72,900.

21. N. J. Demerath III, "The Rise of 'Cultural Religion' in European Christianity: Learning from Poland, Northern Ireland, and Sweden," *Social Compass* 47 (March 2000): 127–39.

22. Sogyal Rinpoche, *The Tibetan Book of Living and Dying* (New York: HarperCollins, 2002).

23. See Dzogchen Beara, "Spiritual Care," *Tibetan Buddhist Retreat Centre*, accessed August 1, 2014, http://www.dzogchenbeara.org/index.php?pid=22.

24. Steve Bruce, *God is Dead: Secularization in the West* (Oxford: Blackwell, 2002), 3.

25. No person who offers faith-based social service has received a Person of the Year award between 2009 and 2013. In the same time, Michael O'Brien (2009) was conferred for his dignity and raw honesty in recounting traumatic childhood experiences at Ferryhouse Industrial School (Rosminians); Christine Buckley (2009) was conferred for her courage and tenacity in exposing one of the darkest chapters in the history of modern Ireland at Golden Bridge Industrial School (Sr. of Mercy); and Fiona Doyle (2013) was conferred for her courage, determination, and bravery in fighting for her own rights and the rights of survivors of abuse (her father).

26. See both Berman Morris, *Wandering God: A Study in Nomadic Spirituality* (Albany, NY: State University of New York Press, 2000); and Robert Wuthnow, *After Heaven: Spirituality in America since the 1950s* (Berkely: University of California Press, 1998), 3.

27. See "National Pilgrims Path Day," *Pilgrims Path*, accessed March 1, 2014, http://www.pilgrimpath.ie/pilgrim-paths-day/. The Paths are: (1) St. Kevin's Way, Wicklow; (2) Turas Cholm Cille, Gleann Cholm Cille, County Donegal; (3) St. Finbarr's Pilgrim Walk from Drimoleague to Gougane Barra, County Cork; (4) Kilcommon Pilgrim Loop. County Tipperary; (5) St. Declan's Way, County Waterford; (6) Lough Derg Pilgrim Path, County Donegal; (7) Tochar Phadraig Pilgrim Path, County Mayo; (8) Clonmacnoise Pilgrim Path, County Offaly; (9) Rath/Dysert Clare Pilgrim Way; (10) Cosán na Naomh, Kerry.

28. Lieven Boeve, "Religion after Detraditionalisation: Christian Faith in a Post-Secular Europe," *Irish Theological Quarterly* 70 (2005): 99–122.

29. Bernadette Roberts, *The Experience of No Self: A Contemplative Journey*, rev. ed. (Albany, NY: SUNY Press, 1993), 13–14.

Appendix 1

Church, State, and Society in Ireland

1929	Diplomatic relations established between the Irish State and the Holy See
1937	Constitution of Ireland; affirms the special position of the Catholic Church in Irish society
1953	The Irish government's proposed Mother & Child Scheme providing health services to pregnant women is opposed by the bishops due to what they regarded as the State's violation of Catholic principles of subsidiarity
1978	Contraception legalized for married couples with bona fide family planning intentions
1983	Pro-life amendment inserted into the Irish Constitution
1984	New Ireland Forum on the future of North-South relations; Catholic bishops presented eloquent arguments in favor of the differentiation of Church (Catholic moral teaching) and State (civil laws)
1986	Divorce amendment—to legalize divorce—failed, by a two to one majority
1992	Irish Supreme Court rules (in the X case) that legislation should be enacted to allow abortion in cases where a woman's life is at risk (including risk of suicide)
1996	Divorce legalized
2006	Census 2006: 86.8 percent of people in Ireland identify as Catholic
2009 (November)	Murphy Report on sex abuse cases in the Dublin Archdiocese

2011 (January)	Civil unions (civil partnerships) legalized in Ireland as a result of Civil Partnership Act
2011 Census	4.6 million people in Ireland (the highest in 150 years); non-Irish nationals account for 12 percent of the population
2011 (July)	Cloyne Report on sex abuse cases in the Diocese of Cloyne
2011	Census 2011: 84.2 percent of people in Ireland identify as Catholic
2013 (August)	Abortion legalized in Ireland for exceptional cases in which the mother's life is endangered (including by threatened suicide)
2014 (April)	67 percent of the Irish electorate indicated they would vote in favor of same-sex marriage (MRBI/Ipsos poll)

Appendix 2

Contemplative Movements in Ireland

WCCM	**Contemplative Outreach**	**Plum Village**
John Main / Laurence Freeman	Thomas Keating	Thich Nhat Hanh
1. Argentina	1. Argentina	*1. Argentina*
2. Australia	2. Australia	*2. Australia*
3. Barbados	3. Austria	3. Austria
4. Belgium	4. Bahamas	*4. Belgium*
5. Brazil	5. Belgium	5. Bermuda
6. Canada	6. Brazil	6. Botswana
7. Chile	7. Canada	*7. Brazil*
8. China	8. Colombia	*8. Canada*
9. Colombia	9. Costa Rica	9. China
10. Curacao	10. Cuba	10. Costa Rica
11. Czech Republic	11. Croatia	11. Czech Republic
12. Denmark	12. Denmark	*12. Denmark*
13. Ecuador	13. Dominican Republic	13. Dominican Republic
14. Fiji	14. El Salvador	*14. Finland*
15. Finland	15. Finland	*15. France*
16. France	16. France	16. Germany
17. Germany	17. Ghana	*17. Great Britain*
18. Great Britain	18. Great Britain	*18. India*
19. Haiti	19. Greece	19. Indonesia

20. Honduras
21. Hong Kong
22. India
23. Indonesia
24. Ireland
25. Italy
26. Latvia
27. Lithuania
28. Malaysia
29. Mauritius
30. Mexico
31. Netherlands
32. New Zealand
33. Nicaragua
34. Norway
35. Pakistan
36. Paraguay
37. Peru
38. Philippines
39. Poland
40. Portugal
41. Russia
42. Singapore
43. Solomon Islands
44. South Africa
45. Spain
46. Sri Lanka
47. Switzerland
48. Tahiti
49. Taiwan
50. Tanzania
51. Thailand
52. Trinidad—West Indies
53. Uganda
54. Ukraine
55. United States
56. Uruguay

20. Guam
21. Honduras
22. Hungary
23. Iceland
24. India
25. Ireland
26. Israel
27. Italy
28. Malaysia
29. Mexico
30. Netherlands
31. New Zealand
32. Nicaragua
33. Peru
34. Phillipines
35. Poland
36. Puerto Rico
37. Singapore
38. South Africa
39. South Korea
40. Spain
41. Sweden
42. Switzerland
43. Tanzania
44. Thailand
45. Trinidad & Tobago
46. United States
47. Venezuela
48. Virgin Islands

20. Ireland
21. Israel
22. Italy
23. Japan
24. Malaysia
25. Mexico
26. Netherlands
27. New Zealand
28. Norway
29. Poland
30. Portugal
31. Russia
32. Singapore
33. South Africa
34. Spain
35. Sweden
36. Switzerland
37. Taiwan
38. Thailand
39. United States
40. Vietnam

57. Venezuela
58. Zambia

Note: Countries listed in italics in the far right column are those in which all three groups are located.
Note: John Main/Lawrence Freeman's Christian Meditation movement has groups in every county in Ireland north and south, with more than forty individual groups in Dublin. While Thomas Keating's Contemplative Outreach Ireland society is less numerous, it has thirty venues throughout Ireland.

Appendix 3

Buddhist Centers in Ireland

	1986 Sogyal Rinpoche TIBET	1977 Chojc Akong Tulku Rinpoche TIBET	1990 Ven. Panchen Ötrul Rinpoche TIBET	2004 Chogyam Trungpa Rinpoche TIBET	1990 Triratna Buddhist Community (formerly the Friends of the Western Buddhist Order, FWBO) No Lineage	1978 Ven. Mahasi Sayadaw / Bhante Bodhidhamma / BURMAE/ THAILAND	1997 Ringu Tulku Rinpoche TIBET	1991 Taisen Deshimaru / Kodo Sawaki JAPAN	2004 Sayagyi U Ba Khin INDIA	2007 Thich Nhat Hanh / Plum Village VIETNAM	2009 Kelsang Gyatso Gen Kelsang Tsering TIBET
Cork	Rigpa	KAGYU SAMYE DZONG				PASSADDHI		SOTO		Little Acorn Sangha & UCC Chaplaincy & Clear Mind, Joyful Heart Sangha	
Galway								SOTO		Elderflower Sangha & Plum Tree Sangha	New Kadampa Tradition
Mayo											
Donegal	Rigpa										
Kerry	Rigpa					Mahasi Vipassana Insight Meditation				Clear Loving Link to the Heart Sangha	
Tipperary											
Clare						Mahasi Vipassana Insight Meditation					
Limerick	Rigpa										New Kadampa Tradition
Roscommon											
Wexford										Three Jewels Sangha	
Meath								SOTO			
Kilkenny						Mahasi Vipassana Insight Meditation					
Wicklow										Full Moon Sangha & Old Heart New Heart Sangha	
Offaly											
Cavan			JAMPA LING								
Waterford	Rigpa										
Westmeath	Rigpa										
Sligo										Peaceful Lake Sangha & Open Circle Sangha	
Laois											
Kildare										LifeFlow Sangha	
Leitrim											
Monaghan											
Longford											
Dublin	Rigpa	KAGYU SAMYE DZONG		SHAMBHALA	BODHICHARYA Local Centres not listed	Mahasi Vipassana Insight - Meditation	Bodhicharya	SOTO	Vipassana	Open Heart Sangha & Suaimhneas Sangha,	New Kadampa Tradition
Carlow										Anam Cairde Sangha	
Louth									Vipassana		

Bibliography

"A Big Heart Open to God: The Exclusive Interview with Pope Francis." *America*, September 30, 2013. Accessed 7 June, 2014. http://americamagazine.org/pope-francis-interview.

"A True Fighter for the Faith." *The Catalyst*, March 12, 1994.

"A Winnable Referendum," *The Irish Times*, April 7, 2014.

Alba, Richard. "Bright vs. Blurred Boundaries: Second-Generation Assimilation and Exclusion in France, Germany, and the United States." *Ethnic and Racial Studies* 28 (2005): 20–49.

Alba, Richard. *Remaking the American Mainstream: Assimilation and Contemporary Immigration*. Cambridge, MA: Harvard University Press, 2003.

Alba, Richard and Victor Nee. "Rethinking Assimilation Theory for a New Era of Immigration." *International Migration Review* 31 (1997): 826–74.

Alexander, Jeffrey. *The Civil Sphere*. New York: Oxford University Press, 2006.

Allen, Kieran. "The Irish Political Elite." In *Are the Irish Different*? edited by Tom Inglis, 54–64. Manchester: Manchester University Press, 2014.

Anglican-Roman Catholic International Commission, *The Final Report, Windsor, September 1981*. London/Cincinnati: SPCK/Forward Movement Publications, 1982.

Annerman, Nancy. *Everyday Religion: Observing Modern Religious Lives*. Oxford: Oxford University Press, 2006.

"Anti-Partition Meeting." *Irish Press*, April 19, 1952.

Auge, Andrew, Louise Fuller, John Littleton, and Eamon Maher. "After the Murphy and Ryan Reports: A Roundtable on the Irish Catholic Church." *New Hibernia Review* 14 (2010): 59–77.

Bampfield, George. *Mixed Marriages: Showing Why the Church Does Not Like Them*. Brooklyn, New York: International Catholic Truth Society, n.d.

Barnard, L. K. and J. F. Curry. "The Relationship of Clergy Burnout to Self-Compassion and Other Personality Dimensions." *Pastoral Psychology* 61 (2012): 49–163.

Barnhart, Bruno. *The Future of Wisdom: Toward a Rebirth of Sapiential Christianity*. New York: Bloomsbury Academic, 2007.

Bartkowski, John P., Aida I. Ramos-Wada, Chris G. Ellison, and Gabriel A. Acevedo. "Faith, Race-Ethnicity, and Public Policy Preferences: Religious Schema and Abortion Attitudes among U.S. Latinos." *Journal for the Scientific Study of Religion* 51 (2012): 343–58.

Bateman, Fiona. "Ireland and the Nigeria-Biafra War: Local Connections to a Distant Conflict." *New Hibernia Review* 16 (2012): 48–67.

Bateman, Fiona. "Ireland's Spiritual Empire: Territory and Landscape in Irish Catholic Missionary Discourse." In *Empires of Religion*, edited by Hilary Carey, 267–87. London: Palgrave Macmillan, 2008.

Bauman, Zygmunt. *Liquid Modernity*. Cambridge: Polity, 2000.

Beara, Dzogchen. "Spiritual Care." *Tibetan Buddhist Retreat Centre*. Accessed August 1, 2014. http://www.dzogchenbeara.org/index.php?pid=22.

Bellah, Robert N. and Hans Joas, eds. *The Axial Age and Its Consequences*. Cambridge: Belknap Press of Harvard University Press, 2012.

Bender, Courtney. "How Does God Answer Back?" *Poetics* 36 (2008): 476–92.

Bender, Courtney. *The New Metaphysicals: Spirituality and the American Religious Imagination*. Chicago: University of Chicago Press, 2010.

Bender, Courtney. *Religion on the Edge: De-Centering and Re-Centering the Sociology of Religion*. Oxford: Oxford University Press, 2013.

Bender, Courtney. *Touching the Transcendent: Rethinking Religious Experience in the Sociological Study of Religion*. Oxford: Oxford University Press, 2007.

Bender, Courtney and Wendy Cadge. "Constructing Buddhism(s): Interreligious Dialogue and Religious Hybridity." *Sociology of Religion* 67 (2006): 229–47.

Bender, Courtney, Wendy Cadge, Peggy Levitt, and David Smilde, eds. *Religion on the Edge: Decentering and Recentering the Sociology of Religion*. New York: Oxford University Press, 2012.

Bender, Courtney and Pamela Klassen, eds. *After Pluralism: Reimagining Models of Religious Engagement*. New York: Columbia University Press, 2010.

Benedict XVI. "Message to the 2012 Eucharistic Congress, June 17, 2012." Accessed March 19, 2013. http://www.iec2012.ie/index.jsp?p=108&n=144&a=2412.

Benedict XVI. *Pastoral Letter of the Holy Father Pope Benedict XVI to the Catholics of Ireland, March 19, 2010*. The Holy See. Accessed July 31, 2014, http://www.vatican.va/holy_father/benedict_xvi/letters/2010/documents/hf_ben-xvi_let_20100319_church-ireland_en.html.

Bernstein, Jacob. "Bill Donohue: The Catholic League's Attack Dog." *WWD*, February 2, 2007.

"Bill Donohue defends child abuse." YouTube video, 8:34. Posted by encliticcopula, May 30, 2009. Accessed July 11, 2014. https://www.youtube.com/watch?v=dKLlxAgMO-w.

Birrell, W. D., J. E. Greer, and D. J. D. Roche. "The Political and Social Influence of Clergy in Northern Ireland." *Sociological Review* 27 (1979): 491–512.

"Bishop Criticized for Attack on McCarthy." *Franklin* (PA) *News-Herald*, April 12, 1954.

Blejwas, Stanislaus. "A Polish Community in Transition: The Evolution of the Holy Cross Parish, New Britain, Connecticut." *Polish American Studies* 35 (1978): 23–53.

Boeve, Lieven. "Religion after Detraditionalisation: Christian Faith in a Post-Secular Europe." *Irish Theological Quarterly* 70 (2005): 99–122.

Brown, R. Kahari. "Religion, Economic Concerns, and African American Immigration Attitudes." *Review of Religious Research* 52 (2010): 146–58.

Brubaker, Rogers. "The Return of Assimilation? Changing Perspectives on Immigration and its Sequels in France, Germany, and the United States." *Ethnic and Racial Studies* 24 (2001): 531–48.

Bruce, Steve. *God is Dead: Secularization in the West*. Oxford: Blackwell, 2002.

Calfano, Brian R., Elizabeth A. Oldmixon, and Mark Gray. "Strategically Prophetic Priests: An Analysis of Competing Principal Influence on Clergy Political Action." *Review of Religious Research* 56 (2014): 1–21.

Calfano, Brian R., Elizabeth A. Oldmixon, and Jane Suiter. "Assessing Clergy Attitudes: Ideology and Institutional Superiors." *Journal of Church and State* (2013). doi:10.1093/jcs/cst028.

Calfano, Brian R., Elizabeth A. Oldmixon, and Jane Suiter. "Who and What Affects the First Estate? An Analysis of Clergy Attitudes on Cultural and Economic Issues." *Politics* (2014). doi: 10.1111/1467-9256.12063.

Catechism of the Catholic Church. Dublin: Gill and Macmillan, 1995.

"Catholic League Members Rally to the Cause." *The Catalyst*, October 1994.

Cavanaugh, Tim. "E Pluribus Umbrage: The Long, Happy Life of America's Anti-Defamation Industry." *Reason*, December 2002.

Central Statistics Office. *This is Ireland: Highlights from Census 2011, Part 1*. Dublin: Government of Ireland, 2012.

Change, Kyung-Sup. "The Second Modern Condition? Compressed Modernity as Internalized Reflexive Modernization." *British Journal of Sociology* 61 (2010): 444–64.

Christus Dominus, Decree Concerning the Pastoral Office of Bishops in the Church, promulgated by Pope Paul VI October 28, 1965. The Holy See. Accessed July 20, 2014. http://www.vatican.va/archive/hist_councils/ii_vatican_council/documents/vat-ii_decree_1965-1028_christus-dominus_en.html.

Claffey, Patrick. Introduction to *Broken Faith: Re-visioning the Church in Ireland*, edited by Patrick Claffey, Joe Egan, and Marie Keenan. Oxford: Peter Lang, 2013.

Claffey, Patrick, Joe Egan, and Marie Keenan, eds. *Broken Faith: Why Hope Matters*. Oxford: Peter Lang, 2013.

Coll, Niall. "Irish Identity and the Future of Catholicism." In *Irish Catholic Identities*, edited by Oliver P. Rafferty, 362–76. Manchester: Manchester University Press, 2013.

Coll, Niall and Paschal Scallon, eds. *A Church with a Future: Challenges to Irish Catholicism Today*. Dublin: The Columba Press, 2005.

Collins, Stephen. "Over 70% Support X-Case Legislation on Abortion." *The Irish Times*, February 11, 2013.

Collins, Stephen. "Support for Same-Sex Marriage Increasing, Poll Finds." *The Irish Times*, April 7, 2014.

Conway, Brian. *The Vanishing Catholic Priest*. Los Angeles: Sage, 2011.

Conway, Eamonn and Colm Kilcoyne, eds. *The Splintered Heart: Conversations with a Church in Crisis*. Dublin: Veritas Publications, 1998.

Conway, Eamonn and Colm Kilcoyne, eds. *Twin Pulpits: Church and Media in Modern Ireland*. Dublin: Veritas Publications, 1997.

Cousins, Ewert. *Christ in the Twenty-First Century*. Rockport: Element Books, 1992.

Cronin, Anthony. *Dead as Doornails*. Dublin: Lilliput, 1999.

Cronin, Michael. "Fear and Loathing in the Republic: Why Hope Matters." In *Broken Faith: Re-visioning the Church in Ireland*, edited by Patrick Claffey, Joe Egan, and Marie Keenan, 107–22. Oxford: Peter Lang, 2013.

Curran, Rev. Edward Lodge. "Address by Rev. Edward Lodge Curran, Ph.D. before Citizens U.S.A. Committee, Chicago, Illinois, February 22, 1944." Archived at *The Pennsylvania Crier*. Accessed July 11, 2014. http://www.pennsylvaniacrier.com/filemgmt_data/files/Address%20by%20Rev%20Edward%20Lodge%20Curran%20PhD.pdf.

Curran, Edward Lodge. *The Blood Myth, Story of Nazi Germany*. Brooklyn, New York: International Catholic Truth Society, 1935.

Curran, Fr. Edward Lodge. *We Catholics*. Brooklyn, New York: International Catholic Truth Society, 1946.

D'Antonio, William, Michele Dillon, and Mary Gautier. *American Catholics in Transition*. Lanham, MD: Rowman & Littlefield, 2013.

de Certeau, Michel. *The Mystic Fable: The Sixteenth and Seventeenth Centuries*. Chicago: University of Chicago Press, 1998.

de Certeau, Michel. "Mystic Speech." In *The Certeau Reader*, edited by Graham Ward, 188–206. Oxford: Blackwell, 2000.

de Certeau, Michel. "The Weakness of Believing." In *The Certeau Reader*, edited by Graham Ward, 214–43. Oxford: Blackwell, 2000.

Demerath, N. J. III. "The Rise of 'Cultural Religion' in European Christianity: Learning from Poland, Northern Ireland, and Sweden." *Social Compass* 47 (March 2000): 127–39.

Dillon, Michele. "Asynchrony in Attitudes Toward Abortion and Gay Rights: The Challenge to Values Alignment." *Journal for the Scientific Study of Religion* 53 (2014): 1–16.

Dillon, Michele. *Catholic Identity: Balancing Reason, Faith, and Power*. New York: Cambridge University Press, 1999.

Dillon, Michele. "Christian Affiliation and Disaffiliation in the United States: Generational and Cultural Change." In *The Global Handbook of Christianity*, edited by Stephen Dalton. Leiden: Brill, in press.

Dillon, Michele. "Jurgen Habermas and the Post-Secular Appropriation of Religion: A Sociological Critique." In *Probing the Post-Secular*, edited by Philip Gorski, David Kim, John

Torpey, and Jonathan Van Antwerpen, 249–78. New York: New York University Press/ Social Science Research Council, 2012.

Dillon, Michele. "The Orphaned Irish: Church and State in Neo-Liberal Ireland." In *Religion and Regimes: Support, Separation, and Opposition*, edited by Mehran Tamadonfar and Ted G. Jelen, 197–211. Lanham: Lexington Books, 2014.

Dixon, Robert, Stephen Reid, and Marilyn Chee. *Mass Attendance in Australia*. Fitzroy, Australia: Australian Catholic Bishops Conference, 2013.

Djupe, Paul A. and Christopher Gilbert. *The Political Influence of Churches*. New York: Cambridge University Press, 2009.

Dolan, Jay P. *The Immigrant Church: New York's Irish and German Catholics, 1815–1865*. Baltimore: John Hopkins University Press, 1975.

Donohue, William. "The Catholic Mind." *The Catalyst*, January/February 1999.

Donohue, William. "Chris Matthews Insults Bishop Tobin." *Catholic League News Releases*, November 24, 2009.

Donohue, William. "Does the New York Times Employ Idiots or Bigots?" *The Catalyst*, May 11, 1994.

Donohue, William. "Is Bush Catholic?" *The Catalyst*, July/August 2001.

Donohue, William. "Spanish Harlem Welcomes an Irishman." In *Catholics in New York: Society, Culture, and Politics 1808–1946*, edited by Terry Golway, 177–80. New York: Fordham University Press, 2008.

Dorr, Donal. *Mission in Today's World*. Maryknoll, NY: Orbis Books, 2000.

Doughney, Mike. "Justice Sunday—Transcripts, Video, Audio." *Daily Kos*, April 25, 2005. Accessed July 10, 2014. http://www.dailykos.com/story/2005/04/25/109317/-Justice-Sunday-Transcripts-Video-Audio.

Dunne, Seán. *The Road to Silence: An Irish Spiritual Odyssey*. Dublin: New Island Books, 1994.

"Economic and Financial Indictors." *The Economist*, June 14–20, 2014.

Egan, Kevin. *Remaining a Catholic after the Murphy Report*. Dublin: The Columba Press, 2011.

Eliot, T. S. "Little Gidding." In *The Oxford Book of American Poetry*, edited by David Lehman, 369–72. New York: Oxford University Press, 2006.

Elliott, Marianne. *When God Took Sides: Religion and Identity in Ireland—Unfinished History*. Oxford: Oxford University Press, 2009.

"Enda Kenny Speech on Cloyne Report." *RTE News*, July 20, 2001. Accessed June 7, 2014. http://www.rte.ie/news/2011/0720/303965-cloyne1/.

Enright, Anne. *The Gathering*. London, Vintage Books, 2007.

Fahy, Patrick. "Some Political Behaviour Patterns and Attitudes of Roman Catholic Priests in a Rural Part of Northern Ireland." *Economic and Social Review* 1 (1971): 1–24.

Fanning, Bryan, Trutz Haase, and Neil O'Boyle. "Well-being, Cultural Capital and Social Inclusion: Immigrants in the Republic of Ireland." *Journal of International Migration and Integration/Revue De l'Integration Et De La Migration Internationale* 12 (2011): 1–24.

"Father Curran Gives Mac Petition Drive Boost at His Church." *Brooklyn Daily Eagle*, November 22, 1954.

Fay, Liam. "What's the Story?" *Hotpress*, April 3, 1996

"Ferns Report Highlights 100 Cases," *RTE*, October 25, 2005.

Ferriter, Diarmaid. *Occasions of Sin: Sex and Society in Modern Ireland*. London: Profile Books, 2009.

Finke, Roger and Rodney Stark. *The Churching of America, 1776–2005: Winners and Losers in Our Religious Economy*. New Brunswick, NJ: Rutgers University Press, 2005.

Finnegan, Richard B. and Edward T. McCarron. *Ireland: Historical Echoes, Contemporary Politics*. Boulder, CO: Westview Press, 2000.

FitzGerald, Garret. *Reflections on the Irish State*. Dublin: Irish Academic Press, 2003.

Flanagan, Bernadette. *The Spirit of the City: Voices from Dublin's Liberties*. Dublin: Veritas, 1999.

Flanagan, Rev. Padraig S.P.S. Preface to *A New Missionary Era*, edited by Rev. Padraig Flanagan, S.P.S. Dublin: Irish Missionary Union, 1979.

Flannery, Tony. *The Death of Religious Life*. Dublin: The Columba Press, 1995.
Flannery, Tony, ed. *Responding to the Ryan Report*. Dublin: The Columba Press, 2009.
Francis L., P. Hills, and P. Kaldor, "The Oswald Clergy Burnout Scale: Reliability, Factor Structure and Preliminary Application among Australian Clergy," *Journal of Pastoral Psychology* 57 (2009): 243–52.
Francis, Leslie J., Stephen H. Louden, and Christopher J. F. Rutledge. "Burnout among Roman Catholic Parochial Clergy in England and Wales: Myth or Reality?" *Review of Religious Research* 46 (2004): 5–19.
Francis, Leslie J. and Christopher J. F. Rutledge. "Are Rural Clergy in the Church of England Under Greater Stress? A Study in Empirical Theology." *Research in the Social Scientific Study of Religion* 11 (2000): 173–91.
Friel, Brian. Brian Friel Papers. National Library of Ireland.
Fuller, Louise. "Identity and Political Fragmentation in Independent Ireland, 1923–83." In *Irish Catholic Identities*, edited by Oliver J. Rafferty, 307–20. Manchester: Manchester University Press, 2013.
Galush, William. "Both Polish and Catholic: Immigrant Clergy in the American Church." *The Catholic Historical Review* 70 (1984): 407–27.
Ganiel, Gladys. "What Irish Priests Really Think? Moncrieff Show's National Priest Survey 2012." *Gladys Ganiel: Building a Church Without Walls*, March 8, 2012. Accessed August 4, 2014. http://www.gladysganiel.com/irish-catholic-church/what-irish-priests-really-think-moncrieff-shows-national-priest-survey-2012/.
Garesché, Edward Francis. *Dialogue on Mixed Marriage*. Brooklyn, New York: International Catholic Truth Society, 1932.
Gaudium et spes, Pastoral Constitution on the Church in the Modern World, promulgated by Pope Paul VI December 7, 1965. The Holy See. Accessed July 31, 2014. http://www.vatican.va/archive/hist_councils/ii_vatican_council/documents/vat-ii_const_19651207_gaudium-et-spes_en.html.
Gilbert, C. P. *The Impact of Churches on Political Behavior: An Empirical Study*. Westport: Greenwood Press, 1993.
Glenn, Norval. "The Trend in 'No Religion' Respondents to U.S. National Surveys, Late 1950s to Early 1980s." *Public Opinion Quarterly* 51 (1987): 292–314.
Glick Schiller, Nina. "Situating Identities: Towards an Identities Studies Without Binaries of Difference." *Identities* 1 (2012): 520–32.
Glick Schiller, Nina and Ayse Caglar. "Toward a Comparative Theory of Locality in Migration Studies: Migrant Incorporation and City Scale." *Journal of Ethnic and Migration Studies* 35 (2009): 107–202.
Glick Schiller, Nina, Ayse Caglar, and Thaddeus Guldbrandsen. "Beyond the Ethnic Lens: Locality, Globality, and Born-Again Incorporation." *American Ethnologist* 33 (2006): 612–33.
Glick Schiller, Nina and Thomas Faist, eds. *Migration, Development, and Transnationalization*. Oxford: Bergahn Books, 2010.
Goldstein, Patrick. "A Film is Condemned, Sight Unseen, Yet Again." *Los Angeles Times*, August 12, 2003. Accessed July 7, 2014. http://articles.latimes.com/2003/aug/12/entertainment/et-gold12/2.
Gordon, Milton. *Assimilation in American Life: The Role of Race, Religion and National Origins*. New York: Oxford University Press, 1964.
"Grammy Nominee Joan Osborne 'Relishes' Controversy." *The Catalyst*, April 12, 1996. Accessed July 11, 2014. http://www.catholicleague.org/grammy-nominee-joan-osborne-relishes-controversy/.
Greeley, Andrew. *American Catholics since the Council*. Chicago: Thomas More Press, 1985.
Greeley, Andrew. *The Catholic Imagination*. Berkeley: University of California Press, 2000.
Greeley, Andrew. *Religion in Europe at the End of the Second Millennium*. New Brunswick, NJ: Transaction Books, 2003.
Guth, James L., John C. Green, Corwin E. Smidt, Lyman A. Kellstedt, and Margaret M. Poloma. *The Bully Pulpit: The Politics of Protestant Clergy*. Lawrence: University of Kansas Press, 1997.

Habermas, Jurgen. "Notes on Post-Secular Society." *New Perspectives Quarterly* 25 (2008): 17–29.

Hassett, Maurice. "Labarum (Chi-Rho)." *The Catholic Encyclopedia*, Vol. 8. New York: Robert Appleton Company, 1910. Accessed July 15, 2014. http://www.newadvent.org/cathen/08717c.htm.

Heaney, Seamus. "Pilgrim's Journey." *Poetry Society Bulletin* 123 (Winter 1984).

Heaney, Seamus. Seamus Heaney Literary Papers. National Library of Ireland.

Heaney, Seamus. *Station Island*. London: Faber and Faber, 1984.

Hederman, Mark Patrick. *Underground Cathedrals*. Dublin: The Columba Press, 2010.

Herberg, Will. *Protestant, Catholic, Jew: An Essay in American Religious Sociology*. Garden City, NY: Doubleday, 1955.

Herron, Thomas J. "Answered Prayers: Bill Donohue's Catholic League Whacks *Culture Wars*." *Culture Wars*, October 2004. Accessed July 10, 2014. http://www.culturewars.com/2004/CatholicLeague.html.

Hoban, Brendan. *Change or Decay: Irish Catholicism in Crisis*. Kilglass: Banley House, 2005.

Hoban, Brendan. "Disenchanted Evenings—The Mood of Irish Diocesan Clergy." *The Furrow* 64 (2013): 604–19.

Hoban, Brendan. *Where Do We Go from Here? The Crisis in Irish Catholicism*. Dublin: Banley House, 2012.

Hoban, Brendan. *Who Will Break the Bread for Us? Disappearing Priests*. Dublin: Banley House, 2013.

Hogan, Edmund. *The Irish Missionary Movement: A Historical Survey 1830–1980*. Dublin: Gill & Macmillan, 1990.

Hout, Michael and Claude Fischer. "Why More Americans Have No Religious Preference: Politics and Generations." *American Sociological Review* 67 (2002): 165–90.

Hout, Michael and Andrew Greeley. "The Center Doesn't Hold: Church Attendance in the United States, 1940–1984." *American Sociological Review* 52 (1987): 332.

Hu, Winnie. "An Outspoken Church Defender." *New York Times*, November 2, 1999.

Huckfeldt, R., E. Plutzer, and J. Sprague. "Alternative Contexts of Political Behavior: Churches, Neighborhoods, and Individuals." *Journal of Politics* 55 (1993): 365–81.

Humphreys, Joe. *God's Entrepreneurs: How Irish Missionaries Tried to Change the World*. Dublin: New Island, 2010.

Inglis, Tom. "Catholic Identity in Contemporary Ireland: Belief and Belonging to Tradition." *Journal of Contemporary Religion* 22 (2007): 205–20.

Inglis, Tom. "Irish Civil Society: From Church to Media Domination." In *Religion and Politics: East-West Contrasts from Contemporary Europe,* edited by Tom Inglis, Zdzislaw Mach, and Rafal Mazanek. Dublin: University College Dublin Press, 2000.

Inglis, Tom. *Moral Monopoly: Catholic Church in Modern Irish Society*. Dublin: Gill and Macmillan, 1987.

Inglis, Tom. *Moral Monopoly: The Rise and Fall of the Catholic Church in Modern Ireland*. Dublin: University College Dublin Press, 1998.

"Ireland Lies about the Holy See." *The Catalyst*, October 2011.

Irish Episcopal Conference. *Summary of the Church's Position on Mass Offerings*. Dublin: Irish Catholic Bishops' Conference, 2010.

"Irish-Catholic Pundits Take Aim at Catholicism." *The Catalyst,* March 2002.

Jaspers, Karl. *The Origin and Goal of History*. New Haven: Yale University Press, 1953.

Jelen, Ted. "Notes for a Theory of Clergy as Political Leaders." In *Christian Clergy in American Politics,* edited by Sue E. S. Crawford and Laura R. Olson, 15–29. Baltimore: Johns Hopkins University Press, 2001.

Joseph, Eugene Newman, Patrick Luyten, Joseph Corveleyn, and Hans De Witte. "The Relationship between Personality, Burnout, and Engagement among Indian Clergy." *International Journal for the Psychology of Religion* 21 (2011): 276–88.

Kane, Fr. Michael CSSp. Interview by Maurice O'Keefe, 2011, Kimmage, Dublin, CDIMU 01-52, IMU Missionary Stories Project. *Irish Life and Lore: An Oral History Archive of Irish Voices.*

Kasper, Walter. "On the Church." *America*, April 23, 2001.

Keenan, Marie. *Child Sexual Abuse & the Catholic Church: Power, Gender, and Organizatinal Culture*. Oxford: Oxford University Press, 2012.

Kelly, Michael. "Irish Bishops Decide not to Publish Responses to Synod Questionnaire." *National Catholic Reporter*. March 12, 2014.

Kelly, Michael. "Irish Priestly Vocations in Worrying Decline," *The Catholic World Report*, October 30, 2012.

Keogh, Dermot. "The Catholic Church in Ireland since the 1950s." In *The Church Confronts Modernity: Catholicism since 1950 in the United States, Ireland, and Quebec*, edited by Leslie Woodcock Tentler. 93–149. Washington, DC: Catholic University of America Press, 2007.

"Kerry Kennedy Catholics." *The Catalyst*, November 2008.

Klimczak, Magdalena. "Island of Hope: Polish Immigrants in Ireland." *Studies: An Irish Quarterly Review* 96 (2007): 37–45.

Lane, Dermot A. "Vatican II: The Irish Experience." *The Furrow* 55 (2004): 67–81.

Lennon, Brian. *Can I Stay in the Catholic Church?* Dublin: The Columba Press, 2012.

"Letter to the Editor." *Commonweal*, July 18, 1997.

Levitt, Peggy. *God Needs No Passport: Immigrants and the Changing American Religious Landscape*. New York: New Press, 2007.

Levitt, Peggy. "Redefining the Boundaries of Belonging: The Institutional Character of Transnational Religious Life." *Sociology of Religion* 65 (2004): 1–18.

Levitt, Peggy. "What's Wrong with Migration Scholarship? A Critique and a Way Forward." *Identities* 19 (2012): 493–500.

Levitt, Peggy. "'You Know, Abraham Was Really the First Immigrant': Religion and Transnational Migration." *International Migration Review* 37 (2003): 847–73.

Levitt, Peggy and B. Nadya Jaworsky. "Transnational Migration Studies: Past Developments and Future Trends." *Annual Review of Sociology* 33 (2007): 129–56.

Levitt, Peggy and Nina Glick Schiller. "Conceptualizing Simultaneity: A Trasnational Social Field Perspective on Society." *International Migration Review* 28 (2004): 1002–39.

Lipsky, Michael. *Street-Level Bureaucracy: Dilemmas of the Individual in Public Services*. New York: Russell Sage Foundation, 1980.

Littleton, John. "Being a Catholic in Ireland Today." In *Contemporary Catholicism in Ireland: A Critical Appraisal*, edited by John Littleton and Eamon Maher, 12–24. Dublin: The Columba Press, 2008.

Littleton, John. "Catholic Identity in the Irish Context." In *Irish and Catholic? Towards an Understanding of Identity*, edited by Louise Fuller, John Littleton, and Eamon Maher, 12–30. Dublin: The Columba Press, 2006.

Littleton, John and Eamon Maher, eds. *The Dublin/Murphy Report: A Watershed for Irish Catholicism?* Dublin: The Columba Press, 2010.

Littleton, John and Eamon Maher, eds. *The Francis Factor: A New Departure*. Dublin: The Columba Press, 2014.

Lumen Gentium, Dogmatic Constitution on the Church, promulgated by Pope Paul VI November 26, 1964. The Holy See. Accessed March 19, 2013. http://www.vatican.va/archive/hist_councils/ii_vatican_council/documents/vat-ii_const_19641121_lumen-gentium_en.html.

Lunn, Peter and Tony Fahey. *Households and Family Structures in Ireland*. Dublin: Economic and Social Research Institute, 2011.

Lynch, Gordon. *The Sacred in the Modern Word: A Cultural Sociological Approach*. Oxford: Oxford University Press, 2012.

"Mac Would Have Been Welcome as a Colonial Leader—Father Curran." *Brooklyn Daily Eagle*, July 6, 1954.

Macklin, William R. "A Religious Watchdog Bares Teeth at Disney: Catholic League's William Donohue Fights Slurs with Pit Bull Tenacity." *Philadelphia Inquirer*, March 28, 1995.

Maguire, Stephen. "Younger Priests Fear 'Being in Public,'" *Irish Times*, August 5, 2011.

Marchetto, Agostino. *The Second Vatican Ecumenical Council: A Counterpoint for the History of the Council*, translated by Kenneth Whitehead. Scranton: Scranton University Press, 2009.

"Mark Patrick Hederman in Conversation with Shirley Ward." *Inside Out* 62 (Autumn 2010). Accessed August 1, 2014. http://iahip.org/inside-out/issue-62-autumn-2010.

Martin, Diarmuid. *Fostering Faith in the City Centre*. Dublin: Office of the Archdiocese of Dublin, 2014.

Martin, Diarmuid. *The Future of the Church in Ireland*. Dublin: Office of the Archdiocese of Dublin, 2010.

Martin, Diarmuid. *Pope Francis—One Year On*. Dublin: Office of the Archdiocese of Dublin, 2014.

McDonagh, Sean SSP. *The Death of Life: The Horror of Extinction*. Dublin: Columba Press, 2004.

McDonagh, Fr. Sean SSP. Interview by Maurice O'Keefe, 2010, Dalgan Park, CDIMU O1-5, IMU Missionary Stories Project. *Irish Life and Lore: An Oral History Archive of Irish Voices*.

McGahern, John. *Love of the World: Essays*. Edited by Stanley Van der Ziel. London: Faber & Faber, 2009.

McGarry, Patsy. "Clergy 'Appalled' by Handling of Abuse," *Irish Times*, August 1, 2011.

McGowan, Mark George and Brian P. Clarke, eds. *Catholics at the "Gathering Place": Historical Essays on the Archdioceses of Toronto*. Toronto: The Canadian Catholic Historical Association, 1993.

McGuire, Meredith. *Lived Religion: Faith and Practice in Everyday Life*. Oxford: Oxford University Press, 2008.

McMahon, Rev. Lawrence. "The Panlum Dingla." *Far East* XXXIV, No.4 (1951).

McShane, Larry. "Revival of the Catholic League." *The Bismarck Tribune*, May 21, 1998.

Melia, Paul. "Exodus from Rural Areas Revealed." *The Irish Independent*, March 29, 2014.

Merton, Thomas. *Conjectures of a Guilty Bystander*. New York: Image Books, 1989.

Mitchell, Claire. *Religion, Identity and Politics in Northern Ireland: Boundaries of Belonging and Belief*. Burlington: Ashgate Publishing Company, 2006.

Morawska, Ewa. "Immigrant Transnationalism and Assimilation: A Variety of Combinations and a Theoretical Model They Suggest." In *Integrating Immigrants in Liberal States*. Edited by Christian Joppke and Ewa Morawska, 133-76. New York: Macmillan/Palgrave, 2003.

Morris, Berman. *Wandering God: A Study in Nomadic Spirituality*. Albany, NY: State University of New York Press, 2000.

Nemoianu, Virgil. "The Church and the Secular Establishment: A Philosophical Dialog between Joseph Ratzinger and Jurgen Habermas," *Logos* 9 (2006): 17–42.

"New York Times Features McCourt Insult." *The Catalyst*, July 2009.

Nones on the Rise: One-in-five Adults Have No Religious Affiliation. Washington, DC: The Pew Forum on Religious and Public Life, 2012. Accessed April 10, 2014. http://www.pewforum.org/files/2012/10/NonesOnTheRise-full.pdf.

O'Donohue, John. *Anam Ċara: Spiritual Wisdom from the Celtic World*. New York: HarperCollins, 1998.

O'Driscoll, Dennis. "Missing God." *New Hibernia Review* 6 (2002): 48–50.

O'Driscoll, Dennis. *Stepping Stones: Interviews with Seamus Heaney*. London: Faber & Faber, 2008.

O'Dwyer, Rory. *The Eucharistic Congress, Dublin 1932*. Gloucestershire: The History Press Ltd, 2009.

O'Dwyer, Rev. Dr. Michael. "Letter." *Far East* XXXIII, No. 3 (1950).

O'Faolain, Sean. "An Enduring Friendship." In *Collected Stories of Sean O'Faolain*. Boston: Atlantic Little Brown Books, 1983.

O'Gorman, Colm. *Beyond Belief*. London: Hodder and Stoughton, 2009.

O'Hanlon, Gerry. *A New Vision for the Catholic Church: A View from Ireland*. Dublin: The Columba Press, 2011.

O'Hanlon, Gerry. *Theology in the Irish Public Square*. Dublin: The Columba Press, 2010.

Olson, Laura R. *Filled with Spirit and Power: Protestant Clergy in Politics*. Albany, NY: State University of New York Press, 2000.

O'Mahony, Eoin. *Practice and Belief among Catholics in the Republic of Ireland*. Dublin: Irish Catholic Bishops Conference, 2011.

O'Toole, James M. *The Faithful: A History of Catholics in America*. Cambridge: Harvard University Press, 2008.

Orsi, Robert A. *Between Heaven and Earth: The Religious Worlds People Make and the Scholars who Study Them*. Princeton, NJ: Princeton University Press, 2007.

Orsi, Robert A. *The Madonna of 115th Street: Faith and Community in Italian Harlem, 1880–1950*, 3rd rev. ed. New Haven: Yale University Press, 2010.

Orsi, Robert A. *Thank You St Jude: Women's Devotion to the Patron Saint of Hopeless Causes*. New Haven: Yale University Press, 1996.

Ouellet, Marc Cardinal. Untitled Address. IEC 2012 Theological Symposium, Saint Patrick's College, Maynooth, Ireland, June 6–9, 2012. Accessed March 18, 2013. http://www.iec2012.ie/index.jsp?p=108&n=4866.

Park, Robert E. "Assimilation, social." In *Encyclopedia of the Social Sciences*, edited by Edwin R. A. Seligman, Vol. 2, 281–83. New York: Macmillan, 1930.

Park, Robert E. "Human Migration and the Marginal Man." *American Journal of Sociology* 33 (1928): 881–93.

Park, Robert E. and Ernest W. Burgess. *Introduction to the Science of Sociology*. Chicago: University of Chicago Press, 1921.

Parker, Michael. *Seamus Heaney: The Making of a Poet*. Iowa City: University of Iowa Press, 1993.

Parot, Joseph John. *Polish Catholics in Chicago, 1850–1920*. Dekalb, IL: Northern Illinois University Press, 1981.

Peillon, Michel. *Contemporary Irish Society*. Dublin: Gill and Macmillan, 1982.

Phadraig, Maire Nic Ghiolla. "Religion in Ireland: No Longer an Exception?" *Access Research Knowledge*, Research Update 64, 2009. Accessed January 14, 2014. www.ark.ac.uk.

"Phil Donohue and Rosie O'Donnell on Display." *The Catalyst,* April 2003.

"Playboy Unearths Bobblehead Ex-Priest." *The Catalyst,* September 2002.

Pontifical Committee for Eucharistic Congresses, *Statutes, promulgated by Cardinal Bertone, Sec. of State, Vatican City, January 7, 2010*. The Holy See. Accessed March 19, 2013. http://www.vatican.va/roman_curia/pont_committees/eucharist-congr/documents/rc_committ-_euchar_doc_20091224_statuto_en.html.

Quas Primas, Encyclical of Pope Pius XI on the Feast of Christ the King, 1925. The Holy See. Accessed July 31, 2014. http://www.vatican.va/holy_father/pius_xi/encyclicals/documents/hf_p-xi_enc_11121925_quas-primas_en.html.

Raftery, Mary. *Do They Tink We're Eejits? A Selection of the Irish Times Columns 2003–2009*. Dublin: The Irish Times, 2013.

Randall, Kelvin J. "Clergy Burnout: Two Different Measures." *Pastoral Psychology* 62 (2013): 333–341.

Ratzinger, Cardinal Joseph. "The Ecclesiology of Vatican II." Opening address at the Pastoral Congress of the Diocese of Avila, Italy (September 15, 2001). *L'Osservatore Romano, Weekly Edition in English*, January 23, 2002. Accessed March 19, 2013. http://www.ewtn.com/library/curia/cdfeccv2.htm.

Ratzinger, Joseph. "On the Local and the Universal Church." *America*, November 19, 2001.

Ratzinger, Cardinal Joseph with Vitterio Messori. *The Ratzinger Report, An Exclusive Interview on the State of the Church*, translated by Salvator Attanansio and Graham Harrison. San Francisco: Ignatius Press, 1985.

Reigel, Ralph. "Cloyne Parishes to Hold Meetings over Abuse Report," *The Independent*, August 14, 2011.

Rinpoche, Sogyal. *The Tibetan Book of Living and Dying*. New York: HarperCollins, 2002.

Rizzo, J. R., R. J. House, and S. I. Lirtzman. "Role Conflict and Ambiguity in Complex Organizations." *Administrative Science Quarterly* 15 (1970): 150–63.

Roberts, Bernadette. *The Experience of No Self: A Contemplative Journey*, rev. ed. Albany, NY: SUNY Press, 1993.

Roche, Anthony. *Brian Friel: Theatre and* Politics. London: Palgrave Macmillan, 2011.

Rohou, Jean. *Catholiques et Bretons Toujours? Essai sur L'histoire du Christianisme en Bretagne*. Brest : Éditions Dialogue, 2012.

Ryan, Aidan. "Clergy Morale." *The Furrow* 57 (2006): 677–82.

Ryan, Liam. "Church and Politics: The Last Twenty-Five Years." *The Furrow* 30 (1979): 3–18.

Sacred Congregation for Divine Worship. *The Rite of Baptism for Children*. London: Geoffrey Chapman, 1970.

Sacrosanctum concilium, Constitution on the Sacred Liturgy, promulgated by His Holiness Pope Paul VI December 4, 1963. The Holy See. Accessed July August 1, 2014. http://www.vatican.va/archive/hist_councils/ii_vatican_council/documents/vat-ii_const_19631204_sacrosanctum-concilium_en.html.

Seitz, John C. *No Closure: Catholic Practice and Boston's Parish Shutdowns*. Cambridge: Harvard University Press, 2011.

Seyer, Loretta G. "Interview with Catholic League President William A Donohue." *Catholic Twin Circle*, January 9, 1994.

Shaughnessy, Gerald. *Has the Immigrant Kept the Faith? A Study of Immigration and Catholic Growth in the United States, 1790–1920*. New York: Macmillan, 1925.

Shaw, George Bernard, "John Bull's Other Island." In *Bernard Shaw: Complete Plays with Prefaces*, vol. 2. New York: Dodd, Mead, and Co., 1963.

Sheridan, Kathy. "The Fearful Fathers," *The Irish Times*, July 23, 2011.

Simmel, Georg. "A Contribution to the Sociology of Religion." *American Journal of Sociology* 11 (1905): 359–76.

Simmel, Georg. *On Individuality and Social Forms*, edited by Donald N. Levine. Chicago: University of Chicago Press, 1971.

Smith, Gregory. "The Influence of Priests on the Political Attitudes of Roman Catholics." *Journal for the Scientific Study of Religion* 44 (2005): 291–306.

Smith, Robert C. "Diasporic Memberships in Historical Perspective: Comparative Insights from the Mexican, Italian and Polish Cases." *International Migration Review* 37 (2003): 724–59.

Smyth, James M. *Ireland's Magdalen Laundries and the Nation's Architecture of Containment*. Notre Dame: University of Notre Dame Press, 2007.

Solari, Cinzia. "Transnational Politics and Settlement Practices: Post-Soviet Immigrant Churches in Rome." *The American Behavioral Scientist* 49 (2006): 1528–53.

Statistics and Research Agency. Northern Ireland Census, 2011. Accessed March 20, 2014. http://www.ninis2.nisra.gov.uk/public/Theme.aspx?themeNumber=136&themeName=-Census%202011.

"Still the Irish Voice." *The Catalyst*, June 2000.

"Taoiseach Enda Kenny: Cloyne Report." YouTube video, 12:13. Posted by RTE, July 21 2011. Accessed June 7, 2014. http://www.youtube.com/watch?v=mo5MXrqbDeA.

Taylor, Charles. *Dilemmas and Connections: Selected Essays*. Cambridge, MA: Harvard University Press, 2011.

The Eucharist: Communion With Christ and One Another: Theological and Pastoral Reflections in Preparation for the 50th International Eucharistic Congress. Dublin: Veritas, 2011.

"This Week They Said." *Irish Times* [Dublin], May 31, 2007.

Trevor, William. *A Bit on the Side*. London: Viking, 2004.

Trzebiatowska, Marta. "The Advent of the 'Easy Jet Priest': Dilemmas of Polish Catholic Integration in the UK." *Sociology* 44 (2010): 1055–72.

Trzebiatowska, Marta. "Habit Does Not a Nun Make? Religious Dress in the Everyday Lives of Polish Catholic Nuns." *Journal of Contemporary Religion* 25 (2010): 51–65.

Tweed, Thomas A. *Our Lady of the Exile: Diasporic Religion at a Cuban Catholic Shrine in Miami*. New York: Oxford University Press, 1997.

Twomey, D. Vincent. *The End of Irish Catholicism?* Dublin: Veritas Publications, 2003.

"U.S. Congressmen's Views on Partition." *Irish Independent*, October 23, 1953.

"U.S. Support in Unity Plan Promised." *Irish Independent*, April 23, 1953.

Wald, Kenneth D., and Allison Calhoun-Brown. *Religion and Politics in the United States*. 6th ed. Lanham, MD: Rowman & Littlefield, 2011.

Wald, Kenneth D., Dennis E. Owen, and Samuel S. Hill. "Churches as Political Communities." *American Political Science Review* 82 (1988): 531–48.

Weber, Max. *The Protestant Ethic and the Spirit of Capitalism*. New York: Scribner's and Sons, 1958.

"Well-Known American Worker in Ireland's Cause: Visit of the Very Rev. Dr. E. Lodge Curran." *Ulster Herald*, October 17 1953.

Whyte, J. H. *Church and State in Modern Ireland, 1923–1970*. Dublin: Gill and MacMillan, 1971.

Wilson, George B. *Clericalism: The Death of Priesthood*. Collegeville: The Liturgical Press, 2008.

Wuthnow, Robert. *After Heaven: Spirituality in America since the 1950s*. Berkely: University of California Press, 1998.

Yeats, William Butler. *Later Poems*. London: Macmillan, 1922.

Yeats, William Butler. *Michael Robartes and the Dancer*. Dundrum: Cuala, 1921.

Index

About the Contributors

Andrew J. Auge directs the Irish Studies Program at Loras College and has published numerous essays on Irish literature in journals such as *An Sionnach*; *LIT: Literature, Interpretation, Theory*; *Contemporary Literature*, and, *New Hibernia Review*. His recent book, *A Chastened Communion, Modern Irish Poetry and Catholicism* (2013) is available from Syracuse University Press.

Brian R. Calfano is associate professor of political science at Missouri State University. His research interests include religion and politics, media effects, and elite cue theory. He has published in journals including *Political Communication*, *Political Behavior*, *Political Research Quarterly*, *International Studies Perspectives*, and *Politics and Religion*. He is the co-author (with Paul Djupe) of *God Talk: Experimenting with the Religious Causes of Public Opinion* (2013), and is the editor of *Assessing MENA Political Reform, Post-Arab Spring: Mediators and Microfoundations* (2014).

David Carroll Cochran is professor of politics and director of the Archbishop Kucera Center for Catholic Intellectual and Spiritual Life at Loras College. His main areas of teaching and scholarship are religion and politics, racial and ethnic politics, and the morality of war. His most recent book is *Catholic Realism and the Abolition of War* (2014). In addition to his academic writing, he frequently writes about politics and culture for magazines such as *America* and *Commonweal*.

Michele Dillon is professor of sociology at the University of New Hampshire. Her publications include *American Catholics in Transition* (with W. D'Antonio and M. Gautier; 2013), *In the Course of a Lifetime: Tracing*

Religious Belief, Practice, and Change (co-author Paul Wink; 2007), *Catholic Identity: Balancing Reason, Faith, and Power* (1999), *Debating Divorce: Moral Conflict in Ireland* (1993), *Handbook of the Sociology of Religion* (editor; 2003), *Introduction to Sociological Theory* (2010), and over fifty research articles and book chapters. She has served as president of the Society for the Scientific Study of Religion, chair of the American Sociological Association Section for the Sociology of Religion, and president of the Association for the Sociology of Religion.

Bernadette Flanagan is director of research at All Hallows College (Dublin City University). Her publications include *The Spirit of the City* (1999); in collaboration with Una Agnew and Greg Heylin; *With Wisdom Seeking God: The Academic Study of Spirituality* (2008); and, in collaboration with Michael O'Sullivan, *Spiritual Capital* (2012). She has served on the governing board of the international Society for the Study of Christian Spirituality and is a non-resident faculty scholar of the Duke University Center for Spirituality, Religion and Health. She has recently been researching the subject of women and new monasticisms, and her book on this subject, *Embracing Solitude* (2013).

John Littleton, a priest of the Diocese of Cashel and Emly in Ireland, is director of The Priory Institute, Tallaght, Dublin. Previously, he taught theology and religious studies in several colleges and institutes in Ireland and the UK. He served as president of the National Conference of Priests of Ireland (NCPI) for six years (2001–2007). Fr. Littleton has co-edited six books dealing with various aspects of Irish Catholicism. Among his other recent publications are *The Fulfilment of God's Saving Promise* (2012) and *Encountering God and Discovering Our True Identity* (2013). He also writes a weekly column in *The Catholic Times* and works in parish and retreat ministries.

Eamon Maher is director of the National Centre for Franco-Irish Studies in IT Tallaght (Dublin), where he also lectures in humanities. He is editor of the highly successful *Reimagining Ireland* book series, and he has also published a number of books in this series. One of his primary research interests is the portrayal of Catholicism in the novel and he is currently preparing a monograph on the Catholic novel in the twentieth century. Maher has co-edited five books on contemporary Irish Catholicism with John Littleton. His most recent publication (co-edited with Eugene O'Brien) is: *From Prosperity to Austerity: A Socio-cultural Critique of the Celtic Tiger and Its Aftermath.*

Matthew J. O'Brien is professor of history at Franciscan University of Steubenville, Ohio. He has co-edited a volume of essays with James Rodgers, *After the Flood: Irish America 1945–1960*, and has contributed articles to a number of scholarly journals, including *Eire-Ireland, Etudes-Irlandaises, U.S. Catholic Historian*, and *New Hibernia Review*.

Elizabeth A. Oldmixon is associate professor of political science at the University of North Texas. She is formerly a Fulbright Scholar at University College Cork (fall 2010) and an American Political Science Association Congressional Fellow (2001–2002). Her research and teaching interests include legislative policymaking, religion and politics, and Irish, Israeli, and American politics. Her work has appeared in *Politics and Religion, Journal of Church and State, Review of Religious Research, Social Science Quarterly, Social Science Journal, Foreign Policy Analysis, Legislative Studies Quarterly*, and *Political Research Quarterly*, and she is author of *Uncompromising Positions: God, Sex, and the U.S. House of Representatives* (2005).

Agata Piękosz is a PhD candidate in the Department of Sociology, concurrently in the Ethnic and Pluralism Studies Program at the University of Toronto. She focuses on the relationship between migration and religion by taking a qualitative methods approach that incorporates migration theory and the conceptualizations of Georg Simmel. Her dissertation explores the religious and migrant lives of Polish Catholic priests in Canada (the classic immigrant receiving nation) and in Ireland (the contemporary immigrant receiving nation). She is currently an active member of the Critical Catholic Studies Working Group at the Department of Anthropology at the University of Toronto, and a part-time lecturer of social theory at the University of Western Ontario.

James Silas Rogers edits *New Hibernia Review* and is director of the Center for Irish Studies in Minnesota. He was president of the American Conference for Irish Studies in 2009–2011. His scholarly publications focus on Irish-American literature, including two contributed volumes, *After the Flood: Irish America 1945-1960* (2009) and *Extended Family: Essays on Being Irish American* (2013). His collection of essays on poems about cemeteries, *Northern Orchards: Places Near the Dead* was published in May 2014. His essays and poems have appeared in many literary publications, including *Poetry East, National Catholic Reporter*, and *Spritus*, and have been read on Garrison Keillor's "Writer's Almanac." His essay "Outside Metaphor" (which first appeared in *Ruminate: Chewing on Faith and Art*) was selected as a notable essay of the year in the current Best American Essays.

John C. Waldmeir is professor of religious studies and theology, Loras College. He has published four books, including the most recent title, *Cathedrals of Bone: The Role of the Body in Contemporary Catholic Literature*

(2009). In 2011–2012 he held the John Cardinal O'Connor Chair of Catholic Thought at Loras and arranged for Loras students and faculty to attend the Eucharistic Congress in Dublin.

Lightning Source UK Ltd.
Milton Keynes UK
UKOW04n0327270917
309911UK00004B/57/P

9 781498 502528